Building and Managing Your Private Practice

by

Daniel L. Richards, Ph.D.

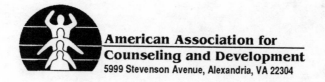

American Association for
Counseling and Development
5999 Stevenson Avenue, Alexandria, VA 22304

American Association for Counseling and Development
5999 Stevenson Avenue
Alexandria, VA 22304

Cover Design by Sarah Jane Valdez

Library of Congress Cataloging-in-Publication Data

Richards, Daniel L.
    Building and managing your private practice/Daniel L. Richards.
      p. cm.
    Includes bibliographical references
    ISBN 1-55620-071-4
    1. Mental health counseling—Practice.   2. Counseling—Practice.
I. Title.
RC466.R53   1990   89-18565
616.89′14′068—dc20   CIP

This publication reflects the opinions of the author, and examines one
possible course of action an individual may choose to follow. It does not
necessarily reflect the opinions of the membership of AACD. The
publisher is not rendering legal advice. It remains the responsibility of all
readers to seek the advice of an attorney or other qualified professional
before proceeding with actions suggested in this publication.

Printed in the United States of America

*To Betty
and my two sons,
Michael and Matthew*

CONTENTS

SECTION FIVE

Marketing: The Key to Success 129

PREFACE

The number of clinicians considering entering private practice is growing each day. With the changes in health delivery systems, more and more clinicians are turning to private practice as a way to do the work they were trained to do. The difficulty for many is that they have little or no understanding of the business requirements and personal involvement that a private practice will necessitate.

When I started my practice I had no idea what would be involved and there weren't many books to read, workshops to attend, or colleagues willing to discuss what they were doing that made them successful. Consequently, I began alone with only my knowledge of business management and my clinical skills to guide me. Over the years my practice grew, and so did the problems. I've made great strides in being successful as a private practitioner, and I've made a great many mistakes along the way.

Six years ago I was asked by the American Association for Counseling and Development to do a workshop entitled: How to Establish and Maintain a Private Practice in Counseling. That workshop was only 1 day long because that was all I knew! Since then I've done over 100 lectures, workshops, seminars, and speeches, and 3 years ago I began publishing a newsletter for private practitioners. Subsequently many have asked me, "When are you going to write a book and 'tell all'?" Here is the book. This book is everything I've learned and experienced, complete with successes and painful learning experiences.

This book will address the need for a therapist to be not only a good clinician, but also a motivated entrepreneur. In today's marketplace it's almost impossible to develop a successful practice without being an entrepreneur.

What does it take to be an entrepreneur? Entrepreneurship is the spirit of growth, change, and free enterprise. Entrepreneurs hold the vision of the future, and in our field, visionaries are necessary—people who are willing and eager to create better ways of helping people grow and change. To be an entrepreneur is to have a dream, but not a dream with an end. It is to have a dream that is constantly renewed, that branches out like the limbs of a tree from the trunk. To be successful, a person must be a dreamer.

To be an entrepreneur is to take risks. By their nature, entrepreneurs are willing, and in some cases overeager, to take risks and challenge the unknown. Entrepreneurs don't ask *Why?*, they ask *Why not?* They are not satisfied with *Why?* because it doesn't translate into action, but becomes theoretical. But *Why not?* brings about change. (Why should we do it this way? Because we've always done it this way, this way works; let's stick with it. But why not change the way we've always done things and try it a different way? Well...yes, why not?) Entrepreneurs are eager to ask *Why not?* Implicit in the idea of *Why not?* is risk. Risk causes changes; simply asking *Why?* allows the asker to avoid challenge and the risk of changing the certainty, the established way.

To be an entrepreneur is to be bored. Yes, bored. Entrepreneurs are not happy when change has been accomplished. The entrepreneurial spirit needs a constant challenge. It lives not for stability, success, complacency, and stagnation, but for challenge. Once a challenge has been accepted, a plan developed and implemented, and success or failure achieved, then boredom will set in, unless a new question is asked and a new challenge is presented.

What is your entrepreneurial spirit? How much of a dreamer are you? Is *Why?* the question you ask most often, or are you plagued by the deeper, riskier question, *Why not?* I believe that you are entrepreneurs, you are the dreamers and the doers of our profession. You are the risk takers, the ones who ask *Why not?*, the ones who will change the face of mental health counseling, training, and health assistance programs in the future.

I say this because you have purchased this book with the hope of more success: success for your clients and success for yourself as a self-employed private practitioner. Throughout the text I have used the terms *therapist, practitioner*, and *counselor* interchangeably, purely for ease in reading. This book will not give all the answers on how to be successful, but it will motivate, challenge, and confront many of the ways private practice is done in this country.

I am deeply committed to success, not from the win/lose idea, but to success that both parties win: clients win/you win. Clients win because their therapists stay in practice, grow, and improve the therapy process, and therapists win because they are successful at what they do.

This book is written for the graduate student who is thinking of going into private practice someday, for the therapist working in an agency or educational setting who longs for the chance to go it alone, and for the clinician who has been in private practice, limited or full-time, for 1 year or for 10, who wants to be more successful.

I've written this book as a step-by-step process with as much detail as I can give. A complete reading offers a sequential process for success and specific details to allow the book to be a reference to guide you, the practitioner, as your practice grows and changes in the years to come. You may not need everything you read initially, but over time you'll refer to specific sections.

The book is divided into eight sections, with the final one offering my personal reflections.

Section 1, "Rationale for Private Practice," begins by establishing the basic foundation of a successful practice: the therapist. Why go into practice? What is a private practice? Why do some fail? And what will be the future? With these issues confronted, the focus moves to the personal questions involving clinical skills, supervision, risk taking, emotional investment, and financial stability. We also examine the differences between a limited and a full-time practice, and the basic questions involved in knowing oneself. For those who have never gone into therapy, or who have never looked at therapy in a private practice setting, there are some helpful suggestions. The section ends with 10 specific steps to a successful start as well as the role of goal setting.

Section 2, "The Business Aspects of a Private Practice," begins the step-by-step process of establishing a practice with the development of a three-member business team (accountant, lawyer, and banker) and the role and use of each. Next, the need for credentials and what they mean for a private practitioner leads into the advantages of being a specialist or a generalist. The last of this section is devoted to the scope of a practice: sole proprietorship, partnership, joining an existing practice, or incorporation.

Section 3, "Setting Up the Practice," presents specific information about the choice of location for an office. Should it be in the home, or should office space be sublet or rented? The pitfalls of each situation are discussed in detail, and the effects each choice would have on a private practice are examined. I have also included a handy checklist and specific information about rental space, as well as secrets involving successful negotiating. The question of whether to use an answering machine or service are discussed in relation to the effect each has on a practice's growth. A complete explanation of the role of a fee in private practice and the proper way to establish a fee to maximize the financial stability of the practice are given. The section ends with a thorough look at the various insurance needs: malpractice, bodily injury, renters', equipment, workers' compensation, and income protection.

Section 4, "Opening the Practice," begins with the importance of the practice's name and the establishment of a time line. Detailed information is included regarding how to save money and increase the effectiveness of printing, yellow page directories and newspaper advertisements, logo development, and business cards and stationery. The importance of a self-disclosure brochure as a marketing tool as well as its specific content are explained. The section closes with information about the role of a secretary in a successful practice and ideas for finding and hiring a good secretary.

Section 5, "Marketing: The Key to Success," includes a well-organized marketing plan. All the methods and materials included in this chapter have been shown to be effective. Practical examples are provided, beginning with a marketing plan and a detailed marketing analysis. Some topics addressed are: getting your name in print, public service announcements, press releases, getting free radio and television exposure, public speaking, and the highly successful technique of giving free presentations. A discussion of how to use business lunches effectively to gain new referrals and the often forgotten value of thank-you forms and cards addresses the value of referral sources. Open houses are excellent ways to increase the referral base of a practice, and the proven secrets are shared in this section. The pressure to keep ahead of the competition is dealt with by citing specific examples of increasing a practitioner's exposure professionally, such as holiday acknowledgments and professional follow-through. The development and marketing of a successful workshop is also included in this section, along with the role of practice newsletters. All this material is presented in a organized way for proven success. The section ends with ways to keep postal costs down and a final marketing technique: the end-of-the-year statement.

Section 6, "Running the Practice," begins by going through the intake process from the business and marketing standpoint with information that clinicians never recieve in their training. Detailed information is provided about collecting the fee, missed appointments, late sessions, phone consultation, insurance forms, collection procedures, and the importance of a business receipt system. Third-party reimbursement is critically involved in most practices today. Consequently, it is necessary to make a thorough analysis of eligibility, payment, the ethical and legal concerns involving diagnosis, fraud and theft by deception, the hazards of co-signing, as well as questionable billing practices.

This section also goes into the tools to build a sound financial base: checking systems, the accounting process, and credit cards. The need to keep proper records and an explanation of what records must be kept and for how long should help if the Internal Revenue Service ever should ask for documentation. This is followed by suggestions for tax preparation and planning. The section ends with an evaluation process for the practice.

Section 7, "Expanding the Practice," offers insights into how to expand an existing practice. It begins with the development of a plan and gives details about subletting, partnerships, investing in property, or selling products.

Section 8, "Reflections," offers some concluding thoughts about being in private practice.

I hope you will find this book helpful, stimulating, and meaningful. Nothing would please me more than to hear 5 years from now that your copy of my book is dog-eared and marked up because you have constantly taken it down from the shelf and referred to it as you have opened and run your successful private practice. Drop me a line and let me know when that happens!

—*Daniel L. Richards*

ACKNOWLEDGMENTS

I wish to acknowledge a few specific people whose support and encouragement have contributed to this book: Alice Hellstrom, whose editorial skills and commitment to this book kept me going; Bobbie Pappa, my secretary of 7 years, who believed in and supported my practice; Kate O'Halloran, editor of *Private Practice News*, who honed my writing skills; Judy Vaughn, MA, NCC, and Theron M. Covin, EdD, for their invaluable comments after reading the manuscript; the many readers of *Private Practice News* and workshop attendees who have shared their successes and failures in private practice with me; my many clients who have taught me the humility of being a counselor and have given me the privilege of being present during the healing change therapy brings—to all of these, my heartfelt thanks.

ABOUT THE AUTHOR

Daniel L. Richards, PhD, NCC, is in private practice at Southern Maine Counseling Center in Portland, Maine.

He has served as state president, regional chairperson, and on the governing council of the American Association for Counseling and Development. He is the director of Private Practice Institute and was editor of *Private Practice News*.

Over the last 7 years he has lectured, presented workshops, and published on the issues confronting private practitioners and is recognized as an expert in the field.

Rationale for Private Practice

WHY GO INTO PRIVATE PRACTICE?

Over the years that I've traveled and lectured on private practice, I've met with hundreds of individuals and talked with them about why they have entered private practice. The various reasons seem to be clustered around two central concepts: autonomy and income potential.

The freedom to control one's own professional development is appealing to many who have worked under a variety of training experiences in which their professional development was controlled and perhaps stifled by the supervision and policies of the agency. It is my firm belief that as the field of private practice continues to grow, we will see more and more creative contributions to the healing of individuals and more improvements in the discipline of psychotherapy.

The current literature in this field is, more often than not, written by people in private practice. (Lerner, 1985; Levine, 1982; Lew, 1988; Small, 1982.) The reason is simple: Private practice affords the opportunity to explore new boundaries and new areas with clients, a freedom that would not necessarily be present in an agency setting. This also creates a moral and ethical dilemma. As professionals we may need to look more clearly at the control process in private practice. At this point, it is enough to say that many people go into private practice in order to control their own professional development. They can choose the type of workshops and training activities they want, seek the type of supervision that is most suitable for clients, and be free to select their clients. Self-employed professionals can also hone their skills with the client population of their choosing.

The second major reason for choosing to enter private practice is increased income potential. Private practice offers an opportunity to control one's own financial destiny. Yes, private practice affords the individual an opportunity to make a great deal of money, but it also increases the risk of losing a great deal of money. The gamble and the responsibility for private practice is solely up to the individual private practitioner. The major limitation to income potential is a lack of knowledge of marketing and business skills. Those are the topics this book will address specifically.

I feel strongly that most private practitioners are not equipped to pursue the business aspects of their practice, but when opportunities are made available, most are willing to seek the kind of counsel and help they need to establish good business management policies.

The income potential for private practice is alluring and often causes people to get involved in unethical and illegal practices simply because of ignorance. Fees, sliding scales, insurance, and co-signing and bartering practices are all areas where private practitioners can get into dilemmas that those working under agencies or schools do not face. But, no doubt, private practice affords the opportunity to build a strong financial base and to ensure income potential.

It is also important to note that because private practice is solely a fee-for-service type of industry, if one does not work, one does not get paid. That means that although private practitioners have an income potential far in excess of that in an agency or school, they do not have paid vacations, paid holidays, sick time, or disability time—which all has to be factored in when fees are determined and client loads are established. Whereas looking forward to several weeks' vacation is the norm in an agency setting, a private practitioner does not always have that luxury. Taking 13 or 14 paid holidays a year is another luxury that people in private practice do not often have. It is extremely important for practitioners to balance the long-term, yearly income needs with the weekly client load. Clearly, entering private practice offers both autonomy and income potential, but it holds many pitfalls.

WHAT IS PRIVATE PRACTICE?

Often, people wonder exactly what a private practice is. The idealists think of private practice as sitting in an office, having clients come to the practitioner, providing good therapy, and collecting a fee for the service. But, realistically, private practice today is not that simple. Private practice is like any other small business. Simply put, there is little difference between someone in private practice and someone who opens a hamburger shop, clothing store, or any other kind of retail business. Practitioners would like to think that they are special and different. But the reality is that they are running a small business. Clients will come for therapy, pay a fee, and assume that the fee will be used appropriately to maintain the integrity and sound business principles necessary for the therapist to stay in business for the length of time the clients need the service.

One of the most difficult things for people in private practice to understand is that when clients pay a fee, they are paying for a long-term service. They assume implicitly that the private practice will be run on good, sound business principles. They hope that practitioners live on a budget, make projections, ensure financial stability, and more than anything else, remain healthy enough, both personally and financially, to stay in business for the length of time that the clients will need the service. The difficulty for most private practitioners is that they have little understanding of business management and financial planning. Most people who enter private practice do so because of their clinical skills, not their business skills.

On the other hand, entering private practice with good business skills and no clinical skills does not guarantee success at all, and may, in fact, be detrimental to clients. It is important that one first have solid clinical skills that have been proven over time, developed through supervision, and honed through life experiences, and that these skills be accompanied by sound management and financial practices. There are private practitioners who are excellent clinicians, who know their work and how to help clients, but they don't know how to market their services or handle their money. Consequently they find themselves burned out, angry, disillusioned, and resenting the concept of private practice.

PRIVATE PRACTICE FAILURES

Private practices fail at the same rate as any other business ventures. The difficulty in understanding that concept in private practice is the very isolated nature of private practice. Many begin private practice on some limited basis, seeing a few clients on the side, while still maintaining full employment elsewhere. They consider themselves in private practice, but they have not made the necessary financial and personal commitment.

But as the practice begins to grow, and as practitioners begin to feel a little more comfortable in developing their practice, they add a few more clients. As time goes on, they have built enough of a client load to consider starting a full-time practice. In most cases, they may decrease their full-time employment to a limited basis, working 2 or 3 days a week or taking a leave of absence from their job. As they do this, they increase their client load, thereby increasing the financial obligations and commitments to their practice. As their confidence grows and their referral bases increase, they may finally choose to make the plunge into full-time private practice.

Sadly, many practitioners do not understand the principles of managing a business, marketing their services, or competing in an aggressive marketplace. They may find themselves depending too heavily upon insurance reimbursement, not having diversified their income sources or maintained a consistent marketing campaign, or having overextended themselves financially. Combined with the constant battering and stress that accompany a successful private practice, they become disillusioned and resentful. At this point, practitioners often begin to expand into some other area, such as consulting or training, part-time employment, or teaching at a university, not to increase the success of their practice but to escape from their practice. As they begin to cut their practice down because they find more security in those other areas, their client loads begin to diminish, until finally they find themselves back where they began, in some type of full-time employment with a limited client load on the side. Often they are angry and resentful of the competition, the large groups of new people entering private practice, the unethical practices of colleagues—whatever kind of justification they can find for failing to realize their dream of full-time private practice.

The risk of failure in private practice is high. In a 5-year period, between 50% and 60% of therapist who enter private practice with the dream of an independent business will not fulfill that hope. This is sad and harmful, for the clinician who has lost a dream, for clients who needed the clinian's help, and for the profession that has lost a potential positive force for change in the human condition.

I believe that many of these failures can be reversed and that with help and support, more and more clinicians can experience success with the dream of a full-time private practice. When that happens we all succeed. This book is designed to help increase the success rate in private practice.

FUTURE DIRECTIONS OF PRIVATE PRACTICE

Often I'm asked, "What's the future direction of private practice?" Depending on people's experiences, location in the country, and their own professional training backgrounds, a wide range of answers are possible. Many traditional groups have long believed that only their credentials, training, or circumstances have qualified them for private practice. These groups often have negative feelings about private practice. In certain areas of the country, fees have been so inflated that only a limited number of people are able to pay them. In other areas of the country, practitioners do not market their services as aggressively as do new professionals entering the business, who are more willing to push the limits on marketing and are more assertive in seeking clients.

More recently we have seen the introduction of health maintenance organizations (HMOs) and preferred provider organizations (PPOs), which have attempted to limit the cost of mental health services. Many private practitioners have accepted these payment schedules in the belief that these organizations would provide them with a stable client base; unfortunately, many practitioners have found the financial base of their practice in jeopardy (Beck, 1988b).

Insurance companies are also questioning the cost of mental health services (Remley, 1988; Richards, 1988). Formerly, a very select group of practitioners were able to collect from the insurance companies. Their fees were in more limited ranges and insurance companies had some type of control over the fees and the number of providers. During the last 10 years, there's been a great influx of new professionals entering the third-party reimbursement system because of licensing laws that cover not only psychologists and psychiatrists but also social workers, marriage and family counselors, psychiatric nurses, and professional mental health counselors. Consequently more and more practitioners rely unduly on insurance companies for payment. Insurance companies base their rates on projections of dollars to be paid out for claims. With the increased proliferation of information available to the public about the need to see a professional counselor or therapist, and the wider variety of professionals accepting insurance, the insurance industry faces a two-pronged problem today. Larger numbers of people are choosing to avail themselves of professional help and more professionals are available to provide this help. This all translates into more insurance dollars being spent. All of this is causing a great deal of strain on an already overburdened health care system. As a result, many question how much longer private practice as it is today will continue, and whether the marketplace can sustain a greater influx of mental health care providers (Beck, 1988a; Wiggins, 1988).

In my opinion, the future is still bright for private practice. There **will** be changes. The HMOs and PPOs have, in fact, increased people's awareness of the cost of mental health services. Insurance companies are clearly attempting to contain costs by placing a limit on reimbursement. Many insurance companies have instituted a flat sum available for mental health services each year for each subscriber. Subscribers are then free to choose whatever type of professional they wish to see, but the insurance company will pay only a certain amount. It has been my experience that insurance reimbursement policies create an opportunity for a great deal of abuse by private practitioners and also can hinder the effectiveness of therapy (Richards, 1989).

Suffice it to say, changes **are** occurring. The private practitioner who controls the practice by managing fees and by being open and honest with clients and who markets and is willing to be aggressive in the marketplace has an excellent future. But for those who have rested on their laurels for years, or who have inflated their fees exorbitantly, the future looks bleak.

EFFECTS OF RECENT CHANGES ON PROFESSIONALS

How are these recent changes affecting professionals? Increasingly private practitioners are taking into account the needs of the public instead of considering the needs of an exclusive group. Professional organizations are more willing to work together. States are actively looking to a single board or regulatory body for all the professions rather than to a separate board for each group. The public is becoming more aware of the credentials and cost of private therapy. No longer is the therapist perceived as the all-knowing, perfect, problem-solving individual. More is being published about the pitfalls of being a therapist (Dwinell, 1987; Kopp, 1985; Kouzmanoff, 1988; Schoff, 1988.)

The public is becoming more aware of what it takes to be a therapist, and many more therapists are facing their own issues as well as those of their clients. The future for private practice is excellent for those who are well trained, well qualified, and knowledgeable about their own particular marketplace. These practitioners are setting fees appropriately, marketing and advertising aggressively, and adhering to strong ethical and legal guidelines. Moreover, they are willing to grow personally themselves.

KEY ISSUES TO CONSIDER BEFORE ENTERING PRIVATE PRACTICE

Credentials: What They Mean in Private Practice

Who is qualified to go into private practice? What type of credentials are needed? Credentials indicate levels of expertise or training. The credentials themselves are not the service performed. In theory, the type of credentials attained assist the private practitioner to be more skilled and to offer more complete service.

The reality is that most training in college settings today does not adequately prepare the therapist for the types of dilemmas that private practice presents. I have always believed that therapists must be comfortable with their own levels of expertise and training. No outside body can judge a private practitioner's comfort level in areas of expertise, but attempts are made through licensing, certification, and legal requirements. Therapists themselves must determine what level of academic training is necessary to be competent and honest in the presentation of skills and abilities. Is it necessary to have a PhD or EdD? Perhaps a degree in psychology is necessary. What about an MSW or an RNMS? Clients almost never judge a therapist by a set of certifications or academic degrees hanging on a wall. Clients assume that their therapists are qualified to do what they claim to be able to do. So who really protects the clients? Who protects the profession?

My next comment is controversial, but I feel strongly that it needs to be said. Licensing boards and boards of regulation simply recognize professional identity; in my opinion, they do not protect the client. Abuse of a client can occur whether the practitioner is licensed or not, and in most cases, the only action a board can take is to revoke a license. Just because a person is licensed as a psychologist or social worker or counselor doesn't mean that what goes on behind closed doors between the therapist and the client is guaranteed to be ethical, legal, and morally sound. Consequently, I think we need to explain to the public exactly what a license does and does not do. Sad to say, "Let the buyer beware" is still the reality in mental health services. I am not saying that licensing and regulation are unnecessary. Just the opposite is true. I believe licensing, certification, and regulations **are** necessary. The credentials allow a regulating body to assess at some minimum level the competence and expertise of the therapist, but credentials do not protect the public.

Credentials are not the key to successful practice either. Credentials are a necessary and important part of entering private practice, but they will not guarantee success. A person can spend long periods of time getting training and expertise, receiving multiple degrees, going through lengthy certification processes and, once these goals are achieved, expect a certain degree of success in private practice. The anticipation is that clients will flock to the door because of the credentials listed after the therapist's name. The truth is that the public never distinguishes appropriately and adequately between a therapist's academic degrees and a therapist's training and experience. The public expects that if therapists represent themselves as trained and qualified professionals that they will, in fact, be able to perform the services offered. Clients expect therapists to be able to assess accurately their particular problems and work with them in a therapeutic relationship or refer them to a more appropriate therapist.

Who protects the public? Individual therapists do, when they make the decision that they are qualified to do what they say they can do, work under ethical guidelines, are aware of their own personal conflicts and stresses, and take care to address their own needs. Therapists who do not avail themselves of personal therapy and support during times of crises or change are putting themselves and their clients at risk. The best protection for the public is a healthy therapist.

Therefore, I often say that there is a myth around credentials. The myth is that the greater the credentials, the more successful the therapist will be in private practice and the more comfortable clients will be in the therapy process. If people are qualified therapists, they will act that way. If they have received the training and achieved the expertise necessary to perform as therapists, they will act accordingly. In reality, certification boards and professional organizations do not protect clients. Therapists entering private practice need to understand the limits of their credentials and how their credentials qualify them. The private practitioner must be willing and able to continue growing and not assume that just because certain credentials have been achieved that training and growing are completed. Personally, my own level of expertise and training has multiplied tenfold as I have conferred with colleagues in order to do the best possible job for those who come to me for help.

Specialists Versus Generalists

An academic degree or level of expertise in theoretical background does not qualify a person to treat all types of client problems. It has been my experience that it is impossible to treat young children, adolescents, adults, geriatrics, married couples, and families and have all the knowledge and expertise necessary in each of those categories. Just keeping up with the literature on one segment of the population is a difficult task. In my opinion, assuming that a practitioner can successfully treat every category of client and all types of problems presented is unethical and potentially legally risky.

From a marketing standpoint, it's important to recognize that specializing in a given area eliminates being in competition with the general run of other private practitioners. Using the medical community as an example, many years ago physicians moved out of general practice into the specialist mode. Over the years various medical specialties have emerged and have been further refined. As a result, an increasingly defined body of knowledge and expertise is needed to treat certain medical problems. This has allowed more doctors to practice medicine. Why is that the case?

The general practitioners are still there, still the first line of screening for referral to a specialist, and that specialist may refer to an even greater level of specialty. Consequently, there has been an increase in the number of physicians, and the fear that the medical community would become glutted has been dispersed by increased specialization to respond to improved treatment methods. Each specialist in the referral chain realizes that the original client belonged to the general practitioner, thus the generalist and the specialist complement each other. In the field of **mental** health services however, this referral process has not been successful. A number of therapists still consider themselves general practitioners and feel that because a client has come to them, they must treat all that client's problems. Some therapists are afraid to look at themselves as specialists, feeling they can't afford to limit themselves in that way because they really need the clients. Just the opposite is the case.

Narrowing down the types of clients the therapist feels most competent in treating serves the clients better, and in turn the clients who have been helped will become public relations representatives for the therapist. The best promotional work for a practice is satisfied clients. Clients who feel that they have been helped, genuinely understood, and have made progress in their therapy are most apt to refer other people to their therapist.

I learned years ago in my practice that when I did intakes for clients and realized that their particular problems were not within my area of expertise or training, and consequently made an appropriate referral to another therapist far more skilled and qualified in that area, that we both came out winners. Basically clients respect my diagnostic skills and the fact that I referred them to a therapist who was more of a specialist in the problem area. Consequently, people whom I may not even have seen as a client except as an intake still saw me as someone to whom they could refer their friends. Instead of decreasing because I referred clients to other specialists, my practice has grown.

In today's highly competitive marketplace, choosing to be a specialist and to do high quality work ultimately builds a firm base for a practice to grow and expand. Before entering private practice, these questions should be asked:

1. What type of clients does the therapist enjoy working with most?
2. What type of academic training has the therapist had that would lend itself to specialization?
3. What kind of credentials have been obtained in the specialty areas?
4. What kind of personal experience has the therapist had in working in the specialty areas?

Analyzing the answers to these questions will quickly bring the realization that the therapists' life experiences and academic interests have determined the specialty areas of their private practice. The therapists with the greatest interest in a particular type of client issue will be the most effective in working with that issue because those therapists will have undertaken the appropriate training. They will have questioned and resolved any personal issues from their background; therefore, they are the most likely to present the knowledgeable, effective therapy needed. Clients expect their therapists to understand where they are coming from, to be objective, and to have the knowledge and expertise to help them. It is no secret that I advocate today's concept of being a specialist, not a generalist. I think that in today's highly competitive marketplace, being a generalist sets the therapist and the practice afloat without any real direction. Being a specialist allows the development of a marketing plan and a public relations program, and ultimately enhances the success of the practice.

Clinical Skills

The first and most important requirement for private practitioners is confidence in their own clinical skills. Because private practice is an unsupervised, closed-in environment, no amount of training or academic degrees guarantees that a person will be effective in private practice. So the big question is, "Am I clinically qualified to do what I say I'm going to do?" No outside person can judge that. In my opinion, anyone fresh out of a doctoral program or a master's level program does not have enough clinical skills to open a solo private practice. Clinical skills need to be gained through a wide variety of training experiences and personal experiences. The best way to look at clinical skills is to ask a series of questions:

How strong are the clinical skills?.
If questioned on ethical terms, will they stand?
If questioned on legal terms, will they stand?
Can they be defended to peers and the public?
What is the level of commitment to ongoing growth and supervision?

It is imperative that potential practitioners evaluate their own clinical skills in the light of these questions.

Supervision

Entering private practice leaves behind the structure of required supervision in an agency or school setting. Therefore, it's extremely important for new practitioners to have either one or two supervisors available the first couple of years in private practice in order to have direct access to someone with more experience, both in the private practice area and in the clinical area, to continue to polish and hone their skills. Topics will come up in private practice that never would have arisen in an agency or supervised environment. Knowing that a supervisor is available to review the case and provide feedback alleviates the otherwise isolated and dangerous ethical position of a new practitioner.

Risk Taking

Entering private practice is a risky endeavor. Risk-taking skills should be assessed before a decision is made to enter private practice. Decisions about marketing, business growth, or retirement investments require a certain comfort level in taking risks. The importance of balancing personal and professional growth and development is also governed by a person's level of risk taking. Knowing when to ask for help either personally during times of stress, or professionally during times of low referrals and slack times requires risk taking. In a private setting, the practitioner must be a good risk taker, someone who is willing to propose and accept challenges, but also able to keep an accurate eye on the results.

Emotional Investment

Private practice takes a huge emotional investment. If the prospective practitioner is not secure emotionally, if the personal life is in chaos, a job has just been lost, a family is breaking up, or some other high level of stress exists, then going into private practice is not a good idea at that time. Once the private practice is opened, practitioners are expected to have their own personal lives together in order to concentrate on the clients. It is generally recognized that some of the highest suicide rates in the professional community are among members of the helping professions, specifically psychiatrists, psychologists, social workers, and counselors who did not take care of themselves. Increased rates of malpractice insurance indicate that some major ethical abuses and violations of clients' rights also occur in the private practice area. Staying healthy is a necessity in private practice. The underlying causes of abuses and attempts to circumvent ethical guidelines are therapists' personal stress and personal emotional vulnerability. If there is a high level of stress, or the personal life is not settled and stable, it is not appropriate to open a private practice. If stress or disruptions in a practitioner's personal life occur while in private practice, getting help is a necessity.

Financial Stability

Private practice is a financial endeavor in which a lot of money can be made or lost. Running a practice is the same as owning and managing a small business. It is not unusual for a successful private practice to gross between $70,000 to $150,000 a year. This is often more cash than a person has ever had to handle previously. A solid financial plan for budgeting and managing this cash flow is crucial. If the personal financial stability is not there, if entering private practice is seen as a way to get out of debt, the practice should not be opened until the would-be practitioner is financially secure. Generally, new practices lose money temporarily and will have cash-flow problems from time to time.

Budget

Private practice requires a budget. Some therapists enter private practice with no budgets. They've never put themselves on a budget, and they have no idea how to balance a checkbook, schedule payments ahead of time, or put money in escrow or savings accounts. All these must be done when in private practice. The private practitioner cannot wait until the 30th day to pay a bill. Nor can it be assumed that the money will be there when the malpractice insurance bill comes. Private practice requires a 12-month budget, fairly closely adhered to, that responds to what is happening in the practice and provides direction for the practice. The would-be practitioner should live on a budget for at least 6 months prior to opening a private practice so that living under a controlled income and a disciplined expenditure plan is not a new experience.

Importance of a Paycheck

The last issue to consider before entering private practice is the importance of a paycheck. Many people live pretty much on the wire from paycheck to paycheck. These people will face some difficult times ahead. Future expenses—paying for children's education, helping aging parents, and other cast-draining costs—must be anticipated before opening a private practice. Some limited private practices may fail within the first couple of years because the practitioners never committed themselves totally to their practice. They attempted to use their practice as a source of additional income to augment the paycheck. During the first year of a private practice it is wise to assume that the paycheck will be minimal. There will be a large drop in disposable personal income. This is because most of the money received will be invested in buying equipment, paying debt service, or continuing the marketing campaign. If there are no savings or sources of income in reserve, and the prospective practitioner is living from paycheck to paycheck, it might be advisable to hold off opening a practice until there is enough of a reserve to cover 6 months' income.

LIMITED VERSUS FULL-TIME

Many people begin their private practice on a part-time basis. Practitioners in a part-time practice are often frustrated because they don't see it growing at the same rate as a full-time practice would. One of the reasons for the lack of growth is the very fact that it is called a *part-time* private practice.

Beginning part-time practitioners need to visualize how they would feel about going to see doctors or attorneys who told them up front that their practices were only part-time. That implies that there is a full-time job, which, in turn, implies that the full-time job will be getting the full-time commitment and the part-time job will be getting whatever is left over. Often private practitioners don't realize how semantics affect their professional and image credibility. The use of the term *part-time* might be hindering the practice's growth.

When I first began my part-time practice specializing in sex counseling, I could not seem to get the referrals that I knew were available. Finally, one physician offered me an opportunity to speak before all the obstetricians and gynecologists in the greater Portland area. I went to this presentation confidently with a well-prepared package of material on what I did in sex counseling, how a referral could be made, and what the expected outcome of therapy would be. I had handouts for everyone, and I felt that I had done a thorough and competent presentation. At the end of the presentation, many physicians commented on how impressed they were and that I had presented new information to them. I left the presentation feeling that my practice was going to take off. As time went on, I sat home waiting for the phone calls that never came.

Finally, out of desperation, I contacted the physician who had set up the presentation for me, and asked him what had gone wrong. Why hadn't I been receiving more referrals? He looked at me with a straight face and said, "Dan, your referrals are limited because you indicated to all of us that you had a part-time private practice. Many of us also teach at the hospital or do some other type of professional work, but we never indicate that we have a part-time practice, rather that we have a limited practice. Others of us have taken the plunge, invested the $100,000 to $200,000 necessary to set up a full-time practice. When someone like you says that you have a part-time practice and are seeing clients in your home, what we hear is that you have minimal overhead, minimal risk, and we feel uncomfortable referring our patients to you."

As I thought about what he was saying, I began to realize that he was exactly right. From then on, I stopped calling my practice *part-time* and began saying I had a *limited* practice. The words *part-time* and *limited* give the public certain images. In reality I was limiting my practice to the number of hours I would work, to the number of clients I would see, and even to the type of clients I would see. So, in fact, that physician was right. I was running a limited practice for my own personal reasons, which were of no importance to the clients. When I began to explain to my clients and other professionals that I had a limited practice in sex counseling, my practice began to grow. Subsequently, it grew so much that I expanded to a full-time practice and have gone on from there.

CREDIBILITY

What are the differences between the terms *limited* (*part-time*) *practice* and *full-time practice*? The first is credibility. It has been my experience that those who indicate that they have a part-time practice in today's competitive marketplace are not considered as credible as those who are in a full-time practice. If the practice is limited, there is a need to be specific about the reasons. With the increased public awareness of what to expect from a therapist and the increased pressure on referral sources from a constant bombardment by new people opening their practice, it's important that new practitioners be credible. Those who say they have a full-time practice have more credibility in today's marketplace than those who say they have a limited or part-time practice.

Many other factors contribute to a practitioner's credibility; these will be discussed in more detail throughout the book. For the purpose here, being in full-time practice as defined by the practitioner gives an emotional advantage because of the assertiveness and confidence projected.

RETURN

There are two types of return from private practice: a financial return and a personal return. In a limited practice the financial return is also limited. People who are in a limited practice because they are still maintaining a full-time position often find themselves burned out, frustrated, and angry because they do not realize the financial return that they had hoped, unless they are working with a specific plan of action toward turning that limited practice into a full-time business. The idea of seeing two or three extra clients, or four or five clients, or even ten clients and still trying to maintain a full-time position can be overwhelming. Even though there may be substantial extra income coming into a practice, by the time the rent, the malpractice insurance, and other expenses are paid, the end financial return is minimal. That is one reason part-time practitioners often question the energy it takes to continue their practice.

Helping people is a personally rewarding experience. To watch clients grow, to be a part of their lives, perhaps for several years, gives me a great deal of satisfaction personally. When I was practicing on a limited basis, I was torn between the energy I wanted to put into the needs of my clients and family and the demands of my regular full-time job. When I had made the move to a full-time practice, I was able to involve myself totally in my work and my family. I was no longer being torn in three directions. All my other professional endeavors evolve around the personal satisfaction I receive from working with my clients and being in private practice.

THE FUTURE

The marketplace has become increasingly competitive during the last 10 years. More therapists are entering private practice on a full-time rather than on a limited basis. They are willing to make the commitment, develop marketing techniques, be aggressive in the marketplace, and form group practices when appropriate. Today the public is more knowledgeable about what to expect from a therapist. People have specific demands about what they expect from their therapists and are able to shop around to find the one they want. Those therapists who commit themselves to full-time practice are going to experience continuing success in the marketplace, whereas those who attempt limited practice often will be frustrated at not receiving the returns they envisioned. Because referral sources are beginning to realize that there is an abundance of full-time practitioners, why would anyone refer to a therapist with a limited practice? However wrong the idea may be, the public may question the quality of the therapy a part-time practitioner offers versus the quality of the full-time practitioner.

EMOTIONAL INVESTMENT

Private practice is a personal journey. Often therapists think about going into private practice without fully understanding the emotional investment involved. Once a private practice has been opened, the therapist becomes personally and intimately involved in a number of people's lives, causing a number of key questions to surface in the therapy process. This personal involvement is different than when working in an agency, organization, or school because of the time involved in therapy. Countertransference can become a real possibility in the therapeutic process in long-term approaches to helping clients. Consequently, there are some key personal questions to ask before entering private practice.

Who Am I?

Who the therapist is is an integral part of the therapy given in private practice because the question involves basic understanding of human dynamics, first, the therapist's own, and then others'. Because private practice is intensely personal, therapists learn more about themselves mostly because clients help point out blind spots in the therapy process. Hence, it is critically important to maintain an active personal growth life outside of the private practice setting, and active personal therapy and supervision when needed. Often in private practice the therapist sees as many as 10 or 12 clients a day, back to back, sometimes 4 or 5 days a week. With this type of work load, it becomes easy to get lost in the clients' identity. So the very essence of "Who am I?" is something that must be maintained at all times if private practitioners are to be effective.

What Do I Want?

Therapists' own wants are what drives them into private practice, and their own wants are what drives them as they strive to become the complete person that they could be. It is also through their wants that they often view their clients. Without a clear understanding of one's own wants, the private practice will amble along, not reaching its full potential, and the therapist will not be effective with clients. Consequently, an initial and continuous assessment of the therapist's personal, financial, physical, familial, professional, and spiritual needs and wants will help to keep a separation between clients' needs and wants and the therapist's needs and wants.

What Are My Fears?

Fears accompany the process of growing up. Fears also limit success. Before entering private practice, the therapist should ask:

- What are my fears?
- Do my fears involve financial security?
- Do my fears involve lack of trust?
- Do they involve engaging in intimate relationships?
- Do they involve my health?
- Do they involve my safety?

Whatever fears therapists have, they will be played out with their clients in a private practice. In a private practice colleagues and supervision are not as readily available as they were in training and preparatory work. Fears can begin to control the therapy process. Fears can sabotage a private practice. If one of the fears is major financial insecurity, new private practitioners may not take the financial risks necessary to establish a practice on a firm base. If the fear is one of intimacy with people, new practitioners will withhold themselves from clients or, even worse, will seek a false, unhealthy intimacy with clients. If the fear is that of public speaking, therapists will tend to avoid lecturing, training, and speaking before civic groups and organizations— all of which are necessary to build name recognition. If the fear is that of being abandoned, practitioners will tend to avoid engaging in support groups and other peer-supervision groups that are needed to hone skills. In essence, whatever the fears, they need to be addressed continually as the practice begins and grows.

How Much Work Is Too Much?

This is the most difficult question for people in private practice to answer. In training, the caseload was determined. The hours of work were determined. Vacations were determined. Holidays and sick days were determined. The difficulty in private practice is that none of these factors are controlled by anyone else but the therapists themselves. Reserving large blocks of time for personal renewal becomes difficult when facing the financial stresses of a private practice. It's easy within an agency setting to talk about "my week's vacation" and know that you will get paid for that week. In private practice no work equals no pay. It's easy and helpful to think about all the days off and the holidays, but in private practice each holiday taken may cost $500 to $1000, depending on the client load. There would be 13 paid holidays in an agency or school setting. In a full-time private practice, a realistic look reveals that 13 paid holidays may represent $10,000 worth of income over a year. A decision has to be made about the number of holidays to take. What happens when the growing practice reaches its capacity? A well-established practice may have far more referrals than needed. Deciding when the practice schedule is full and beginning to limit the caseload is difficult. Often people going into private practice are also workaholics; that is, they are driven by the need to work.

Many practitioners begin private practice while maintaining a full-time position elsewhere. I was working as a director of guidance services, at least a 50-hour a week job, while building my private practice on the side. It took an average of 20 clients a week before I finally left the school job. Add 50 hours' worth of work a week for the school job to 20 hours' worth of seeing clients. Then add hours of supervision, consultation, and writing and it's easy to see what was happening. I was really over-working; consequently, I was not effective in any area. Private practice can become a wonderful escape for workaholics. The new practitioner needs to be aware of this potential danger.

SITTING ON THE OTHER SIDE OF THE COUCH

Private practice demands a great deal emotionally. The therapist's health has a direct effect on the clients. Does one need to undergo therapy to be a therapist? Is it necessary to have experienced a psychotherapeutic relationship to offer therapy? Some would answer both questions with a firm "No." Opinions range from "You don't need to be divorced to do divorce counseling" to "You don't need to be a recovering drug addict to be a substance abuse counselor" to "You don't need to go to therapy if you don't have a problem." Therapists and counselors expound the virtues of their profession. Many therapists would say, "Everyone could benefit from some therapy in their lives—but not me, not right now." Being a therapist demands 100% commitment. Emotionally, the therapist struggles with the clients' concerns and shares their joys and sorrows. Then, at the end of the day, the therapist joins that struggle, entering the world that he or she has tried so hard to help clients understand.

Therapists owe it to themselves to take the time to deal with their own human limitations, their own vulnerability, spirituality, conflicts, and concerns of intimacy. The client who has the strength to admit weakness is admired. Therapists must cultivate that strength in themselves, for they are stronger and more human when they recognize their need to talk with someone in a therapeutic relationship. Private practitioners are not immune to the issues that affect their clients. Of course, it is to be hoped that therapists have a good understanding of their own emotional systems, but these can still be overloaded by divorce, death, illness, abuse, ambition, and insecurity, just like everyone else's. Going into therapy also allows therapists to step back and look at private practice through the eyes of a client.

The following set of questions is designed to evaluate the private therapy process from the point of view of the therapist who has decided to seek therapy. There are two purposes for this: the first is to assist the therapist in thinking through the process of selection, and the second is to offer the practitioner a way of looking at the selection process the way a client might. Whom do professionals call for professional help?

- What standards, both personal and professional, do they use?
- What cost is appropriate?
- What about using insurance?
- How much control will be needed over time of appointments, sitting in a public waiting room, and leaving messages with secretaries and answering services?
- How open will they be with friends, family, and others about their own need for therapy?

To help with these decisions, here is a list of further questions about the various issues of therapy.

What About Standards?

To begin the process of choosing a therapist, consider what standards will be applied to the selection, including degrees, credentials, professional identification, and experience. How important are they, and why? How are a therapist's credentials measured? In trying to select a competent, qualified human being as a therapist, other levels of competence and qualifications must be judged by the therapist-turned-client's personal standards.

When examining these personal standards, the therapist may find some surprising issues. For example, is it important whether the therapist is male or female, married, single, or divorced? What about age? If the therapist chosen is not personally known, and the first contact is either over the phone or in the first visit, what judgments will be made about the therapist based on voice, physical appearance, dress, personal mannerisms, and openness to needs?

Fee

The cost of therapy will also be a factor in the decision. Therapy is not cheap; what role does cost play? Are a practitioner's qualifications, competence, and experience judged by the fees charged? What is the therapist-turned-client's personal budget for therapy? How long is therapy expected to continue, and what effect will it have on the monthly bills? What payment plan is best, weekly or monthly? If cost is a factor in deciding to go into therapy, there must be a willingness to discuss it with the therapist. Should the fee be paid to the therapist or the receptionist? What about being charged for a missed appointment, short sessions, or sessions that don't start on time?

Insurance

Therapists all fight for clients' rights to use their insurance. If the therapist is the client, should insurance be used to pay for therapy? If not, why not? What factors govern that decision? How many therapists are available whose fees are low enough to avoid insurance coverage? Does the therapist have options, such as a payment plan or reduced fees? If it is decided to use insurance, how informed will the therapist-turned-client be about the diagnosis, and if a mental health status report is requested, how informed will the therapist-turned-client want to be? Will copies of all insurance correspondence be volunteered or will they have to be requested? If the counseling is in the area of marriage or family, what will be the determination of "identified client," and will that be appropriate? The "identified client" is the person labeled with a psychiatric diagnosis because insurance does not cover marriage or family counseling.

Which Professional?

Next comes the question of whom to call for professional help. Here again, there are many choices. Should it be a friend or a stranger? Should recommendations be sought? Would a colleague to whom clients are referred be a good choice? Should the first contact be a professional call, or a meeting, lunch, or other situation where the topic can be brought up only when a positive response is assured? What if the call is made and the answer is that the colleague is not taking on more clients, or does not think he or she could work with the therapist on that issue, or doesn't want to change the professional or referral relationship to a client relationship? In short, the caller is rejected. What are the options? More importantly, what assistance will the therapist called give in helping to find someone else?

Booking the First Appointment

Next, evaluate the issues brought up by the actual scheduling of an appointment. What will the appointment needs be—morning, afternoon, evening, before or after client hours, or on a different day? How flexible does the therapist seem to be in meeting the needs for appointment times, and how much flexibility is needed? Is there a wait of more than a week to see the therapist? Can appointments be as frequent as needed? What about emergency sessions? Should the appointment be made directly with the therapist, through a secretary, or a combination of the two? If there is a secretary, how informed does that secretary seem to be? Does the therapist use an answering service or answering machine, and if so, what feelings does that bring up? How long does it take to get a return call?

The Therapist's Office

Is there an area where clients can wait before an appointment, and if so, what effect does its appearance have? Is it neat, clean, and comfortable? If it's a group practice, are there other clients waiting to see other therapists? Would a private entrance alleviate any embarrassment in being there? Does it make a difference? Why? Are there forms to fill out while waiting, and if so what are they, when should they be filled out, where are they located, and what is their purpose?

The Need for Privacy

The concern for privacy is always an important factor in selecting a therapist. Clients should always feel that their privacy will be protected. Consequently, how soundproof is the office space? Does the entrance design take into consideration the needs of privacy when clients enter or leave the office? Does the therapist seem to be sensitive to privacy issues in the waiting area and in phone conversations?

On the personal side, how private should the therapy be for a therapist-turned-client? What type of response should be given when colleagues or clients ask why the practitioner is seeing a therapist? In short, what are the concerns for privacy and why?

When a therapist becomes a client and experiences the world of therapy as a struggling human being, with all the needs and sensibilities, how aware does the therapist become? Going through the process allows the therapist to sit on the other side of the couch—to see, experience, and judge what being a client means. If the only benefit received from a few sessions is some insight into making clients more comfortable, improving the professional image, and setting a more productive environment for therapy, then a great deal has been gained. As a group, therapists are no different from the public they serve. Therapists talk about improving their professional image; they fight for recognition, proclaim to the public that therapy helps to make people's lives fuller and richer, yet some are still fearful of their own profession.

TEN STEPS TO SUCCESSFUL START-UP

There are 10 essential steps for starting a small business. These steps are not cure-alls; they are simply sound, basic ideas for creating a successful small business and keeping it successful. They are just as relevant to the mental health professional in private practice as they are to any other small businessperson, and can be tailored to meet therapists' needs.

1. The private practitioner must be a technician and a manager.

If a practice is to grow and be successful, the therapist must be a technician, an expert in the field. This does not mean the therapist must be a national expert, just knowledgeable and having something unique to offer. At the same time therapists will have to do some things they may not really enjoy, such as marketing the practice. Marketing efforts will bring clients to the door and boost the success of the practice.

Private practitioners must also be the managers of the practice. As the practice expands and people are employed, a spectrum of new problems and issues will arise. The therapist must learn about management techniques and become the best manager possible. The ultimate success of a practice will be based on expansion and the proper utilization of other people.

2. The private practitioner must know the competition.

In private practice, competition is a fact of life. This can be a very positive thing, keeping therapists alert to the needs of people in the area and keeping them from getting stale. It also means that other practitioners' ads in the newspapers, yellow pages, and other advertising need to be evaluated to see how their marketing is being done. Practitioners must keep up on the latest trends and marketing ideas, comparing their practice to that of doctors, lawyers, dentists, chiropractors, and other professionals. The therapist must see how others are marketing themselves. Often marketing techniques can be adapted from other professions. The more knowledgeable the practitioner is about what is happening in the field of expertise and with the competition, the more successful the practice will be.

3. Private practitioners must constantly evaluate the business, the market, and themselves.

Being in private practice does not provide an opportunity to sit back and let things take their course. Private practitioners must continue to learn about the people they serve, about the theory of their work, and about business trends, but most of all, therapists must stay in touch with themselves. They must set aside time to ask themselves, "How well am I doing in my practice? How well do I serve my clients?" If a therapist does not see as many clients as desired, or if they do not keep coming back, it is not because of the competition. Therapists should be willing to look at their own weaknesses and constantly try to overcome them. Being in private practice means going to even more workshops, conferences, and professional meetings than when working for someone else. To give the best possible service to the community, private practitioners must constantly assess themselves.

4. The private practice *is* the practitioner; there should be pride in it.

A private practice is a business. The customers are the clients, and the physicians, lawyers, and other professionals who refer to the practice. The product is the therapy, consultation, or training provided. If therapists feel strongly enough about the services they provide to risk their livelihood, their income, and their personal well-being, they should make their practice something of which to be proud. When a practice is opened, professional and financial risks are taken. There must be pride of ownership. The practitioner's confidence will build the basic foundation for the practice.

5. Know the customers' needs and how to meet them.

Private practitioners must be able to tell who the clients and referral sources are, and they must be able to convince them of the value of their product. Advertising is critical in private practice. Word of mouth simply will not bring in the volume of clients needed to give a practice a strong financial base.

Remember that advertising is not just buying space in the yellow pages or mailing out a practice newsletter. To get full value from advertising, there must be good follow-through once the initial contact is made. An advertising program needs to be multifaceted, tailored to the clients, and predicated on providing an excellent service.

6. The business plan is the blueprint of success.

A good business plan is a wonderful achievement. It must be firm and flexible, based on fact and tempered with optimism. It must effectively deal with existing circumstances, but be able to adjust to change. New needs in the community and new changes in the marketplace may alter the original direction of the practice. A successful private practice is always adapting to needs and changes. A business plan should be updated on a regular basis so both the cash flow and promotional efforts can be determined. A good business plan should take into consideration both long-term and short-term cash flow patterns and capitalization based on normal fluctuations in a practice. For example, for some practices the Christmas season is a very slow time, whereas for others the stress of holidays brings in large numbers of clients.

7. The solo practitioner is not alone.

Going into private practice means being willing to work day and night, whether the practice is set up as a partnership or a sole proprietorship. Even though the final responsibility rests on the therapist's shoulders, he or she does not need to feel alone. Help of many kinds is available from individuals and organizations, whether it's meeting a colleague for breakfast as an emotional pick-me-up, or attending a tax seminar at the chamber of commerce. A therapist must decide what kind of help is needed, ask for it, and be ready and willing to accept the advice received.

8. Select staff carefully.

Employees reflect their employer's business. Treat them well and reward them for good work. As the practice grows, inevitably secretarial and other clerical help will be needed. Take a long-term view of the practice. Make it an attractive place to work, with good benefits and excellent human relations. If the receptionist or secretary is happy, it will show. The secretary will work diligently to make the practice successful. Keep the support staff involved, keep them stimulated, and believe in them.

9. Read the newspaper daily.

The practitioner should read the newspaper every day, especially the financial pages, to keep up to date. One should look at the big picture and be prepared for what lies ahead. This is one aspect of private practice that practitioners tend to overlook. Local newspapers are full of small items that can have dramatic effects on a business. For example, perhaps an area close to the office has been rezoned to allow increased multifamily units. Knowing this in advance may stimulate tailoring of marketing for that area, because the new housing may contain many clients who could use the services of the practice. Or the local school district may be planning to start a drug awareness or family awareness program. An expert in that area could approach the school and seek some ongoing contact on a planning or advisory committee, thus enhancing visibility in the community.

Reading the financial pages also gives information about major national employers and trends in the economy. Although many practices try to build themselves on the third-party reimbursement model, clients still need to be able to pay their percentage of the fee. Knowing that a company may be planning a large layoff may suggest some free seminars or workshops on job change or transition, giving the aware therapists an edge on their colleagues.

10. Join local, state, and national professional organizations.

A therapist must be actively involved in professional associations. Private practitioners should lead the way in professional organizations. It is reasonable to expect that the use of private mental health services will increase, and that there will be an increased need for legal and ethical guidelines and for active professional growth and improvement. Being involved does more than increase the professional image; it ensures being aware of change in the professional organization.

Success in business is not a mystery; it's an awareness based on sound principles. Incorporating these principles into every facet of a practice will increase the chances for success, and each success increases the probability of success for all private practitioners.

GOAL SETTING

A successful practice will require successful goal setting. Individuals who have set up successful private practices are those who have established personal and financial goals. These people seem to be satisfied with their personal and financial situation; they have a clear path to success. The ability to set goals becomes directly related to the chances of success in private practice. In private practice the therapists are the only ones influencing and controlling their personal and financial destinies. Unless the therapist has a clear idea of what it means to achieve success, the practice will never fulfill personal and financial needs.

How to Set Goals

It seems strange to have a section about how to set goals in a book written for clinicians who spend their time helping clients establish goals. Goal setting is critical for the private practitioner. Once a goal has been set, it should be written down to make a firmer impression on the mind. It's easy to set a goal mentally, but it's only when it is written down on paper that it becomes a constant reminder of the commitment to meet that goal. Reviewing goals on a regular basis, giving a time line for accomplishing the goals, and reviewing the progress made is necessary in developing a successful private practice. Just establishing a goal is useless. There needs to be an action plan to accompany the goal. It is important not to discuss goals with others too soon. Too often private practitioners set unrealistic goals for their practice and tell everyone what they are going to do. Unrealistic goals are unattainable, and broadcasting them leads to a failure cycle both for the practitioner and the clients. To avoid this, the practitioner needs to establish a set of goals that are attainable (both emotionally and physically), write them down, review them periodically, and **then** share these realistic goals with others.

The Role of Excuses

The best way to approach opening a private practice is to leave the word "excuses" out of the vocabulary. There can be no excuses for what is done in private practice, only learning experiences. Each attempt to establish a practice, market the practice, deal with a new client population, or try out a new technique with clients is a learning experience. The goal setter is the only one who can judge a failure or turn an excuse into a failure. A constant evaluation of goals is necessary. The goal setter needs to ask about the realistic nature of the goals and the expectations toward completing them, and when a goal is not achieved, look at it not as a failure but as a learning experience. Many opportunities will not measure up to expectations. Setbacks are normal and natural. They are also part of the goal-setting process. If one can understand that the field of private practice is not an exact science, it becomes possible to turn setbacks into advantages. Each setback I have experienced in my private practice has prompted me to do a self-examination focusing on the different aspects of the unmet goal and to consider if these were areas in which I needed improvement or if they were out of my control. It is often said that failure contains the seeds of greater opportunities. The essence of a goal-setting process is to set specific, realistic goals for a practice. Goals should be established for weekly, monthly, and yearly time frames and reviewed regularly. As each goal is achieved, success in the practice will increase.

SUMMARY

It is important to know why one is going into private practice, to understand the rationale for it, and to be able to assess in clear terms what a private practice is and why a private practice fails. The future directions of private practice are many. There will be many changes over the next few years in the way practices are developed and in the types of individuals going into private practice as many of the ethical and legal guidelines are reshaped. Key factors need to be considered—such as what type of clinical skills are needed, the role of supervision, the need to be a risk taker, the emotional investment that will be required, and financial stability—before taking the plunge to open a private practice. The need to understand one's own financial needs and live within them are also primary considerations before opening the door. The decision of whether a private practice should be a limited or a full-time practice and what the returns are is critical at the outset. Most people beginning private practice choose to start on a limited basis. Without clear goals and direction as to when the practice will become full-time, it can become a frustrating and ultimately a disappointing experience. The emotional investment in private practice is extremely significant and must be taken into account. The need to have worked through one's own wants and fears as well as deciding how much work is possible must be addressed, and the therapist is the only person who can make those decisions.

The issue of whether one should have been in therapy before going into private practice is a question that will be debated in many sectors of the professional community. But if nothing else, one's going into private practice without ever having been a client in a therapeutic process limits both one's own understanding of what it takes for a client to come for therapy as well as the potential learning experience of observing another practitioner run a private practice. The realization that success depends on clear steps and actions of the practitioner is vital as each clinician begins the process of deciding whether to go into private practice. A private practice is basically no different than any other type of business venture in that the practitioner is basically supplying a product and service to the public for a specified fee. Knowing the specific steps to take to accomplish that enhances the success of a practice. Understanding that a practice will need goals and that these goals will need to be established at specific intervals, reviewed, and changed will become the lifeblood of a successful practice.

SECTION TWO

The Business Aspects of a Private Practice

THE NEED FOR A BUSINESS TEAM

The key ingredients in setting up a private practice are recognizing one's limitations in business skills and understanding that a private practice is a small business. Most people in private practice don't realize they are running a small business, consequently they don't observe the normal business practices that would be expected if they were opening a grocery store, clothing store, or any other type of business.

There are three major players on the business team: an accountant, a lawyer, and a banker. No one should go into business today without consulting an accountant to make sure that proper business procedures are in place. Equally, no one should enter any type of small business, especially a private practice, without consulting a lawyer to ensure that legal safeguards and responsibilities have been met. In private practice as in any other business there will be times of inconsistent cash flow. A business banker can help prepare for those times and plan accordingly.

Because I had a business background, when I began my private practice I was aware of the importance of these three people. Luckily, throughout the years, I made the correct decision to involve them and form what I call "a business team." Over time, they have proven to be very effective and helpful.

Your Accountant and You

How important is an accountant to the success and growth of the new private practice? The best answer to that is another question: What degree of success is desired and how much growth is anticipated? If the practitioner wants to maintain a limited practice and doesn't plan to make a living from the practice, an accountant will be needed only at tax time. On the other hand, if making a full-time living from the practice or diversifying into

31

other products and services is anticipated, then an accountant is vital.

An accountant can save a client time, energy, and money by helping to give the direction and self-confidence needed to manage and expand the practice. A knowledgeable accountant has the training to advise on taxes, financing, bookkeeping, and a wide array of financial systems.

What to Look for in an Accountant

In my opinion, the ideal accountant has these top seven characteristics, listed in order of importance:

- has the proper credentials (is a CPA);
- completes tasks on time; specializes in health-related businesses;
- is able to assist in general business planning;
- is located in the same community as the practice;
- is knowledgeable about local banking personnel; and
- has an affordable fee.

These characteristics are equally important whether the business in question is a counseling or consulting practice. Time is critical in making business decisions, making expert help essential.

Finding an Accountant

As with any other professional service group, word of mouth is the prime source of referral for accountants. Colleagues and business friends should be willing to supply the names of their accountants, which provides a list of possible candidates. The practitioner should shop around and not choose an accountant just because a friend uses the same one; each client should establish a relationship of his or her own with the accountant, making candor and confidence the cornerstones of that relationship. The accountant should become a trusted advisor and a vital member of the management team.

The Interview

If an accountant is interested in working with the practitioner, an initial meeting should be set where needs can be outlined and a mutual decision can be made whether to work together or not. Three questions need to be answered at this initial meeting:

- What kind of services does the accountant perform?

- What is the quality of those services?
- What is the fee structure?

Services

Most accounting firms have printed material to explain their services, and the accountant should be able to elaborate if there is any question about any area. The prospective client's needs will be based on the list developed prior to this meeting, but a few key areas of interest to remember for a mental health practitioner are: What does the accountant see as the role regarding bank financing, buying and leasing property, financial planning, and the preparation of business plans?

Quality

One of the most valued characteristics in an accountant is the ability to complete tasks on time. Practitioners' needs will be varied, but they should have a clear idea about their tax preparation schedule and completion of accounting projects. A list of the accountant's clients should be available as references and the practitioner should call these clients. The practitioner should evaluate all the written material, or lack of it, offered by the accountant. The attention to detail shown in the accountant's advertising brochures and other written material will give an idea of the attention to detail in general.

Fee

Some accountants charge by the hour or partial hour; others use a retainer system. The accountant should be able to explain clearly how the fees for services are assessed. Most accountants have standard *understanding of arrangements* contracts that set forth the client's responsibility, the accountant's responsibility, and what the financial arrangement will be. Overall, accountants' fees are similar to those charged by other professionals, ranging from $50.00 to $125.00 per hour.

Contracting

Once an accountant has been selected, a second meeting should be set to discuss specific needs. At that meeting, the accountant's time clock will be running and a fee will be charged. It is wise to bring a written proposal explaining the services needed, such as:

- bank financing to expand the practice;
- evaluation of tax liabilities with strategies to lower them;

- changing the business structure of the practice; and
- purchasing a computer and developing a better billing and accounting system.

The last 3 years' tax returns should be taken to that second meeting, as well as written material about the practice, training, consulting, or products, and the present cash flow situation (accounting sheets and checking ledger). These documents will give the accountant the information to provide the services needed, and will give a complete picture of the health of the practice.

Ongoing Update

The accountant will rapidly become a valuable member of the team. To increase the involvement and make it as efficient as possible, the therapist should provide a monthly report listing the billable income, actual income, expenses, and any new short-term or long-term debt. A meeting should be held every few months to review the practice and business plan. The more aware the accountant is, the better the service will be and the more effective the tax planning will be.

How to Choose an Attorney and What to Expect

A large number of private practitioners have never consulted an attorney despite the many legal ramifications of being in private practice. I was very lucky when I started my practice because one of the first things I did after hiring my accountant was to ask his advice in finding a lawyer who would also work with me. There have been many times that I have received the benefits of having an attorney on retainer, able to advise me at a moment's notice if I were beginning to get into some kind of legal difficulty. A private practice is a small business and must adhere to certain laws and requirements of the local community, the state, the nation, and professional organizations.

An attorney is a legal representative, an advisor, a sounding board, and a mentor as the practice grows, expands, or decreases. I have sought the advice of my attorney often over the years. For example, bringing partners into my practice, buying property, starting new business ventures, ending business ventures or selling property, or decreasing the number of my associates—all have been occasions to consult my attorney. Because of my attorney's advice, I have avoided legal hassles that would have cost me time, money, and frustration.

Things to Have a Lawyer Check Out in the Beginning

When considering setting up a private practice, it is worth spending the money for an initial consultation and review of the proposed practice. If the practice is already open, it is not too late to select an attorney for a consultation and review of the existing practice. Here are some specifics to discuss:

Right to Practice

Each state has unique requirements as to what may be done in the scope of a private practice. There are also ethical guidelines of the various professional organizations. In addition, there are understandings of competence. Having a license does not give a person the right to practice, nor does the lack of a license exclude a person from practicing.

Scope of Practice

States have different laws for the different professional groups. There may be laws covering psychiatrists, psychologists, mental health counselors, psychiatric nurses, and social workers. Each law is written for a specific group of professionals and usually has a section on rights of practice or scope of practice.

Most professionals simply look at the law as it relates to their particular profession, not in relation to the other licensed professionals in their state. It is important for an attorney to make sure that what a therapist does in a practice is directly covered by the particular licensing law and is not in conflict with another licensing law. For example, a licensing law may state that a certain professional has the right to diagnose. Another licensing law for a different professional may state that this particular professional does not have the right to diagnose. If the question of insurance reimbursement arises, and the professional enters a diagnosis on the form, there may be a conflict between the law governing the therapist and the other licensing law because that law did not give the right to diagnose. It could then be interpreted that the therapist might be acting in the disguise of a different professional and violating the other professionals' licensing law. Some states have no licensing of a particular professional entity. Consequently, the question is raised as to whether the practice may be opened or not. An attorney reading over each of the laws will be able to advise what professional designation may be used and the types of therapy that may be offered in the practice that are not in conflict with another existing law. This will ensure that what the therapist does in practice is directly covered by the licensing law and is not in conflict with another licensing law.

Ethics

Each professional organization has developed a certain code of ethics. In most cases a practitioner gives this code of ethics a cursory reading upon joining a professional organization, and that's as far as it goes. It is wise to have an attorney review the professional ethical guidelines and discuss any gray areas in relationship to the existing state laws to gain specific knowledge of how to interpret the guidelines that must be followed.

Understanding of Competence

When a private practitioner is sued, certain assumptions will be made in a court of law that the practitioner's attorney will attempt to defend. Those assumptions will involve competence. Often private practitioners operate without proper training or expertise with certain client problems, assuming that because they hold a license and the license implies that they can practice, that will be adequate defense in a court of law. As an example, part of my own background is in sex counseling; consequently, I have joined the appropriate national professional organization, and adhere to its training and ethical standards.

I watch a number of people in my state offer sex counseling who do not belong to the appropriate professional organization and infrequently see clients on the issues of sex. These people assume that because they hold a license and a certain professional title, they are not excluded from practicing sex counseling. They feel they are protected and that what they do in therapy is within the scope of the practice. The practitioner who does not belong to, or hold certification in, an area where a standard does exist, may find his or her professional competence questioned. The difficulty is that when one is in front of a judge and jury, the major question that will be asked is in the area of competence.

Competence is judged by academic training, clinical training, and ongoing professional development relevant to a particular area. I have talked with professionals who have said that they adhere to a certain theoretical background of working with people and because of that theoretical background, they obviously can handle any type of client problem. Defending that in a court of law is almost impossible. A jury and a judge may not understand the complexities of theoretical abstractions such as theories of counseling or therapy; therefore, they may be confused in attempting to understand whether a practitioner is, in fact, competent to practice. It is important to discuss with an attorney the particular types of clients that would be seen in the practice, what experience the practitioner has had in working with such clients, and how that would be defensible in a court of law.

Clinical Notes

One of the things I realized early in my practice that has proven to be important was that the type of notes I had been taking for training and supervision were not the kind of notes that would be in the best interests of a client or myself in a court of law.

The therapist should take a de-identified sample of clinical notes to an attorney for review. The attorney should be asked to highlight any part of those notes that could be interpreted as self-incriminating for either the practitioner or the client if a suit were filed. Most private practitioners do not understand that clinical notes become both the best defense of a practice as well as the best offense for prosecuting attorneys. Clinical notes are totally available in a court of law. A judge can make them public to the press or anyone else who should want to see them.

It is extremely important that clinical notes be solely clinical and nonbiased, nonsexist, nonjudgmental, and nonincriminating for both the client and the practitioner. An attorney should be able to review a practitioner's notes and give specific guidelines as to what would be viewed as acceptable in a court of law. The type of clinical notes taken for training or supervision will not be the type of notes the attorney will advise as being appropriate before a court of law.

Filing Documents

To open a private practice, a number of documents must be filed and licenses must be obtained. One of the first things to check is the name of the practice. Business names are usually filed with the state for a nominal fee, and the owner has an exclusive right to that name. When I set up my counseling center, I wanted simply to call it "Counseling Center." When I checked that name, I found I could not use it. Another organization already was using the name "Counseling Center." So I filed the name, "Southern Maine Counseling Center," and was in compliance with the law.

Within each state and city, various other licenses must be obtained. In many local communities vendors' licenses or county licenses are issued to each business. A therapist shouldn't underestimate the need to comply with these local ordinances. A case in point is a woman who was in practice as a Jungian analyst. She had been in a successful practice for 14 years, and one day was presented with a "cease and desist" order from her local sheriff because she had neglected to pay a $5.00 fee. In her local parish, a fee was required to do business. It didn't make any difference if the business were a restaurant, psychotherapy office, or whatever. There was a $5.00 filing fee. Someone told the local commissioners that she did not have a proper license to be in business. A subpoena was served and she was told that she could not practice her business until she had gone to court. It took her 30 days to get to court. During that time she was not allowed to see any clients or practice her business in any way, all because of a $5.00 filing fee. It's a good idea to consult with an attorney to find out whether any fees or licenses in addition to the license to practice may be necessary.

Legal Implications of Fee and Fee Structure

Discussing with an attorney exactly what can or cannot be done with a fee in exchange for services may save untold hours if a complication occurs. Most therapists I have talked with have just assumed that they can decide arbitrarily what fee to charge clients, to collect the fee or not, to barter, to reduce the fee, and to bill the insurance company as well. A fee is a legal contract between the therapist and a client and, if reimbursement is involved, the legal contract includes the insurance company also. There are certain guidelines and principles that must be followed to avoid committing fraud or theft by deception. The therapist must discuss the fee with an attorney to learn what it means to have a sliding scale, what it means to collect fees directly from clients, what the billing process means, and what the rights of collection are. Therapists who don't like to collect the money just assume that a client will pay. When a client doesn't pay, or if the client doesn't show up, what are the legal rights of collection? Can that be turned over to a collection agency? Can a client be taken to small claims court? An attorney can explain specifically what rights exist in these areas.

Business Structures

Often people begin private practice either by themselves as a sole proprietorship, or as some kind of quasi partnership. There have been a number of incidences of individuals who never considered themselves to be in a partnership because they had no written document, and they just assumed that because they had no written agreement, they did not have to take legal responsibility for the other person's actions. However, in most states, a legal document in fact provides protection. By not having one, the therapist in a "loose" partnership can be held responsible if a legal or ethical problem should arise from the other person's practice.

What are the implications of a sole proprietorship? Many people open private practice as sole practitioners but call themselves "John Jones Associates," or "John Jones Counseling Center," when it is, in fact, a solo practice. This may or may not be legal. The terms "associates" and "center" imply more than one therapist and may constitute fraud. The public may incorrectly assume that the practice has more than one therapist. It is important to examine the state's business structures with an attorney before materials are printed and marketing begins in order to save untold embarrassment and legal problems later.

Leasing Space

Most private practitioners will rent space. Many just assume that if a landlord gives them a lease and it makes some sense and seems fairly simple, they should sign it. A lease is a legal document with certain requirements for a specified time, possibly years. An attorney can read the lease and explain the lessee's rights, the lessor's rights, how the lease can be broken, and if the space can be sublet. Leases generally protect the lessor.

Review of Liability Requirements

Many private practitioners assume that a professional liability policy from a professional organization is adequate coverage, without checking that assumption. Each organization negotiates a policy based on what it assumes its members need. The difficulty is that professional liability policies vary from one professional organization to another. It is also important to remember that the professional liability policy protects the insurance company.

The therapist needs to review the various professional liability policies available with an attorney. Having additional liability policies would be wise, such as bodily injury, workers' compensation, and disability. Each one of these policies has certain legal requirements also, and an attorney can help to ensure there is complete coverage and keep the costs down. Liability suits for bodily injury by a client or employee are common.

Other Ways to Use an Attorney

As a practice grows, the practitioner may want to bring in associates or form a corporation or partnership. The documentation for those different entities is extremely important and should be handled by an attorney. Making an assumption that two people sharing office space is not a partnership is dangerous. All arrangements should be in writing. It is not unusual to hear of good professional friendships being dissolved and unprofessional comments being made in the community when two therapists who were coleading groups and workshops decided to break up over money issues. It is always better, when entering any kind of arrangement involving finances, to draw up some kind of simple, clearly written document explaining the rights and responsibilities of both parties.

Purchasing Property

As a practice grows and the practitioner's private life grows, often either a home, office building, or a condominium will be purchased. It's extremely important to have the attorney for the practice review the documentation for the home purchase also, and act as the legal representative in negotiations, ensuring that both the practice and personal assets are adequately protected. The mortgage document is the lifeblood and strength of that major investment. Having an attorney review the documentation will protect the investment. If the purchase is an office building or condominium, it is especially important to have an attorney involved. Dealing with the bank about commercial use is always difficult, and negotiating is part of the process. The therapist must not depend on a real estate agent to act in his or her behalf.

Requirements of Hiring Employees or Subcontractors

Each state has requirements regarding employees and subcontractors. If a practitioner has someone doing typing or clerical work, can that person be considered a subcontractor rather than an employee? If someone coleads groups with the practitioner, is that person a subcontractor or a partner? Consulting with an attorney before becoming involved in a working relationship with any other person is extremely important to delineate the arrangement between the two parties and prevent potential problems. It's usually advisable to have someone considered a subcontractor versus an employee for services. There are both IRS requirements and state law requirements for employees (see "Who's an Employee?" later in this section for more information). As an example, in Maine, if an employee is hired for more than 32 hours, the employer must make health insurance available to that employee. That can be costly, but not knowing that can cost more and cause legal complications later.

Privileged Communication

Privileged communication is a right extended by the legislature in each state. However, a therapist cannot assume that he or she has privileged communication. Often certain exclusions or other laws supersede privileged communication. A practitioner must know in detail what the state requirements are regarding privileged communication before saying to a client, "What you say in my office will be held in confidence." When the right to privileged communication is challenged, an attorney who has been working with the practitioner since the inception of the practice will have already advised the practitioner beforehand, saving time and money.

A number of times I have been contacted by attorneys wanting information regarding clients. These attorneys may have been involved in divorce situations or injury cases, and were attempting to gather as much information as possible to represent the client. It has always been my policy to refer all questions about my records to my attorney first. It has also been my policy not to testify in any court hearings regarding divorce settlements. When I am contacted by an attorney, I do not personally respond. I simply contact my attorney and have him respond. In most cases, we have been successful in preventing my notes from being released.

Preparation for Court: Expert Witness

Therapists are perceived as experts in a given field and may be asked to present testimony in court. What is involved in being considered an expert witness? An expert witness must be able to convince the judge that he or she is indeed an expert in order to collect the fee. The testimony presented to a jury must be believable. Consulting an attorney prior to offering services as an expert witness is advisable. Becoming an expert witness can be a lucrative part of a practice if done correctly.

When Rights Are Questioned

Legal disputes will undoubtedly arise between the practitioner and the government, landlords, banks, or licensing boards. An attorney who is familiar with the practitioner can be asked to serve as the middle person. Many times these disputes can be settled fairly quickly and easily if an attorney is involved, mostly because the attorney will know what legal standing the agency, landlord, or licensing board actually has.

Because of the complicated licensing laws in different states and the importance of the license in a practice, anytime a licensing board has a question, the practitioner's attorney should be contacted immediately for advice before answering questions from the licensing board. The license is a critical part of a practice and the practitioner should always know what the legal standing is.

Tax and Estate Issues

An attorney should be available to advise the practitioner regarding tax laws and tax requirements. A will and some kind of estate planning is also advisable. An estate is not only the assets owned but the liabilities accrued. Having a will and keeping it updated is advisable because the stability of the therapist's practice and family is based on good documentation of all legal transactions involving the therapist. It's been my policy that all written contracts, all leases, and all purchase agreements are always reviewed by my attorney first, and he keeps copies in his office. If there is ever a dispute or question, my attorney has the necessary information at hand. If I should die unexpectedly my attorney has all the information that he needs to administer my estate properly.

How to Find an Attorney

I have been asked many times, "How do I find an attorney?" Finding an attorney is similar to finding an accountant. First ask the other members of the team—the accountant and the banker. Whom do they use as attorneys? What attorneys in town do they recommend? Do they know any attorneys who handle similar private practices?

Often the working relationship between the practitioner's accountant and attorney is a delicate balance. They are both looking out for the practitioner's best interests and it helps if they know each other. "Should I have both, or should I have one?" is a question I am often asked. The answer to that is simply, "Two heads are better than one." It has been my experience that having a separate attorney and a separate accountant allows me to consult with each separately and get two opinions. I can then make the decision that is in my best interest.

Another way of finding an attorney is to ask professionals in other health care fields. Doctors, dentists, chiropractors, and other health care professionals usually have attorneys.

Qualifications an Attorney Should Have

It is my opinion that the best attorney is one who is part of a large firm. I believe in specialization, and I think that in the counseling profession, one person cannot know everything there is to know about treating clients. I feel the same way about law. It has been my experience that having an attorney who is part of a large firm makes a variety of expertise available. For example, my attorney does not do my estate planning, but there is another attorney in the firm who handles that task. When a family member was injured in a car accident, we learned that my attorney was not the appropriate one to handle the legal work resulting from the accident for he does not specialize in that type of litigation. In publishing a newsletter, *Private Practice News*, issues of copyright have arisen. I was able to consult an attorney in the firm who handled copyright documentation and knew what specific things needed to be done. An attorney who is part of a firm will provide access to not only that personal attorney's expertise, but the expertise of all the colleagues in the firm.

Additionally, the attorney should have a thorough understanding of the legal needs of professionals in private practice, and the nature of private practice itself. It is not in the private practitioner's best interests to have to educate an attorney about those facts. For example, in bringing clinical notes to an attorney for review, if the attorney has never taken anyone into court over mental health services and has no idea of the concept of notetaking, then valuable time will be spent educating that attorney. However, if the attorney has handled that kind of litigation as either a defender or prosecutor, many of the mental health practitioner's questions will be within the attorney's area of expertise.

Personal Feelings

The attorney is going to become a valuable member of the team, and the skilled clinician and interviewer should feel totally comfortable with the answers the attorney gives. The attorney should be willing to talk, have time available, and instill confidence and trust in the potential client. A good question to ask after interviewing an attorney as a potential team member for a private practice is, "If this person were representing me in court, would I be favorably impressed with the professionalism, appearance, and actions?" I remember that early in my career I used an attorney with whom I felt comfortable and liked very much. Later on, in a court dispute as he was representing us on an issue, I realized that his demeanor was not effective in the courtroom. Consequently, he was not able to defend us in the court the way we had wanted. It's extremely important to judge the attorney as an active professional, not just as a friend and someone who gives comfortable advice.

Fee

When the attorney team member has been selected, often a retainer will be requested. This will be a certain amount of money in advance that will be credited to an account. Once the retainer is depleted, fees for services will be billed as they accrue. Attorneys' fees are high, but so are mental health fees. Attorneys have many costs similar to those of mental health professionals, such as malpractice insurance and secretarial costs. I'm appalled when I hear that therapists are upset when they think about paying an attorney $75 to $100 an hour and then turn around and feel very comfortable charging clients the same amount. Basically the fee buys the time of a skilled professional. And as with all professionals, the fee reflects what the marketplace will bear and the expertise of the professional. The therapist should take the time to look for the best attorney who meets the criteria before opening a private practice.

Selecting a Banker

The final member of the private practice team is the banker. People have asked, "Dan, I understand about an accountant; I understand about a lawyer; but I don't see the need for a banker. I don't want to borrow any money." That's a major mistake. Any new business is going to have cash flow problems from time to time. A new business must have a firm financial standing in the beginning to sustain its development and survive the crucial first few years. It is possible and probable that the first year's gross income of a full-time private practice will be over $50,000, and over $100,000 the second and third years. These figures may be higher in different parts of the country depending on the fees charged, but I offer them as an average. It is wise to separate the personal financial history from the business financial history. Choosing a bank to work with and to help establish a sound financial base is not the same as opening an account at the branch nearest the office. It is a process.

Choosing a Bank

Banks are set up with two different divisions; one handles consumer accounts and loans and the other handles business accounts. The banker who handles the practitioner's personal and family transactions is not the banker for the practitioner's private practice. What is needed is a commercial loan officer. If the practitioner's local personal bank cannot help or if the practitioner doesn't have a personal banker and if a referral is needed, ask the accountant to recommend a commercial loan officer whose bank is aggressive in the marketplace. Banks are like any other industry in that their areas of interest vary. Some specialize in various types of commercial transactions, but the new private practitioner should look for a bank that traditionally funds small businesses.

Once two or three banks have been selected, preliminary meetings should be scheduled with a representative of each. This meeting should focus on the type of practice the therapist has and the therapist's particular interest. The therapist should try to ascertain the bank's philosophy toward dealing with a small mental health practice.

After that initial meeting, if it seems that one of the banks is interested in a working relationship, a second meeting should be set to go over profit and loss statements, projections, and net worth statements, along with materials about the practice such as brochures and press releases. The more professional the business package is, and the more clearly it is presented to the bank, the better are the chances in negotiating the type of arrangement desired. Bankers are professionals and time is valuable to them; a presentation that is well thought-out, in both the written and oral aspects, will go a long way toward expediting the banking relationship.

Format for the Meeting

Begin the meeting with a thorough explanation of the materials regarding the practice. Allow time for the banker to ask questions and probe the strength of the practice. When the banker has a thorough understanding of the practice, present specific needs.

Business Needs

The first need is to establish a business checking account and money market savings account. The business checking account will usually be a noninterest-bearing account and, if a minimum balance is maintained, a nonservice charge account. This account establishes a relationship with the bank. The money market savings account will afford a way to move cash above the minimum to an interest-bearing situation.

The next item is a bank credit card to be used in tracking travel, entertainment, supplies, and additional purchases. At least a $3,000 credit line should be available, but any amount above that would be helpful. This MasterCard or Visa will be used exclusively for the practice, and will again allow the bank to have a clear picture of the practice's expenses.

I do not recommend an American Express or Diners' Club card because of the higher yearly fee and the inability to spread payments over several months if needed. These bank credit cards have no connection with a local bank, and consequently no credit history advantage.

The cornerstone of the small businessperson's relationship with the bank is a commercial loan. Many people beginning a small business are reluctant to borrow, especially if, through savings or other means, they have enough capital on hand to start the business themselves. There are, however, considerable advantages to borrowing instead of using savings for financing. I will explain a few advantages, but it should be noted that the decision to start a practice and raise the needed capital should be made only after consulting many advisors. Borrowing the needed capital or taking it from savings should be discussed thoroughly with a financial advisor or accountant.

Why Borrow?

As an example, consider a mental health counselor with $10,000 in savings who wants to start a private practice. That $10,000 could be used to buy equipment, lease an office, and make up the shortfall before client income meets all the monetary needs, but it would leave the counselor with nothing for emergencies. If the practice should fail there would be no savings and no liquidity. Compare this situation with one where the practitioner borrows $10,000, leaving the $10,000 savings in the bank. The furniture and equipment bought with the $10,000 become collateral for the loan and the practitioner is free, in an emergency, to use the savings. Although payments must be made on the borrowed money, these payments are extended over time. In this case, even if the business fails, the practitioner is not immediately left without assets—the savings. If desired, the $10,000 savings can be used to pay off the rest of the loan, or time pay-

end of the year, sole proprietors must file a tax form known as "Schedule C." This form will be used to list all income of the practice and deductions for all expenses. The profits or losses from the business are then transferred over to the therapist's 1040 form and taxes are calculated. If the therapist is not working at any other job where a paycheck is received and withholding taxes are deducted, the entire withholding amount will be taken from the earnings of the sole proprietorship. If a sole proprietorship loses money the first year, that loss will be subtracted from any other income, including any spousal income, and taxes will be calculated accordingly.

The bookkeeping and record keeping for a sole proprietorship are minimal. They are not as complicated as they are in a corporation or a partnership, because basically the sole proprietor and the business are one and the same. A general ledger system is usually adequate for a sole proprietorship. A general ledger system consists of a checkbook and a page for posting debits and credits.

The records kept in a sole proprietorship are uncomplicated; the legal costs and accounting costs are not great, and basically the paperwork is simple. Clients are seen, fees are collected and deposited in a checking account, and bills are paid. It's important to note that all fees collected **must** be kept separate from personal funds. All expenses **must** be paid out of a checking account specifically used for the practice. If a therapist doesn't keep separate accurate records, an IRS audit could be a nightmare. Some states require a separate income tax form on the business, and an accountant will be able to ensure that any other forms are properly filed.

Many private practitioners choose to have a sole proprietorship because it is not very complicated, and they are in total control of their practice. An accountant will know what kind of books and records need to be kept. In most cases a sole proprietorship will earn less than $100,000 a year.

Partnerships

As a marriage counselor, I constantly see people caught up in the human struggle to remain separate, but together. I often help people understand the traumatic emotional and financial consequences of a marriage gone bad. A partnership can be like a marriage. It can be the best business move of your career, bringing the financial and personal health desired, or it can be the worst possible decision. Marriages are not made in heaven, nor are business partnerships.

Build on a Sound Base

Too often people form partnerships based on little more than a feeling that the two individuals will get along well together and, therefore, the business will prosper. That is not necessarily a proper assumption. Deciding to form a partnership is an important decision and should not be entered into lightly. (For more information regarding partnerships refer to section 7.)

Joining an Existing Practice

The third way of starting a private practice is to join an existing practice. One thing to be aware of when doing this is the method of joining. The therapist should never join an existing practice without having a legal agreement specifying exactly what is involved. If the existing practice is a sole proprietorship and is going to become a partnership, then that's what needs to be specified. If the therapist is joining the existing practice as an associate, a type of subcontractor or renter arrangement needs to be established and put in writing. But in both cases, the therapist would also be maintaining the legal entity of a sole proprietorship.

When I started Southern Maine Counseling Center, I had an agreement with each of the people who joined the center specifying that each one joined as a sole proprietor having a rental arrangement with me. It simply meant that I did nothing with their billing or handled any of their income whatsoever. That meant that they were not my employees. One of the important issues is what the IRS considers subcontracting. The IRS subcontracting definition is fairly simple and clear. To be considered as a subcontractor, a person must have his or her own work space, control the hours, and have a written agreement specifying the contractual arrangements under which services are provided. Also the person in the hiring position should not contribute to health or life insurance for the subcontractor.

Who's an Employee?

The determination of who is an employee is made under common law rules, and in Revenue Ruling 87-41 the IRS lists 20 factors as guides for making that determination. These factors are:

1. **Instructions.** A worker who must comply with another's instructions about when, where, and how to work is ordinarily an employee.

2. **Training.** If the worker is required to receive training to learn how to do the work, an employment relationship is likely.
3. **Integration.** The more the worker is integrated into the business operations, the more likely that person is to be an employee.
4. **Services.** If services are rendered personally, this tends to indicate an employment relationship when required.
5. **Right to terminate.** If the worker can terminate services without liability, this indicates an employment relationship.
6. **Continuing relationship.** A continuing or recurring nature of work suggests employment.
7. **Set hours of work.** If hours are established by the business, this tends to indicate employment.
8. **Payment of traveling expenses.** An employer generally retains the right to regulate the employee's business activities.
9. **Doing work on business premises.** If this is required, it suggests control by the employer.
10. **Order of sequence set.** The more this is controlled for, instead of by, the worker, the more employment is suggested.
11. **Reporting.** The more the worker must report, or the greater the control of those supervising him, indicates employment.

On the other hand, independent contractors usually meet the following criteria:

12. **Payment by job, not time.** Independent contractors are more often paid by the job.
13. **Hiring, supervising, and paying assistants.** If the worker is responsible for assistants, this is indicative of independent contractor status.
14. **Furnishing tools.** Independent contractors often furnish their own tools and materials.
15. **Investment.** Independent contractors often invest in facilities that are used in performing services.
16. **Realization of profit or loss.** A worker who can realize a profit or loss from the services is generally an independent contractor.
17. **Working for more than one firm at a time.** An independent contractor will often perform services for more than one business at a time.

18. **Making service available to the public.** This indicates the status of an independent contractor.
19. **Right to discharge.** An independent contractor cannot be discharged so long as the result of the work meets contract specifications.
20. **Full-time required.** An independent contractor has more freedom as to when and for whom the work will be done.

In the end, if the question has to be asked whether or not someone is an employee, the person probably is.

Rental Arrangement

A rental arrangement is slightly different. What I had done at the counseling center is set up a rental arrangement, (see appendix A, form 1), which meant that people had an agreement to rent space from me, for which they paid a certain amount and received certain services in return. The services were spelled out clearly in the contract, and included use of their space 24 hours per day and use of a secretary to book their clients for them, but not to do any billing. They were free to hire the secretary to do personal typing or billing for extra pay. They also had use of a phone for local phone calls, with all long-distance phone calls being charged to their own credit cards. They had use of the waiting room facilities and the right to use the name "Southern Maine Counseling Center" on their stationery. In fact, I supplied them with stationery and common envelopes. The key to the arrangement was that we had a legal contract specifying that I did not supervise them in regard to any of their clients. This is very important. Set up a rental arrangement that clearly specifies that it is a rental arrangement, not some type of associate relationship or employee relationship. My own contract specified that I did not meet with the renters to discuss clients, but that I did meet with them to discuss common strategies for the counseling center and marketing ideas, even though I made all the decisions. There was no implied assumption that these people would be discussing cases with me or that I would have any responsibility for their cases. I did have phone coverage with a couple of the therapists who were in the practice, so that on vacations or holidays I covered their clients or they covered mine. The arrangement we had was specifically written out, explaining all the ramifications and responsibilities each side had, and that I exercised no control over or responsibility for any of their clinical work. Had I not done this, I could have been held legally responsible for any malpractice claims against them.

A 30-day clause in the written agreement gives each party an out if one is desired. The 30-day clause allows a practitioner to get someone out of a practice if anything unethical or illegal is going on. Equally important is that the other party has a right to leave if it is felt the practitioner is doing anything unethical or illegal. Make sure it is understood ahead of time how the contract can be broken. Too often when people join existing practices, they are optimistic about how wonderful everything will be and how everything will work. In reality, joining an existing practice is going into business with someone else. That involves money and one's own personal issues. It's always good to have a clear clause that states "this is how the contract can be terminated; these are the rules under which it can be terminated; these are the responsibilities of both parties."

Going into a rental arrangement maintains all of the advantages of a sole proprietorship such as control of clients, hours worked, fee setting and collection, and financial flexibility. It also adds colleague contact, cross-client referrals, and possible co-therapy groups or workshops without giving up the freedom of working solely for oneself.

Incorporation

When should a practitioner incorporate? The rule of thumb is that incorporation should not occur before gross receipts reach $100,000 a year. The reason is that a corporation becomes a free-standing separate entity. When a corporation is formed a clone of the practitioner is formed. The practitioner becomes the employee of the corporation. Therefore, separate books must be maintained and separate income tax forms have to be filed. A corporation is a legal entity that can borrow money, lend money, hire and fire employees, and incur debt. In reality, the corporation is the practitioner. If the practitioner does something unethical with a client or something happens with a client in a personal injury suit, the client is not going to sue only the practitioner but also the corporation, incurring additional legal costs.

There are two types of corporate structures: sub-chapter S corporations and C corporations.

A sub-chapter S corporation is a recognized legal entity designed to allow the profits and losses of the corporation to flow directly to the stockholders. In a sole proprietorship, if any profits remain after the schedule C form is filed, they are transferred onto a regular 1040 form and are taxed accordingly. If there are any losses, they go onto the regular 1040 form and are subtracted from any other income. The same principle applies to a sub-chapter S corporation. Both profits and losses of the corporation are entered on the 1040 form and taxed accordingly. The advantage of a sub-chapter S corporation is that in the first few years when corporations often experience losses, those losses will be taken off the practitioner's personal income tax.

A C corporation is in essence a double-taxing process. Any profits made in the corporation are taxed on the corporate form, and any excess money is paid as dividends to the stockholders. The major stockholder is usually the practitioner, and in a C corporation, the stockholders pay taxes on those dividends. In addition, the taxes for the corporation are much higher than personal income taxes. An accountant can provide definitive answers on specific issues. There used to be an advantage in forming a corporation, because when taxes could be as much as 70% of the income under the old tax laws, a corporation would limit the taxes. Many people formed corporations as a way to control their tax liabilities. Under the new tax laws this is a questionable concept. When I first formed my corporation, I formed a C corporation. When the tax law changed, my knowledgeable tax accountant called me and suggested I convert my corporation to an S corporation because of the difference in the way profits are handled.

Another confusion about a corporation is that the president of the corporation has a tax-free salary. In reality, the money received from a corporation is either salary or profit. In the case of an S corporation, if practitioners pay themselves salaries, then whatever the salary amount is, it is going to be taxed on the 1040 form. As the employer of the practitioner, the C corporation must deduct withholding, unemployment taxes, and whatever local and state taxes that may be required. Those are considered business deductions because they reduce the gross receipts of the corporation.

In the case of the C corporation, the practitioner is paid a salary; the corporation must take that as a deduction, so the practitioner moves his or her income onto the 1040 form and pays taxes accordingly. In neither case does the practitioner avoid paying taxes. The salary is going to be taxed, either on the corporate level as profit, or on the personal level as income. Before forming a corporation, consult an attorney and an accountant, and be sure that both agree that the time is right.

If the practice has gross receipts of over $100,000, forming a corporation of some sort is definitely worth investigating. If a substantial amount of personal private property is owned, it is appropriate to discuss forming a corporation in order to limit liability. If buying property is anticipated, it may be advantageous to buy property in the name of the corporation instead of in the practitioner's own name. Much real estate is held by corporate entities. Many who are considering entering private practice are erroneously advised to form a corporation to free themselves from personal liability. My own decision to form a corporation was made when I brought other people into my practice. When I was working as a sole proprietor, there was no need for a corporation. When I began to have renters in my practice and began hiring other people to work for me as consultants, I formed a corporation, making it clear that those people were working for the corporation, not for me.

SUMMARY

In summary, being able to establish a successful practice will necessitate starting with a firm management base. No company planning sales of over $100,000 and anticipating being in business for a number of years would consider opening the doors without establishing a management team. An accountant will prove to be an excellent resource for the practice, both in establishing the firm financial and bookkeeping base, and also in planning for the tax liabilities of a practice. A lawyer is critical to the success of the practice. Being in practice without legal advice is like crossing the Atlantic in an 8-foot boat; it's possible, but extremely dangerous and potentially deadly. With the many complex legal situations involving rights to practice, competence, clinical notes, fees, contracts, and liability, I can't see why so many practitioners go it alone. The few dollars saved by not consulting an attorney can be quickly spent in a legal battle; spending them on preventive advice from an attorney might have kept the situation from arising in the first place. The issues I've raised in this section and the process I've outlined are extremely valuable to establishing a solid legal base for the practice.

The banker is often totally overlooked, but as a practice grows, especially one based heavily on third-party reimbursement, cash flow problems are inevitable. Having a healthy relationship with a commercial bank where credit has been established and where a long-term plan has been developed for the health and growth of the practice will keep the practice on a firm financial base. The need to keep cash in reserve is a necessity in the beginning of a practice; consequently, realizing that the development and growth of a practice will necessitate some borrowing is part of the reality of today's competitive market.

Finally, the choice of what type of practice to have—sole proprietorship, partnership, joining an existing practice, or incorporation are all individual choices but extremely important to the practice. The pitfalls and benefits of each are known and explained. The progression of a sole proprietorship to a partnership or corporation is extremely important and should be done only with consultation of the business team. Success in private practice becomes more likely when the proper business decisions are made in the beginning. Taking the time to plan and consult with experts greatly enhances the chances for success.

Setting Up the Practice

THE HOME OFFICE

When I first went into private practice, I maintained full-time employment because I was not in a financial position to abandon my regular paycheck. The type of job I held (director of guidance) and its distance from my home meant that I spent a great deal of time away from my family. I knew I wanted to start my practice part time, specializing in sex counseling. At that time there were few counselors around who were interested in sharing an office. All things considered, an office in my home seemed the logical choice; I'd heard about all the tax advantages, and how the deductions would probably mean a tax loss to offset my taxable income from my job. I didn't want to take more time away from my family, and felt that I could work my clients around my family needs. Because I had a large home in a good area, all I had to do was turn the basement into an office.

These arguments will sound familiar. What are the advantages and disadvantages of a home office?

Tax Issues

When I began my practice, I knew I didn't have a lot of money to invest, and because the practice was limited to part-time, I didn't expect to make a lot of money either. My hope was to build up a referral base with the intention of going full-time at some point in the future when the practice was established. A friend had told me that if I had a home office used solely for my practice, I could take tax deductions for the office space. I decided to build a separate room in the basement that would meet the IRS rules. The room would become the seventh room in the house, and I could deduct one seventh of the heating and electrical expenses, taxes, and depreciation of the house, as well as all the costs of building the room. As I added up the deductions, the total was pretty sizeable, especially as I would pay almost all those bills anyway. It seemed like a good deal to me. So I built my office, opened it, used it for 5 years, and felt that I had made a sound business decision.

From a tax standpoint, it had been a good decision. There was only one important point that I was not aware of concerning depreciation deduction. Basically, I had purchased a home at a very reasonable price 5 years before opening my practice. I fixed the house up, adding equity to it, and ran my practice from it for 5 years. Then I moved the practice to an outside office, and continued adding to my home. Finally, I sold the house for approximately four times the amount I paid for it, and used the profits toward my new house.

I thought I was within my rights in doing this. Then tax time came, and my accountant told me that I had to pay capital gains tax on a percentage of the equity gain on the sale of the house. I had forgotten that from the tax liability standpoint, the government had allowed me to deduct expenses and depreciation, considering one seventh of the house as a business. Consequently one seventh of the profit was taxable under the capital gains rules.

The lesson is to be sure to understand IRS rules regarding home offices. When in compliance, a therapist with a home office should take all the deductions allowed, but be careful with the rules regarding the depreciation deduction, especially if:

- the house has a great deal of prior equity buildup;
- the house was purchased some time ago for a price substantially lower than the present appraised value;
- the practitioner plans to live in the house for at least 5 more years; and
- the house is in an area where houses appreciate quickly.

If some or all of these apply, an accountant should be consulted as to whether the business depreciation of the house is a sound business decision.

The law has changed since I had my office in my home, and I expect the law will change again. An office in the home should not be opened without fully discussing all tax implications with an accountant. For most, a home is the major retirement investment; jeopardizing it for a short-term tax deduction could be a costly mistake.

Family

Because I was working an 8-hour day and spending another 2 hours traveling each day, I wanted to be able to spend more time at home. Locating my practice in my home seemed a logical choice. However, having an office at home had an unexpected effect on my family. At the time I opened my practice, I had two sons, age 4 and 7, and my wife was also working full time. We soon began to have family conflicts over space and privacy. Even though clients did not come into the main part of the house, the whole family was aware of their presence and knew that noise inside or outside the house might detract from the counseling process. Imagine two young boys trying to amuse themselves without making noise! The needs and rights of the family should receive equal consideration to those given the client in a home office situation.

Life-Style

Like it or not, the appearance of the practitioner's house becomes part of the therapeutic and business relationship with a client. A client who comes to the practitioner's home will immediately make a value judgment about the practitioner, the practitioner's family if there is one, and the practitioner's business. Clients have a need to know their therapists and identify with them. Therapeutically, this involves a variety of issues such as self-disclosure, transference, and countertransference. This means that if the therapist decides to have a home office, the effect that the house and the practitioner's life-style have on the public image and on the counseling relationship should be considered.

Business Issues

Business issues are also involved in having a home office. Observing the therapist's life-style enables a client to make a judgment about the fees charged. The therapist who rents space away from the home would not be subject to this type of evaluation by the clients. When a client pays a fee, it is assumed that a considerable percentage of that fee will go toward the cost of running the practice. With a home office, operating costs for the practice are reduced. Many counselors have told me that clients resent paying the same rate to see them at home as they would to see them in a rented office.

Another aspect to consider is whether clients will be gained or lost by having a home office. This may not be a big issue for some because the clients gained often balance the clients lost. Some clients, however, feel uncomfortable going to a counselor's home, for a host of therapeutic reasons. This should be factored into the decision of whether to set up the office in the home or away from home.

Finally, the therapist should be able to separate work life and personal life, which includes being able to leave the office at the office. A home office demands a different level of discipline than does a leased office. When the records are in the home and the therapist knows there are reports to write, it may be difficult to leave the office and not return. The therapist with the home office needs to balance home and office, and know when enough is enough. The home office should be treated as an office; the therapist must work the scheduled hours and leave in order to allow for a life outside the office.

Isolation

Private practice is a lonely profession. Most of the therapist's working hours are spent dealing on a one-to-one basis with individuals or couples in demanding emotional situations. Consequently, it is important not to become isolated because a good sense of reality is critical for good work. A few ways to avoid isolation are listed below.

- Plan to take daily breaks to meet with colleagues. One counselor I know eats business lunches every day as a way to get out of the home office.
- Include consulting or training in the practice, which necessitates being out of the office at regular intervals.
- Hire a secretary. Secretarial help is important to every practice, but especially in a home office setup. Besides providing human contact in the office, this help will allow the therapist to have more client contact hours, as well as showing clients and other professionals that the business is run professionally although it is located in the home instead of in an office building.
- Get involved in a peer supervision support group that meets at someone else's office, or rotates from office to office.

Zoning

Every community has ordinances covering business and residential arrangements that allocate land use within the community. This allocation is called zoning. As a community establishes zones, it attempts to meet the needs of both businesses and individuals. Increasingly, zoning boards have attempted to locate the business needs of the community in set geographic areas in the belief that this will facilitate development of adequate services for these businesses.

A private practice in counseling is a business and must obey zoning ordinances. If the plan is to locate the office in the home, the practitioner should first be sure that the zone in which the house is located allows for a professional in-house business. The best way to check this is by going to the local building inspector or town planning office and asking to see the zoning code for the area in question. This code will specify whether a professional office is allowed and, if it is, what the permit and construction requirements are. The home office must be in compliance with these requirements before a permit will be issued. Some of these requirements are:

- a set amount of off-street parking, usually based on the type of business or on the square feet of business space;
- appropriate fire protection, which may include sprinklers;
- at least two clearly marked exits;
- compliance with local rules regarding a sign or public advertising in front of the office;
- specific permits needed for new construction; and
- specific requirements about a bathroom and cooking or eating areas.

If the zoning does not allow a professional office, there is an avenue of appeal; the refusal of the permit application allows an appeal to a local board set up just for that purpose. If it is decided to appeal, here are some suggestions:

- Consult a lawyer to find out the personal and legal steps to take. Meet with the lawyer, or the member of the firm who is most skilled in zoning appeals, far enough in advance to be fully prepared.
- If the neighbors are known, arrange to meet with them and explain the nature of a private practice and why a zoning appeal is needed. Most communities will notify all neighbors of the zone change request hearing and ask for their input. It's always better to be prepared and informed about the neighbors' opinions before the hearing.
- Meet with the building inspector or town planner to be sure the structure of the appeal is understood: time of meetings, number of meetings, voting procedures, what documentation is needed, and how to make a formal appeal.

In most cases, it is not easy to obtain a zoning change because it will set a precedent for the zone, but if this is what the therapist really wants, it is the homeowner's right to appeal. Just be sure to use an attorney and take the necessary time to prepare.

SETTING UP THE OFFICE

When the various aspects of having a home office have been thoroughly considered and the necessary permits have been obtained, it is time to look at the physical space of the office.

Soundproofing

The most critical thing to have in a home office is thorough soundproofing; both counselor and client need an environment free of distraction. Rooms in ordinary houses are not soundproof. They typically have hollow walls and doors, and ceilings are usually uninsulated. Consequently, in constructing the office, particular attention should be paid to using insulation in the walls and ceiling, especially if the plan is to use a basement room. Use solid core doors, not hollow core, and choose an area well removed from family traffic.

Bathroom

Bathroom space is the next item to consider. A bathroom must be available to clients, and it is generally preferable that it be used only by clients. If it is contained within the office space and used only by clients, it is tax-deductible.

Waiting Space

Clients should be able to come early for their appointments and have a comfortable place to wait. This space should be clearly marked, be separate from the rest of the house, and be used solely by clients. This waiting space can also double as secretarial space.

Entrance

Clients will need to know exactly which door leads to the office and to be able to go through that door directly into the office space. Mark the entrance clearly, and make sure it is used only by clients.

Parking

Finally, there should be adequate and appropriate parking. Most zoning requirements will indicate off-street parking needs; don't assume clients can park on the street. The parking provided should be marked for the clients and be well lighted and easily accessible.

Insurance

The worst mistake counselors make with home offices is failing to obtain proper insurance. A homeowner's policy does not cover the practice. A client paying a fee to see a therapist is not a guest in the therapist's home, and is not covered by the accident section of a homeowner's policy. A rider can be added to the homeowner's policy covering the office as a business and providing bodily liability coverage in case of injuries to clients.

A fire and loss rider is also wise. If the home should burn down, the insurance would cover the house and personal contents, but not, in most cases, business contents. A call to the insurance carrier and a consultation with the attorney will ensure that the business is adequately covered in case of fire or theft. The cost of this rider is usually minimal but the benefits are extensive.

SUBLETTING OFFICE SPACE

Most therapists at some time will find themselves either subletting space from someone else or to someone else. The issues around subletting can be complicated if one does not understand the principles behind them.

To begin with, one should understand a simple rule about subletting: Always sublet to or from someone with whom there is compatibility. In any subletting arrangement, the reputation of the therapist is likely to become blurred with the reputation of the person from whom or to whom the space is sublet. This can work on both ends. People who are beginning their practice will find it to their advantage to sublet from someone with an established practice and a good reputation. When practitioners are subletting from an individual with an established practice, or using the same address, there is often a credibility established because of the reputation of the sublessor. Basically three methods are used in subletting space: flat rate, percentage of gross, or per-session rate.

Flat Rate

The flat-rate method is the most commonly used method in subletting. It is a simple concept: a fixed amount of money for a set number of days or times. In a flat-rate situation, there are no implied assumptions about referrals. It is solely the use of an office space when it is vacant. The flat-rate method is usually the least expensive. It is a set amount paid each month, whether the therapist sees clients or not.

Percentage of Gross

The percentage-of-gross method is a tricky and ultimately a no-win situation for both the sublessor or the sublessee. But it is often advocated by various professionals who have licenses, third-party reimbursement, or well-established practices. The therapist should be careful of this arrangement. Basically, percentage of gross is usually a set amount of the total income from clients. It is a contractual arrangement where, for a certain percentage of the sublessee's gross income, the sublessor will supply specific services and space. The difficulty with this concept is that in the beginning it may seem attractive to the sublessee because the income is minimal and the percentage, even though high, does not seem to be a large dollar amount. The problem is that even though the percentage rate stays the same, as the gross income increases, so does the amount that must be paid to the sublessor. These percentages range anywhere from 50% to 70% of gross income. It may seem attractive because generally a wide variety of services such as secretarial, answering service, billing, or co-signing is part of the agreement. An average full-time private practice operating budget is usually between 30% and 40% of gross income for all opereating expenses. Paying in excess of 50% and still having other business expenses on top of that becomes a ridiculous business decision.

Per-Session Rate

The per-session rate is basically a mathematical formula where the sublessee pays on the basis of the number of sessions the office space is used. In the per-session rate, the amount for each session is fixed, but after certain intervals, the fixed amount goes down. This is then a decreasing percentage. It is a process where the sublessee pays only for the time the office space is used, yet the sublessor is able to increase the return on the investment, for as the sublessee becomes busier, the total rent amount increases. In the per-session rate versus the flat rate, usually a wide variety of services is offered under a contractual arrangement. There are advantages to both (see appendix A, form 2).

The advantage to the flat-rate method is knowing the set amount and being able to budget specifically how much is to be paid each month for rent. From the sublessor's viewpoint, an obvious advantage is knowing how much income will be coming in each month for the rental space. A disadvantage to the system is that there is no encouragement for the sublessor to help the sublessee in the new practice such as by referrals or cross-referrals. It is solely an additional income to the sublessor's practice. The per-session rate, though, allows the sublessor, who may have a busy practice, to refer clients to the sublessee, knowing that each time that therapist sees those referrals, a percentage of the fee will be collected. In the per-session rate, one other point is that the sublessor takes no responsibility for the amount charged by the sublessee for the sessions. Determining and collecting the fee is solely at the discretion of the subletting therapist.

Questions to Ask Before Signing the Sublease

- **Has the sublessee's lawyer reviewed the sublease?** In all subletting situations, whether it be flat rate, percentage of gross, or per-session rate, the sublessee should always seek legal counsel to review any documents that will be used in the renting arrangement. Never rent from another individual without a lawyer's reviewing the written document between the two parties. In the case of the sublessee, a copy of the master lease needs to be reviewed. The sublessor may not be the owner of the building. Consequently, there may be a contract between the owner of the building and the person from whom the space is sublet. It is important in any subletting situation to see and have access to the master lease. That contract supersedes any contractual arrangement the sublessee may have with the sublessor. After reviewing the master contract or lease, an attorney should be able to advise of any snags or pitfalls for the sublessee.

Points to look for include clearly defined days and nights of use. A contractual arrangement should state the specific days that the space will be available. This should be spelled out in exact time parameters, not in general statements such as "Mondays, or Tuesdays," and give specific hours. Many therapists who sublease space encounter problems when they want to change their schedules to accommodate school vacations or a different day off. In some cases, the sublessor may have leased the space to another therapist on those days and this wasn't spelled out in the contract. The rule of any contractual arrangement is to make things crystal clear in a written document, thus eliminating misunderstandings later.

- **Is there specific space to store files and other equipment?** In any subletting situation, there should be a designated area on the premises where the sublessee will be able to keep materials such as records, tests, tools, or equipment used in the practice. The contract should spell out that it is an obligation of the sublessor to provide space for the sublessee to store files and other materials.

- **What office furniture will be provided?** The contract should clearly state whether the office is furnished or unfurnished and, if it is furnished, whether the sublessee can bring in other furniture, pictures, or items such as pillows used in the practice. Often people assume that when they have leased a space they are free to bring in their own furniture or equipment. That may not be the case and should be spelled out clearly prior to signing the contract. Again, it is only the space that is being leased, and because this is a subletting situation, the space may be used by someone else also.

- **What are the rules regarding smoking?** In any contractual arrangement the issue of smoking should be discussed and written into the contract. Smoking affects many clients. The sublessee should clearly understand whether clients are free to smoke if they desire.

- **Is there a space for displaying degrees and credentials?** Degrees are part of the therapist's credentials and demonstrate professionalism. The contractual arrangement should clearly state the therapist's right to display degrees and the location in which they may be displayed. If the office is being shared, the issue of the placement of the sublessee's degrees in relationship to the sublessor's degrees needs to be discussed, settled, and clearly stated in the contract prior to signing.

- **Can the lease be broken?** Just because a good space is available for sublease and everything looks rosy doesn't mean the therapist will want to sublet that particular space *ad infinitum*. An attorney can outline covenants around disagreements on the contract and how those disagreements are to be resolved. If the contract is broken, the attorney can spell out what responsibilities each party will have. Never enter into a contractual arrangement without a clear understanding of how the contract can be terminated or amended and what responsibilities each party has.

- **Can the same space be sublet to another person on the days the first sublessee is not using it?** What effect will this have on the first sublessee? It is important to clarify this in the contract. Sometimes many people will use the same office space over a week's time. Due to personal habits, cleanliness of office space could become an issue, and cleaning arrangements should be spelled out in the contract.

- **If it is decided to refurnish the space, will the sublessee have any input?** When renting a furnished office space, future conflicts will be avoided if the contract spells out clearly what type of input will be allowed. What recourse is available if the sublessee dislikes the refurnishing of the space after it is done? Does the sublessee have any financial responsibilities if the space is refurnished with new carpeting or new furniture?

- **In the sublessee's advertising, may it be indicated that space is being sublet from the sublessor?** Limits on advertising should be clearly stated in the contract. In one situation, a therapist discovered that the sublessees were indicating on their business cards that they were subletting space from him in his office. The problem was that there was nothing in the contract forbidding that, and it was assumed that the sublessor was somehow endorsing the sublessees' practices. That was neither the intent, nor was it acceptable. Find out if the sublessor's name may be used in any advertising the sublessee intends to do. It is important to check if the master lease has any advertising limitations. In many professional buildings, the front marquee is limited in space. It is important for the sublessee to have the practice's name on that marquee, so this question needs to be settled ahead of time. It can be confusing to clients if the sublessees cannot have their practice's name on the marquee and always have to specify that they are subletting from another practitioner. It would be best to have the sublessee's name displayed on the marquee if at all possible.

- **What type of phone service will be provided?** What responsibility should the sublessee take for phone messages for the sublessor? How will the messages coming over the sublessor's phone for the sublessee be handled? Often the solution is an answering machine. This can be difficult for the clients, and sometimes in frustration they will call the sublessor to leave a message for the sublessee. This, of course, is not a good idea and may cause problems.

- **Are kitchen or food storage facilities available?** Due to the long hours a therapist often works, facilities should be available to prepare a meal, or a refrigerator to store lunches.

- **Who will take responsibility for cleaning the office?** Because nothing in a subletting situation should be left to chance, the issue of cleaning should always be discussed and written in the agreement. Will the landlord or lessee clean the office and waiting area, or will the subletter have that responsibility? If the lessor uses a cleaning service, is the lessee responsible for any part of the cost?

Any subletting of space should be seen as a win-win situation for both parties involved. No subletting should ever take place without a clear contract, negotiated by an attorney, with both parties having legal advice on the contract. All assumptions in the contractual arrangement should be discussed and clearly spelled out in writing. Subletting space can be a winning situation. It can be an additional source of income to the sublessor, and it can help the sublessee to establish a new practice. But ignorance is not defensible in a court of law, and the therapist should not enter any subletting situation without adequate legal counsel prior to signing the contract. No matter how well the sublessee knows the sublessor, friendship or verbal agreements will not hold up when a misunderstanding or a legal issue arises. All there is to depend upon is the written contract between the two parties.

HOW TO FIND AND EVALUATE GOOD RENTAL SPACE

For those who choose to practice in a rented space, the choice of location is a vital decision. The purpose of the checklist that follows is to provide a format for evaluating rental space. Most people find a wide variety of rental space available in the community. It is always helpful to have a basis of comparison for rental spaces. Use the following criteria each time you inspect a prospective rental space. Evaluate each criterion on a scale of 1–10. The order of the items on the checklist is in the order of importance as suggested by various therapists interviewed. The list breaks down into two major areas: location and actual space (see appendix A, form 3).

Location

1. Other Professionals

One of the key time-saving and image-building aspects of a practice is locating it near other professionals' offices, for three reasons. First, it will be important to consult with other professionals, to meet them for lunch, for example, to review cases and talk shop. Locating the office in an area where other professionals have their offices will cut travel time to a minimum. This is extremely important as the practice becomes busier and time constraints grow. Second, in most large communities, certain areas of town are considered "professional" areas. It is important to locate the new practice in close proximity to other professionals' offices. Each time clients come to see doctors, lawyers, or dentists, they are made aware of the new practice. If the office is located in a large medical building or mixed-use building, each time people enter the building and look at the central marquee, they become aware of the new practitioner's name. Third, giving directions to the office becomes much easier in terms of its relationship to other medical practices, or other large geographic areas. If the office is located near a major hospital, or if there is an area of town referred to as "Doctors' Park," indicating that the office is located in that area will make it easier for clients to find it.

2. Parking

The second most important criterion is parking. Virtually all clients will travel by car except in large metropolitan areas. But in a suburb or rural area, the parking requirement is extremely important. Clients need to know that there is a designated parking lot or parking area. Indicating parking areas on a map or brochure is helpful, especially in an urban setting.

3. Bus Routes

Bus routes are important even though most clients don't travel by bus. In most communities, especially in areas that have snow and ice in the winter, bus routes are the best maintained roads in the community. They are the first to be plowed, sanded, and repaired. They also are major traffic routes in and out of the community. If possible, locate the office on a bus route rather than on a side street or off the beaten path.

4. Major Highways

Most clients travel from 30 to 45 minutes to visit their therapists, so it is important to be located near major highways. Many communities have beltways or bypasses surrounding the community that facilitate traveling from one part of the community to another. It has been my experience that clients will travel half an hour or even an hour for therapy. In my own practice, clients travel as much as an hour and a half, and some even 3 hours to come for therapy. Being located close to the highway makes it easy to give directions to the office. In small communities, many clients do not want to see a therapist in their local community but are willing to travel to an adjacent community. If that is the case, being close to a freeway simplifies traveling.

5. Easy to Find

The location of the office should be easy to describe. There is a simple rule, the rule of three, in selecting an office. It should be possible to give directions to the office in three ways—orally, in writing, and visually. The other "rule of three" is that giving more than three oral directions at a time is apt to confuse clients and they may simply not show up for the first appointment. I've conducted a number of studies in which I asked "no shows" the reasons for not coming to the first appointment. One of the startling results I obtained was that clients were not able to find the office. If they were not able to find the office on the first session, they simply didn't show, and went home feeling embarrassed or confused and often never called to indicate that. Consequently, the therapist needs to be able to give directions in three ways: orally, in writing, and from a map. The last two can be done in the self-disclosure brochure. When choosing office space, make sure that three easy directions can be given to find the office, that it is on a well-traveled road, and that wherever the office is located, the entrance can be clearly seen from the road.

6. Night Lighting

Usually people look at prospective office space during the day. Any potential office location should be visited at three times of the day: in the morning, in the afternoon, and in the evening. Checking out the location in the morning and evening will reveal what kind of lighting there is. Most new private practitioners will do a lot of evening work. An office building may look attractive during the day, but in the evening it may become a deserted building with an empty parking lot. I have often visited private practice settings in communities when I have been doing workshops, and found myself approaching an office building with only one or two lights on, and questioned whether or not I would want to enter that building if I were a client. The parking lot also needs to be well lit, without shadows and dark corners. Clients coming for the first session judge the therapist by the location of the office and how protected and safe they feel.

7. Entrance

The entrance is an extremely important part of an office setting, for it is often the first impression clients get as they approach the office. The building may be attractive, but if clients cannot reach the office by the front entrance and have to enter through a side entrance, rule that office space out. The entrance to the office should be the entrance to the building. The entrance should be well lit, an open and pleasant area for clients. The therapist may be responsible for the safety of the clients from the time they reach the front door of the building until they leave, and that includes the front entrance. Pay particular attention to the appearance and attractiveness of the office building being considered. It is best to choose a building that has an open and spacious entrance.

Actual Space

When looking at a prospective office space, is always helpful to bring along a colleague or a friend. The therapist will be looking at the space as a therapist, thinking how comfortable he or she will feel working there. The friend will be looking at it as a potential client, imagining how comfortable he or she would feel being here.

1. Soundproofing

The most important consideration in an office space is soundproofing. It must not be overlooked. The integrity of a client's privacy can be compromised by a room that does not have adequate soundproofing. In evaluating office space, the therapist should bring a friend and a radio. The radio gives some idea of the range of sounds. Male and female voice tones carry differently, but a radio will emit a wide variety of voice tones and sounds. If a sound can be heard in the waiting area, clients will be able to hear it also. Ask the friend to go into the room that will be used as the counseling office and turn on the radio. Wait in what would be the waiting area and listen until the radio can be heard through the walls. When that happens, evaluate how high the radio has been turned up in order to be heard in the waiting area. Ask the friend to act angry and enraged, yelling and stomping the feet. Listen in the waiting area to determine if the yelling and stomping can be heard. If new practitioners don't anticipate clients yelling and screaming, it is obvious they are unrealistic about what to expect in private practice, because clients' behavior is unpredictable. A few hints for soundproofing follow. Many office spaces can be soundproofed, and this can usually be negotiated with the owner if the prospective tenant knows what to look for and request.

Carpeting

Is the space carpeted? Hardwood floors may look attractive but cause echoing, therefore carpeting should be considered. If the office has standard commercial carpeting, putting additional carpeting on top of it, such as a Persian rug or scatter rug, will help to muffle sound. Make sure that a chair or couch for clients is never placed against the waiting room wall. If anyone sits with the back to the waiting room wall, it should be the therapist. The farther away clients are to the waiting room area, the chance that their voices will penetrate the wall is reduced. Putting a bookcase or mural, or hanging some type of cloth such as a Persian rug on the wall facing the waiting area, will help to muffle sound. If the building has suspended ceilings, putting insulation in the ceiling 4 feet on either side of the partition will help to prevent sound from traveling up through the suspended ceilings and down to the other side.

In many office buildings, the doors do not close flush with the floor. Installing a door that will close flush with the floor will help keep sound from going under the door. Having doors that are solid core, either all metal or all wood, will also help muffle sound.

The Waiting Area

Soundproofing the waiting area also is important. Playing soft background music in the waiting area will help soundproof the space. Making sure that clients sit opposite the wall that backs up to the counseling office will help ensure that sound from the counseling room will not be heard. If clients in the waiting area can hear what is being said in the counseling room, they know that others waiting will be able to hear them when they are in the counseling room. Adequate soundproofing must be guaranteed to a client.

2. Size of Space

Generally speaking, an office that is 750 square feet would have a waiting room large enough for a secretary's desk, a counseling office, and a bathroom. If the practice is going to include group work, then a larger space will be needed. It's important to estimate space needs correctly, for if the practitioner is leasing space, it will often be for several years. As the practice grows and specialties change, it's better to have more space than not enough. Some therapists find it an advantage to rent enough space so that after the first year they can sublet some of the extra space to another therapist on a limited basis.

3. *Lighting*

Lighting is an important consideration in a private practice setting. Use as much natural lighting as possible for everyone's comfort. Lamps and natural lighting work out extremely well. Fluorescent lighting can be a major problem for both the therapist and the clients. When I first started my practice, I developed eye strain caused by the concentration of looking at a steady flow of clients, day after day, working under fluorescent lights. Fluorescent lights also cause clients to feel uncomfortable; many have told me that they felt they were under some type of spotlight. Natural lighting or indirect lighting by lamps is the better choice.

4. *Private Work Area*

If possible the therapist should have a separate and private place for a desk and work area. The image of the therapist sitting behind a large wooden desk talking to clients is a thing of the past. Most private offices now are comfortable spaces with soft chairs and couches, but there is still a need for space to do paperwork. It is nice to have either a separate room for that purpose or a separate work area within the larger office space.

5. *Waiting Area*

Space for a waiting area is often the last thing therapists look at when they're evaluating office space, and yet it is one of the most important. A bright, sunny, naturally lit, spacious waiting area makes a client feel welcome and comfortable. Too often waiting areas are tiny and cramped, with barely enough room for two or three clients to sit. Even worse is a waiting area that is dark and dingy, with magazines strewn on tables, empty coffee cups, and overflowing wastebaskets, if there is a wastebasket at all. It is important that your waiting area be a bright, cheery area, with magazine racks and plenty of sunlight. Soft music adds a calming effect and, more important than anything else, there should be more chairs than clients. People like to have space. It also gives a nice homey effect to see plenty of chairs available. As the practice develops and group work becomes a part of the schedule, the waiting area needs to have enough comfortable chairs for the group while they are waiting. I usually limit my groups to 8 members, so my waiting area has 10 chairs. Some people like to sit side by side; some prefer to have a space between themselves and another person. If a waiting area could speak, it should say, "Welcome! I'm eager to see you and am looking forward to our time together. Please sit down, relax, and make yourself comfortable."

6. Bathroom Space

When selecting office space, the bathroom facilities tend to be an afterthought. The best situation would be to have an on-site bathroom for the therapist as well as one for clients. The reason is simple. If clients are scheduled on the hour, there is a 10-minute time period between one client and the next. If both the therapist and the client wish to use the only bathroom at the same time, who uses it first? This situation is not covered in the etiquette books! It is a lot easier to have two bathrooms available. Sometimes there is a bathroom within the office space and a public bathroom in the hallway. The bathroom within the office space should be the one that clients use, and the therapist should use the public bathroom. The bathroom space should be pleasantly decorated and well lit, with a working lock on the door.

7. Private Entrance for the Therapist

An office that provides a private entrance for the therapist is ideal. For example, if the therapist is returning from a business lunch and is running a bit late, it isn't necessary to walk through the waiting area and apologize for being late. Clients like to assume that the 10 minutes between the time the previous client's session is finished and their own session begins are used in preparation, not in the therapist's arriving at the office.

8. Private Entrance for Certain Clients

Often in my own practice I've had clients who preferred not to sit in the waiting area. These were people who did not want to compromise their job settings or professional identities by meeting any of their clients or customers in a therapist's office. Respecting their right to privacy by giving them a private entrance proved to be effective and helpful in my practice.

9. Access for the Handicapped

Depending on the type of practice, access for the handicapped can be an advantage. I have often received referrals from doctors or chiropractors wanting a therapist who could see clients who were wheelchair-bound or who had impaired mobility. Therapists should also be aware that clients who are temporarily injured should have access to the therapist's office when they are experiencing mobility problems. Particular concerns regarding handicapped clients are that:

- bathrooms should meet handicapped standards;
- doorways should be large enough and threshold-free;

- floors should be of skid-free material;
- there should be a ramp at the front entry; and
- there should be adequate and proper lighting.

10. Secretarial Space

A secretary is vitally important to a full-time practice. Should the secretary be located in the waiting area or have a separate space? There are arguments on both sides. If the secretary is located in the waiting area, there is someone there to greet clients when they come in, to monitor the waiting area, to help keep it tidy, to take care of any deliveries or service people, and to make sure that no one comes into the waiting area who is not supposed to be there. If the secretary is located in another part of the office suite, obviously the secretary will have more privacy for phone calls and discussions when clients are in a separate waiting area. I've had secretaries in both locations and for me, having the secretary in the waiting area was, by far, the better option. Planning for secretarial space when selecting an office location, even though a secretary is not planned for a year or two, will prove to be effective in the long run.

11. Phone Location

It is best not to have a phone ring in the counseling office. If there is an answering machine, place it in a closet or in another space where it will not distract clients.

12. Location of the Practitioner's Name

The practitioner's name should be clearly visible to anyone entering the office building. If the office space is small, with only one or two offices, it's not a particular problem; the central marquee will work fine. Sometimes in larger office buildings, it is difficult to find one name in the long list posted in the foyer. When clients come to the office building, the first thing they do is come through the front door and make sure they are in the right place. The practitioner's name should be in a logical, clear place so that clients will be able to find it easily.

13. Furnished Versus Unfurnished Office Space

Potential office space should be evaluated in regard to furniture needs. Is it better to rent office space that is furnished? To answer that the therapist needs to know how large the practice is going to be. If it is a very limited practice, it may be best to rent a furnished office suite. But if a full-time private practice is planned, unfurnished space would be better. Buying one's own furniture allows the practitioner to take advantage of tax write-offs and allows the practitioner to design the space.

LEASING: HOW TO GET THE BEST FOR YOUR MONEY

One of the major expenses in a private practice is the cost of office space. As in any small business, selecting office space is one of the key decisions that must be made.

Negotiation

Getting the best for your money is not a mysterious venture. It is based on one principle: negotiation. The renter and the owner both want the best arrangement possible. To accomplish this, terms will need to be negotiated. For the lessee, the key to successful negotiation is knowing what is wanted, what can be spent, and how long the practice is expected to be located there. The owner simply wants to lease as much space as possible for the best price for the longest time.

Before moving to the negotiating stage with owners, therapists should ask themselves what they want in terms of space. The therapist shouldn't take a space and then fit the practice into it. The space is not only the place where the business is run but also a reflection of the therapist. The practitioner leasing space for the first time has likely had to accept working in undesirable space in the past because it was assigned as a part of the job. This time, there is a choice.

Once the the needs for space are established, the decision about how much can be spent must be made. Checking what others are paying for space and comparing that to the budget is a good idea. This is usually 10%–15% of the gross receipts. For example, if the gross income is $50,000 and 15% of that is for rent, the rent allowance would be $7,500 per year, or $625 per month. This sum can be compared to the amount colleagues are paying to determine if the budget is high or low.

The next decision relates to how long the therapist expects to locate the practice in this space. Longevity is the best measure of success; being in the same office location over a period of time lets people get used to where the therapist is, and does not confuse referral sources. Space varies from city to city. At present, many areas in the United States are experiencing office space gluts. Therefore, most owners want the security of long-term leases to avoid costly vacancies.

Rent for office space is based on cost per square foot. To figure the rental of a given space, multiply the total number of square feet in the space by a multiplier. For example, suppose a therapist wants to rent 750 square feet for a counseling office, waiting area, one bathroom, and a multipurpose room to be used by the secretary. The average rental multiplier in your area is $10.00 per square foot per year (750 × 10 = $7,500). Here are some points for negotiating that space.

Making the Best Deal

First, the longer the space is wanted, the better the deal. Most owners will hold the rent figure for 3 years without an increase; over 4 or 5 years the base rent may be cheaper, that is, $10.00 per square foot for up to 3 years, $9.75 per square foot for 4 or 5 years.

Staggered rent is a way to decrease initial rent payments, providing an opportunity to lower the overall rental of the space. A staggered rent works as follows: If the rent is $7,500 per year ($22,500 total over 3 years), the therapist should negotiate to pay $4,000 for the first year, $7,500 for the second year, and $11,000 for the third year. The advantage of this strategy is that if the budget will bear the $7,500 the first year but only $4,000 has to be paid, the other $3,500 can be put in an interest-bearing account at 6%. Thus, a total of $459.77 would be saved over the 3 years, reducing the rent to $9.79 per square foot. Exactly how does this work?

For the first year, the rent would be $333.33 per month; the second year, it would be $625.00 per month; and the third, $916.67 per month. By putting the difference between $625.00 and $333.33 (or $291.67) in an interest-bearing account, a total of $3,615.89 would be saved by the end of the first year. Leaving that money in the account for the next year and letting it collect interest would bring the total to $3,838.90. In the last year, after withdrawing $291.67 per month, there would be approximately $459.77 left at the end of month 36 of the lease. Subtracting this from the total rent of $22,500 paid to the owner gives a new total of $22,040.23; dividing this total by three gives a figure of $7,346.74 per year. This figure divided by 750 (the total area of the office) gives a rent figure of $9.79 per square foot, compared to the original rent of $10.00 per square foot charged by the owner. Staggering the rent payment over 4 or 5 years would result in even greater savings.

When the length of the lease has been negotiated, ask about repairs. Remember, most offices will not be soundproofed. Will the owner pay for that work and put in carpeting? If the owner agrees to this at a rent of $10.00 per square foot, see if the rent can be lowered by offering to pay for the work to be done. How is that an advantage? The base rent goes down and the money put into the soundproofing and carpeting can be depreciated over a specified time. If the money for the repairs is borrowed, the interest is fully deductible as a business expense, consequently lowering the self-employment tax.

Negotiate for the right to sublet the space. If it is not in the lease, don't assume it is legal. Make sure that the sublet does not affect the rental arrangement with the owner. In most cases he or she will only want the sublet or lease to comply with the therapist's, and will want to be notified of all subletting situations. By making a subletting arrangement with a lease for 3 or more years, the therapist can get a good rate while maintaining the right to move out as the practice grows, or to bring in associates.

A final point to ask for is a first refusal option to buy; that is, if the owner decides to sell the building, the therapist would have the first choice to buy it. There are two advantages for the owner in this. First, the owner gets the impression that the therapist is a serious tenant who wants to stay in the building. Second, the owner knows that if the owner decides to sell the building, the therapist will be approached first, thus possibly saving some of the costs of a real estate agent.

There are also advantages to the therapist as the tenant. Of course, if the building is in a good area, the tenant may want to have the right to purchase it if the owner decides to sell, but it also means that the therapist will know at once if the owner intends to place the building on the market so that he or she can make other plans for remaining in the same location.

The decision to lease an office space is not one to be made lightly. A number of issues involved must be addressed: Both the needs of the therapist and of the practice should be thought out; there should be a solid business plan; the therapist needs to be aware of what is going on in the geographic area with regard to the rental market.

Remember, the art of negotiating is the key to a successful renting situation.

MARKETING IMAGE

First impressions are extremely important in any business setting. The private practice is no different. Therapists who locate their offices in attractive buildings in strategic locations but do not pay attention to the impression the clients receive when they walk into the waiting area are missing the point. The professional image begins when a client walks up to the front door of the office. For most therapists, the idea of interior design, color coordination, and proper utilization of space is something of a mystery. In designing the office space, the practitioner should contact two or three major furniture outlets in the local community. In a large community, most furniture outlets will send someone to do a floor plan and layout of the office. This floor plan will locate where different pieces of equipment, furniture, lamps, paintings, and other items should be placed to maximize the use of space and to create a comfortable and soothing atmosphere. Some of the items to be considered in a professional office space will be described (see appendix A, form 4).

Most of these items are self-explanatory. In the case of file cabinets, it is advantageous to have at least one fireproof, theft-resistant file cabinet in which to keep permanent client records and income tax information. In regard to sofas and chairs, it is preferable to use durable furniture, not the type that would be located in a standard house, because there may be much more wear and tear in an office setting. Tables, chairs, and couches from an office furniture company will have the proper construction and fabric to withstand heavy use.

The furnishings of an office should reflect the practitioner's own taste, consider the comfort of the clients, and be easy to clean and maintain. One of the difficulties in a busy practice is the time necessary to keep an office clean. Brass and glass may be very attractive, but dust, coffee rings, or stains can convey a negative impression about the therapist. Wood and neutral colors are easier to clean and maintain.

Computers

Computers are becoming increasingly necessary in an office setting. With the growing use of personal computers in business, buying used computers may be the answer for the new private practice. Used computer dealers advertise in the business or classified sections of most major newspapers, in computer magazines, and in the yellow pages. Established businesses buy and sell used computers, peripherals, and related equipment. There are many advantages to buying from a dealer. Wide selection, competitive pricing, warranties, and service are definite advantages. Buyers will find that dealers have low prices for used equipment and high criteria for acceptance of used machines.

Used computer dealers are springing up everywhere, and there are several well-established chains.

Used computer brokers never actually buy or sell equipment. They find buyers and sellers, match them, and collect a commission from the seller when a deal is struck. Buyers and sellers negotiate their own prices, warranty arrangements, and other details. This way sellers can expect to realize a greater percentage of profit on the sale. Brokers' current price lists are usually available by mail, or via modem or telephone. A local computer users' group is a good place to start.

Whenever purchasing a used computer, use the following criteria:

- Are all the original cartons, packing materials, cables, and connectors included?
- When removing the components from the packing, check for nicks and dents.
- Are the keys, switches, knobs, and drive doors in good working condition?
- Are the connectors in good shape?
- When the cables are inserted, do they fit tightly and solidly?
- Does the system have enough memory to support the applications that will be used?
- Be sure to test the computer thoroughly so there will be no surprises later. Peripherals should be put through a similar inspection.
- Check the warranty and return policy. These important features can be negotiated along with the price.

Copy Machine

With a busy practice and the need for correspondence, insurance forms, and other materials, the idea of purchasing or leasing a copy machine makes a great deal of sense. It is possible to buy copy machines on a lease-purchase arrangement. There are a lot of options in this area and an accountant will help sort out the best choice.

Overall Impression

Having someone come in once a week to clean the office is usually a minimal cost item and provides maximum good appearance. Most practitioners are too busy to do this and the secretary shouldn't be expected to clean up after clients unless this was specified in the job description and discussed during hiring. Clients need to feel comfortable in the waiting area and the bathroom area, not just in the "inner sanctum."

Waiting Area

The waiting area needs particular attention because it is the place where a client makes the first judgment. The waiting area should be made attractive with plants and reading material. However, there are pitfalls with live plants in waiting areas and office space. They are attractive and soothing to clients, but they need to be plants that can be easily maintained and kept well-watered and healthy looking. Silk plants and flowers may be appropriate because they need only an occasional dusting. Plastic plants, however, are considered in poor taste. Many areas have businesses that specialize in "plantscaping" office space, both with real plants and silk plants.

In the case of reading materials in the waiting area, it is advantageous to have two types of materials available: easy to read magazines and picture books. The most-read books in my own waiting area are those that have pictures and scenes of the Maine coast versus *Cosmopolitan*, *Newsweek*, *People*, and other popular magazines. Clients often enjoy flipping the pages in a colorful photography book while waiting to see the therapist rather than reading something mentally absorbing. The magazines in a waiting area should be suited to the clients' interests, not the therapist's interests. It is best to have a variety: some women's magazines, a news magazine or two, and perhaps *National Geographic*, *Popular Mechanics*, or *Sports Illustrated*. Professional journals should be kept in the therapist's office and not in the waiting room.

It is also advantageous to have a table where free community service information and public information materials are made available to clients, as well as practice newsletters and other promotional newsletters from the practice. All this material should be stamped with the therapist's name and the words "compliments of" so that clients will constantly be reminded of the practice. These materials act as a referral source when clients pass on something to a friend that they have found helpful. From a visual standpoint, any displayed material such as magazines or books should be kept in a neat and orderly fashion. If the therapist has a solo practice without a secretary and is seeing 8 to 10 clients one after another, keeping magazines and materials neat is difficult. In that case the materials in the waiting area should be displayed in a rack or in some other way that will ensure that the area will look neat and clean.

Documentation

Documentation and record keeping of all major purchases for the office space is vitally important. Anything purchased for the office space will need to be depreciated on the therapist's income tax form. If the IRS chooses to do an audit, it will need to see the purchase orders and delivery directions. Purchases for the office should always be delivered to the office, not to the home. Materials delivered to the home and taken from there to the office may be questioned by the IRS. Good documentation of all materials purchased for the office will save much time if an audit is ever required.

Miscellaneous Materials

Sometimes therapists assume they can purchase items such as paper, pencils, office supplies, or cleaning materials and take a full deduction for them. To avoid any questions by the IRS about any purchases, all materials, supplies, or equipment should be purchased from a company recognized for supplying services to businesses, and the purchases should be delivered to the office address.

Telephone Answering

The first contact for over 90% of a therapist's clients is that initial phone call. Very few clients walk in unannounced and request information about the practice. As competition in the field of mental health services increases, clients are beginning to realize that they have a choice. Referral sources often give clients more than one name to call for mental health services. A therapist seldom has an exclusive market. A substantial part of a practice's operating budget is dedicated to promoting a professional image. Practitioners are spending an increasing amount of money on display advertising in the telephone directory.

The telephone is the most valuable marketing tool a practitioner has. Potential clients tend to be uncomfortable coming into the office for information and prefer to telephone. As soon as the telephone is answered or not answered, the client begins to form an opinion of the therapist and the services. The manner in which the caller's questions are answered will determine whether an appointment will be set up, or the next number in the book will be called.

Answering Machines

Most individuals in private practice and partnerships with three or fewer members use answering machines on their phones.

The overwhelming justification for this is cost. People feel that a machine is a one-time cost, whereas a secretary or answering service is a regular monthly expense. A struggling new practice needs to keep the overhead down. Before buying an answering machine, the practitioner should ensure getting the best value for the dollar. If the therapist already has an answering machine, the machine should be evaluated. Here are some guideline questions for evaluating the effectiveness of the answering machine:

- How many times does the machine record a call, but no message is left?
- How many times do people leave unclear messages?
- How many times does the caller leave an incorrect or incomplete number?
- How many times is a call returned before making contact with the person who left the number on the machine?

If the answer to the above questions is "fairly often," the machine is not meeting the needs of the practice, and a secretary or service needs to be considered.

Choosing an Answering Machine

The therapist should bear in mind the saying, "You get what you pay for," and should avoid buying a cheap machine. Look for one with a nonspecified time for the message. Voice-activated machines allow the caller to leave as long a message as desired. If the machine doesn't allow the outgoing message to be as long as desired, make sure the outgoing message fills all the time allotted, leaving no "dead time" between the time you stop and the caller begins to speak. Many people grow nervous when they have to wait.

The second feature to look for is unlimited time for the callers' messages. When most people make a telephone call, they expect to speak to another person; they don't have a message prepared, and they need time to formulate what they want to say. With this feature, make sure the recording capacity of the tape is long enough to take the volume of messages that will be left between the times that the machine is checked.

Be sure that the machine allows for changing the message tapes as often as necessary so that the message does not say that the therapist is in session when, in fact, the therapist is out of town.

Make sure there is a good warranty, preferably one that allows for replacement when broken, or guarantees a minimal time for repair. When the machine isn't working, clients can't call.

The Message

The message on the answering machine may provide the first impression prospective clients receive of the practice. Therefore it is important that both the content and the delivery of the message be professional.

First and foremost, the therapist's message should be prepared in advance. Few people can leave a perfect message on the spur of the moment. The message should give the caller any information about the therapist and the practice that would be needed in an initial call. Write the message down, then read it a few times out loud. When you are ready to record it, practicing in front of a mirror is a good idea. Smile . . . it will come across in the recording! If the person recording the message is uncomfortable, that will come across to the caller as well. The message should project clarity, patience, and understanding. Several tapes should be prepared to cover different situations. A message indicating the therapist is in the office but unavailable to take the call is not appropriate when he or she is not in the office and won't be returning calls until the next day. The proper tape in the machine will tell the caller what to expect.

Check-In

An answering machine needs to be monitored constantly for calls. The sooner a message is returned, the less time it will take to return it because callers typically leave the number where they can be reached at the time they make the call. Referral sources often give a prospective client several names from which to choose. The caller will usually book an appointment with the first therapist reached. The same holds true if the caller has found the therapist's name in the phone book. There is no incentive to wait for the first therapist to return the call before calling the second therapist. The longer it takes the first therapist to return the call, the greater the chance the prospective client will be lost. The practitioner should call his or her own number often to check for messages and to make sure that the machine is working properly. A faulty message reflects negatively on the practice.

From a business standpoint, time is money. If more than 2 hours a week is spent returning calls and trying to reach callers, or if more than five hang-ups a week are received on the machine, it may be time to switch to an answering service. The practice could be losing business.

Answering Service

With an answering service, callers are answered by a person, not a machine, which is always preferable. Most communities have a variety of answering services, often catering to specialized clientele, which enables the practitioner to choose one that projects the professional confidence necessary to get maximum impact from that first call.

The therapist should start by developing a list of available services, asking colleagues which service they use and how they feel about the service. The services should be called and askd for a list of references. The references should be contacted and asked whether they are satisfied with the service. Test the service by letting the colleague know in advance, then call the colleague's office and leave a message. This reveals exactly what message is received from the service. The colleague may be surprised when notes are compared.

The therapist should arrange to interview the answering service manager or representative at the place of business. This gives an opportunity to see how clean and professional the office is. The answering service representrative should be asked to explain exactly what services are offered and how they work. This process should yield enough information to lead to an informed decision about which service to select. Once the selection is made, the therapist should let the service know in writing what is expected from it. It is generally a good idea to conduct all communication with the service in writing because most services use part-time people and have a high turnover rate.

Some of the specifics to cover are:

- How the phone should be answered, giving the number, the name of the practice or therapist, or both.
- What information should be given about the practice or the practitioner? (Dr. Jones is a licensed psychologist; Mary Smith is a career consultant; Dr. Jones does accept insurance.)
- What will the practitioner's return call policy be? It helps the service to know each day what the policy for the day will be; for example, "I will be returning calls between 12:00 and 1:00." Then the service can inform the caller, and this helps make efficient use of the practitioner's time.
- What is the policy for emergencies? Answering service employees are not familiar with the profession; they will need specific directions regarding what to say to a caller who is suicidal, or is in some other stressful situation. Some practitioners have a policy that allows the phone to ring

through to the office in an emergency, or they carry a beeper.

- If the practitioner is going to be out of town, the service will need to inform callers when the practitioner will be back and who will cover for the practitioner in the meantime.
- How many times should the service let the phone ring before answering it? Studies have shown that people hang up after three rings. Very few people let a phone ring more than six times, even though it takes only 60 seconds for 10 rings.

After the service has been selected, it would be wrong to assume that everything will go well. The answering service is an employee of the practice, for all intents and purposes except taxes. The practitioner's obligation doesn't end with paying the bill.

Consider visiting the service periodically. Most services would welcome a visit. It gives the people on the switchboard a chance to put a face to a name. Stop by at different times because most services hire people to work short shifts, and the night people are often the ones who get the "panic" calls. The service employees are potential referral sources. Once they have met the practitioner in person, they will be more apt to tell others about the practice and the services the therapist offers.

The service employees should be treated with respect; they have a very demanding job. If there is ever a conflict, it helps to know the management style of the owner or supervisor. The therapist's clarification of issues should always have a positive tone and be put in writing.

Small gifts like flowers, fruit baskets, and cards go a long way in building positive rapport between the therapist and the answering service. We all like to feel that our jobs are special and are recognized as such.

When the practice grows to the point that more than 3 hours per week are spent returning calls, dealing with questions about the practice, or consulting with a service, and two or three prospective clients are lost each week, it might be time to hire a secretary. When the phone time takes away from expanding the practice, a secretary is needed.

The first impression callers receive often determines whether or not they become clients. If an answering machine or service is used when the therapist is not available to answer the phone, the best possible image should be presented to the caller. Selecting a good, clearly programmed machine, and developing a professional business relationship with the answering service are essential to give a good first impression.

Now that the office is ready, how will the therapist pay the bills?

INCOME SOURCES

In planning a private practice it's important to keep in mind that there should be a variety of income sources. Often therapists think of their income in terms of clinical fees only. There are basically six areas of income in a private practice.

The first area is clinical fees. The reality for most private practitioners is that the major source of income to the practice is the clinical fee. Proper attention paid to the establishment of that fee in relationship to the number of billable hours is critical to the solvency of a practice.

The second area is consultation. Consultation can be a lucrative area for private practice, especially if the practitioner is recognized as an expert in a certain area. Many therapists do consulting with business or industry, or the legal system as jury selectors, expert witnesses, court consultants, or evaluators. Testing and clinical assessment in schools or agencies are also forms of consultation. It is important in setting fees for consultation that the practitioner consider what the clinical fee would be, including hours spent in preparation, travel time, and expertise. I know of no set formula for consultation fees other than asking what the marketplace will bear.

The third area is workshops. Many private practitioners find workshops to be a lucrative area if they have skill and expertise in delivering them. Workshops also become ways to recruit clients for individual therapy or other services. Workshops are usually priced by considering the number of people involved in the workshop and the therapist's normal clinical fee.

The fourth source is speaking engagements. These can be lucrative if the therapist has published a book or is known as an expert in a given area. Often speaking engagements have minimal financial gain but excellent marketing and promotional gain.

The fifth area of income is products. A number of private practitioners have developed various products for use in their practice. These products then are sold or wholesaled to other practitioners to provide income for the private practice. Examples are newsletters, printed or written material, tests, audio or visual tapes, or therapeutic products such as puppets.

The sixth form of income source is rental space that can be sublet to another practitioner (see sections 2 and 7).

It is recommended that in considering a private practice there be more than one form of income for the practice. A blending of clinical fees with one or two other sources of income will help to build a more stable financial base for the practice.

The Fee

What fee will be charged for services rendered? This is one of the most important decisions a counselor has to make. The fee is the critical component of a successful practice. Determining the fee is not a mysterious process; it is based on the most fundamental of business principles: Fees generate capital; capital minus expenses equals profit. This means that determining an appropriate fee is critical to the success of the private practice.

Determining the fee is no more complicated than choosing where to locate the office or making any other business decision. Unfortunately, some counselors do not take the time to analyze and structure their fees to enhance the development of their practice, but choose a figure at random and hope it will work. It is easy to set a fee that will contribute to the success of the practice by asking a series of questions about the therapist and the practice. The answers will provide the guidelines needed to set an appropriate fee. The first consideration seems elementary, but it is necessary to ask: "Why charge a fee?"

Therapeutic Aspects

For counseling to be effective, clients need to feel that they are paying the counselor, and that the fee is reasonable for both client and counselor. Most clients who use private counselors realize that they will have to pay all or part of the fee.

Another therapeutic aspect of setting and collecting the fee is the trust and confidence that this process helps to establish between counselor and client. The counselor expects to charge a fee based on preestablished principles: length of session, type of session, time of session, and payment process. The client agrees that a fee will be charged based on these principles and that payment will be expected on an agreed-upon basis. Counselors have also come to recognize that a client's noncompliance with the agreed-upon fee structure indicates a variety of therapeutic issues that should be pursued.

Monetary Aspects

A fee involves an exchange of money for a service; it is a legal contract for services. In its simplest form, the client agrees to pay a set amount of money for a specific service, which the counselor agrees to supply. The fee is based on the value the counselor attaches to that service. The value the counselor establishes is based on the expenses and an expectation of a fair return.

The key point to remember is that a fee involves money, and that money has a variety of meanings for people. Counselors must be aware of what the fee projects about the profession, themselves, and the service (counseling) they supply. When a client who earns $7.00 to $15.00 per hour is asked to pay $50.00 to $150.00 per hour, can that fee be justified? The dollar amount of the fee will be either a source of strength for the practice or a deterrent to its growth. For that reason, determining the fee should be a well-thought-out business decision.

Determining the Fee

The practical side of setting a fee is based on four factors: a survey of the local market costs, business costs, collectibility, and concern for the maximum growth of the practice. The fee is a reflection of the counselor and the service; it needs to be one that is acceptable and will work for the practice.

Surveying Other Professionals

Before launching a new product, successful companies survey the market to see how their product will compare in price to similar products already on the market. Starting a private practice is similar to this; the fee should not be too low, nor should it be so high that the therapist is priced out of the market. A good understanding of the market is necessary, as well as a clear plan for capturing a share of it. A survey is the first and most important step toward this understanding.

The first step in setting the fee is to survey other mental health practitioners in the community to determine the prevailing rates charged. Keep in mind the fact that clients travel for counseling; it is not unusual to have a client travel 30–40 miles for therapy. The survey should take into account the rates throughout the radius the private practice will serve. To collect sufficient data, at least five members of each professional group should be contacted. Seek out new professionals; don't rely only on established professionals.

The different groups to contact are psychiatrists, psychologists, counselors, social workers, and psychiatric nurses. Each should be asked what type of practitioner he or she is, how long he or she has been in practice, what fee is charged, and how long a wait there is for a first appointment (see appendix A, form 5).

The first variable to examine is the length of time the professional has been in practice. It is important to know this for sound comparisons because most private practitioners raise their fees each year; the person charging the highest fee may also have been in practice for the longest time. A therapist who is charging the maximum fee but has only been in practice for a year may not be a good comparison because the life of the practice may not be long.

The next area to survey is the fee charged, which includes information on the type of fee, that is, whether the practitioner charges one fixed fee, a range of fees, or uses a sliding scale. If a sliding scale is used, the inquirer should find out how it is determined, keeping some notation for comparison; most sliding scales are based on the client's income. When the practitioner charges a range of fees, this means that different fees are charged for different services, such as group work, marriage counseling, or family counseling. A fixed fee is just that: the amount charged all clients if the practitioner doesn't use a sliding scale. It's important to evaluate sliding scales carefully because therapists who use them are almost always seeing clients on the low end and hoping for clients on the high end. So use slightly less than the middle as the average fee.

The next variable concerns the use of insurance. Find out whether the practitioner accepts insurance, what client payment is required when insurance is used, and what percentage of clients use insurance.

Finally, see how long it takes to get an appointment with each practitioner. This will help determine how busy the practitioner is and what role the fee plays in the practice. Well-established practices will usually charge higher fees and have longer waiting times.

Business Costs

Once the fee survey is complete, analyze the costs of the practice. Here is a brief explanation of budget categories to help compare budget projections.

- The ongoing cost for case consultation and supervision is a critical aspect of a practice's business expenses. This item also is used to cover the cost of training or supervision needed to gain or maintain licenses or certification.
- Wages cover the cost of a part-time secretary/receptionist for 13–14 hours per week.

- Travel includes costs incurred going to and from local, state, and national meetings and training sessions as well as any travel costs incurred in speaking, counsulting, or workshops.
- Dues/publications includes membership in local, state, and national associations, subscriptions to professional journals, and fees for licenses and certifications.
- Telephone includes the monthly costs, phone rentals or payments, long-distance costs, and telephone book listings.
- Supplies are regular office expenses such as paper, pencils, cleaning supplies, or bathroom essentials.
- Payroll taxes are those associated with wages paid to a secretary/receptionist.
- Rent for office space.
- Postage covers letters sent to clients and referral sources.
- Miscellaneous expenses include service contracts and unpredictable costs.
- Insurance is the cost of coverage for business and professional liabilities.
- Advertising includes the cost of printing, mailing, or purchasing advertising material to promote the practice; business lunches also come under this category.
- Professional fees are costs for legal and accounting services.
- Interest is the cost of credit card and business debts, including start-up costs and ongoing line-of-credit charges.

It is important to note that depending on the location of the practice within the United States and the specific type of practice (such as career or rehabilitation counseling, or a practice that requires technical equipment such as biofeedback machines or computers), the budget figures will need to be adjusted accordingly and additional budget items may need to be added. The sample budget (see appendix A, form 6) is based on a clinical mental health practice in a small state. If the practice is already in existence, these costs already have been established; if the practice is new, the sample budget chart will provide some guidelines for full-time private practice with a part-time secretary/receptionist on the payroll.

It is important to remember that a budget is a projection of costs and therefore will be increased each year. Another point to keep in mind is that most practices make no profit in the first year and are lucky if they break even by the end of the year. The second year should see a small profit, and the practice should be well established by the third year. These are traditionally the projections of any small business (see appendix A, form 7).

The next step in the process is to determine the projected number of sessions in the second year of the practice. The second year is used because once a fee is established, it should stay fixed for at least 2 years. Also, within 2 years a practice should be full. If it isn't, the practice is in trouble and changes, especially in marketing, should be considered. To help clarify this, the billable hours of three fictitious counselors, Drs. Acton, Currer, and Ellis, will be examined.

Dr. Acton works 27 billable hours each week. Based on a 48-week year to allow 4 weeks for vacation and conferences, this averages out to 100 billable hours per month.

Dr. Currer also works an average of 27 billable hours each week, but to balance such a low number of sessions, he is also involved in consulting, teaching, and training. His average gross income per month from these other activities is $9,600 per year, or $800 per month.

Dr. Ellis devotes herself to full-time practice and has no other source of income. She has an average of 30 billable hours each week, or 120 hours per month.

Each counselor's business expenses are related to the time he or she spends with clients to determine the actual business cost of each hour of counseling that must be reimbursed. In Dr. Currer's case, the extra income he makes from other sources is first deducted from the monthly business expenses.

Again, it's important to remember that the second year is used because the first year of a practice is a building year, making it difficult to project the number of sessions accurately. The second year provides a goal to work toward, whereas in the third year the client billable hours will be increased and the fee will be raised (see appendix A, form 8).

Personal Needs

Next, the therapist's personal financial needs must be examined. To be successful in the highly competitive world of private practice, the therapist must first clearly understand the personal monthly financial needs, such as rent, food, and so forth. The practice should generate enough to cover these needs, so they must be taken into account in setting a fee. For purposes here, the figure of $2,000 per month will be used (see appendix A, form 9).

Finally, a profit and return on individual investment should be figured. The assumption is that one of the reasons for leaving the security of a job was to increase income, which must be provided for by adding a measure of profit on top of business and personal expenses. Any loans or other capital financing taken out to start the new business should be included also. It should be possible to repay these in 3 years. If the practitioner didn't borrow to start the practice, but used personal funds such as savings, repayment with interest should be factored into the plan.

The various figures are brought together to give a fee that takes into account business expenses, personal expenses, profit, and individual investment. Thus, for Dr. Acton, who works 100 billable hours per month with no other income, the per-session fee to cover expenses and provide some profit would be $48.00. Dr. Currer, who works the same number of hours but has another source of income providing $800.00 per month, would need $40.00 per session; and Dr. Ellis, working 120 billable hours per month, would also require a fee of $40.00. Thus, the level at which a fee is set will depend in part on the number of hours worked and on whether the fee-generated income is the only source of income.

Compare this figure with the fees listed in the survey. Is $40.00 high, medium, or low for other practitioners in the same field? How does it compare with the fees of practitioners who have been in practice for more than 3 years, and with those who use insurance reimbursement? If the fee is compatible with that of professional colleagues, and if a client could pay the full fee without using insurance, the fee is in a good position in the market. If not, consideration must be given to either increasing outside income or trimming the budget, personal needs, or profit expectation. It is also easy to see that if expenses are higher, either the fee will need to be increased or the therapist will have to work more hours.

Collectibility

The fee must be easy to collect. The practice will need to have a positive cash flow as soon as possible. This is easiest to establish by collecting the full fee from the client at each session. Every dollar allowed to sit on the books is a negative factor in the cash flow projections. It is necessary to have cash to pay the practice's bills; therefore, it is necessary for the client to pay at the time the service is provided.

Sliding Scales

Some mental health practitioners use a sliding scale for fees. The advantage to this approach is that the sliding scale allows clients to come for therapy who otherwise would do without help because they could not afford to pay the full fee. Unfortunately, this means that clients who can pay more than the amount needed (for example, $40.00) would need to pay a higher amount ($50.00) in order to balance the shortfall created by clients who pay less than that amount ($30.00). This is a personal value decision and one that should be weighed carefully. Although using a sliding scale may increase the volume of clients seen, thus helping to build the referral base more quickly than when using a fixed rate, practitioners may find themselves seeing more clients for $30.00 than for $50.00, which will leave the practitioner unable to make up the difference between the lowered fee and the budget needs.

Sliding scales have one other major consideration: the use of insurance. If a sliding scale is used and insurance reimbursement is accepted, the scale must also apply to the clients who will receive insurance reimbursement. Insurance companies usually will not question the fee charged as long as that fee is equal for all clients. If the fee is $40.00 for a client with an annual income of $20,000, the company will reimburse for its part of the $40.00. The therapist cannot decide that because the client is using insurance, a top-of-the-scale fee can be charged. Consequently, sliding scales and insurance reimbursement simply don't mix in most practices.

Insurance Reimbursement

Insurance reimbursement is extremely involved in the delivery of mental health services. If practitioners are not eligible for third-party reimbursement, they should certainly work to obtain that right for their clients. However, they should also be aware of the disadvantages of this type of payment. Foremost among these is the length of time it takes to be reimbursed by the insurance company. Taking into consideration the need for a healthy cash flow, delays in payment can be devastating to the practice. If the practitioner is just starting out and is eligible for reimbursement, one possible approach is to set the fee according to the principles outlined above and offer the reimbursement as a benefit to the client. The client pays the fee at the time the service is provided and then collects directly from the insurance company. This avoids the problem of leaving large amounts of uncollected fees on the books, strangling the cash flow and possibly ruining a fledgling practice. Setting the fee without reference to insurance reimbursement, and not depending on that reimbursement for cash flow, will speed and strengthen the growth of the practice.

Maximum Growth

Deciding what fee to charge is critical to the success of the practice. Consider McDonald's, the fast-food chain. The company's success is based on one good idea. Realizing that it needed repeat business, McDonald's started selling a 19-cent hamburger when other restaurants sold theirs for 25 cents. It stressed attention to detail, whereas other restaurants assumed that customers were happy as long as they didn't complain. The company marketed its 19-cent hamburger until people came to recognize that McDonald's was offering a product at a good price, along with good service and attention to detail.

What does McDonald's have to do with setting the fee? The fact is, its marketing technique can be copied. Demonstrate to the community that the service being offered, although priced lower than others', is of excellent quality, and market the service. The fee can be raised by degrees and clients will accept that, but it is very hard to lower the fee. If the fee is high for the market to begin with, potential clients will associate the service with high cost; even if the fee is lowered, that association will remain.

The keys to setting a workable fee lie in understanding the competition, pricing the service competitively with that of other practitioners, and offering a professional, ethical service. The fee is the cornerstone of the success of a private practice. Once the fee issue has been resolved, the next consideration is insurance.

PROTECTION: INSURANCE

One advantage of being in private practice is having a degree of autonomy; the therapist alone is responsible for hours of work and free time. The therapist selects the office and hires and fires the staff. On the other hand, the therapist alone is responsible for the safety of the clients and staff while they are in the office, and all the bills come to the therapist, whether he or she is sick or well. Exercising proper care will help to minimize accidents, but appropriate insurance is critical to protect the clients, the business, and the practitioners themselves.

Malpractice Insurance

The first type of insurance that most counselors think of is malpractice insurance. With the increase in suits brought by clients who feel they have been wronged by their therapists, adequate protection is essential. At present, malpractice insurance can be obtained only through a group format, which limits the counselor's choice regarding the cost and coverage of the insurance. The practitioner should apply to the professional association to determine what the group has to offer.

One question often asked about malpractice insurance is, "How much should I buy?" When private practitioners need malpractice insurance, they need all they can have. It is not wise to be underinsured. Settlements of a million dollars and higher are not uncommon in today's legal climate.

Bodily Injury Liability

A common area in which legal suits occur is that of bodily injury. If clients come to the office for counseling and sustain a bodily injury, they are entitled to coverage of medical expenses. Furthermore, if the injury was caused by neglect on the practitioner's part, the client may also be awarded an amount based on the injury and the extent of the neglect. The best protection against such suits is a property policy covering bodily injury. Coverage of $300,000 should be adequate for any reasonable claim.

Counselors who run a limited or full-time practice in the home often assume that their homeowner's or renter's policy gives them adequate coverage for bodily injury, but this is not the case. Although this policy will cover injuries incurred by a friend or guest, it will not cover injury to a client. Because the counselor is running a business and charging a fee for services, he or she must have a commercial bodily injury liability policy. In most cases adding a rider to the present policy will suffice, but the rider is necessary to ensure coverage.

Renter's Coverage

Another type of insurance that is a good protection for private practitioners who rent office space is a renter's policy. This policy provides protection in case the counselor is unable to work due to accident or illness. When the majority of the counselor's income comes from the practice, being unable to work means a drastic cut in income, but bills such as rent must still be paid. In such a case, a renter's policy is worth having. Be sure the rental needs and the policy's agreement to pay are understood. A review by a lawyer and an accountant is a must in this type of policy. Don't assume that what the agent says is true. Always approach insurance with the caution of "let the buyer beware."

Equipment Coverage

Counselors don't always think about the equipment they use to carry out their practice as something they need to protect. But what if the rented office were destroyed by fire, or the home office were burglarized? Would the counselor's copy machine, typewriter, dictaphone, and other equipment be covered? Homeowner's insurance does not cover an office in the home if that office is used for commercial purposes. Private practitioners need to make sure they have riders to their homeowner's policies covering equipment loss. In most cases, either the homeowner's rider or standard office policy will include equipment coverage as a part of the personal bodily liability policy, but this has to be checked.

Workers' Compensation

If the practice has paid employees such as a secretary, the practitioner has to have a workers' compensation policy. It's a good idea for therapists to put themselves on the policy as well. Workers' compensation will provide coverage for injuries incurred at work.

For example, take the case of a therapist who, during a session with a client, fell and permanently injured his knee. His medical treatment after the injury included several operations and other in-patient treatment. Fortunately, he was covered by a workers' compensation policy; he was able to collect not only for the medical costs of the injury but also for a long-term disability caused by the accident.

Another example involves a counselor who had a secretary come in one day a week to do typing and billing at her office. A file drawer came off its track while the secretary was filing and injured the secretary's right arm and shoulder. The counselor's workers' compensation policy covered the medical bills and, again, the long-term effects of the injury.

The point here is that employees do get injured on the job; it is wise not to be caught without an adequate workers' compensation policy. These policies are becoming more difficult to obtain in some states, but a good insurance agent will help in developing the best policy to meet the needs.

Income Protection

Many employers offer their employees some provisions in case of sickness. Private practitioners are their own employers and do not have the fringe benefits of sick leave, especially for long-term illness. To protect themselves from loss of income due to sickness or injury, private practitioners should have a personal disability policy. The purpose of this policy is to cover the portion of lost income usually allocated to personal expenses; it does not cover business expenses. This policy does not duplicate coverage under a workers' compensation policy because coverage under a personal disability policy will cover the loss of income for any long-term sickness or injury.

To set up a disability policy, the practitioner needs to know the monthly income. For example, if the monthly draw or salary (gross client income minus operating expenses) is $2,000, the policy should cover that amount. In the case of an injury or illness, the policy will take effect a specified number of days after the onset of the disability, and will usually continue in force until the income is restored to at least 80% of the gross income before the injury or illness.

As an example, take the case of a counselor whose car was hit by a drunk driver. Before the accident, he had a gross client income of $10,000 per month, of which he drew $2,000 per month for personal use. He spent a month in the hospital after the accident, and needed over 3 weeks of recuperation and physical therapy before he could again start seeing clients. It was 6 full months before he was back to his previous client load. His personal disability policy was set up to come into effect 30 days after an injury; on the 31st day, the policy began to pay him $2,000 per month—the same amount he drew from his practice. By then he was out of the hospital, but just beginning the process of recuperation. The payments continued throughout the next 6 months, and ceased only when his income reached $8,000 per month (80% of his former gross income).

As mentioned, the coverage of a disability policy does not overlap that of the other policies recommended here. It provides income for household and personal expenses. A combination of this policy and the renter's policy should cover the practice during a prolonged injury or sickness.

There are a few factors to be aware of in applying for a personal disability policy. The first is the length of time after the onset of disability before the policy comes into effect. Standard starting times are after 30, 60, or 90 days. The longer the elapse before the policy starts, the cheaper the insurance rate and the longer the practitioner must rely on savings before receiving payments. It should be determined in advance whether the lower rate is in fact an advantage.

The cost of the policy will also be affected by a practitioner's age, occupation, and past medical **and** psychological health. In most cases, the practitioner who has used insurance to cover the cost of personal counseling will pay a higher premium than one who hasn't, just as a smoker will pay a higher premium than a nonsmoker.

A third point to be aware of is that the availability of increases to the coverage will be preset at the time the policy is taken out. Practitioners must be sure they understand how they will be affected, what increases they may add to the policy, and what limitations, if any, the insurance company places on increases.

Next, most policies will stay in effect until the income is restored to 80% of the income level before the disability. It should be clear how the 80% figure is determined. Some approaches are to use a 3-month average of gross receipts, a 6-month average of gross receipts, or simply the last month's gross receipts.

The practitioner should also know how social security disability payments will work in the policy. Most policies will pay the full amount stipulated until the policyholder is eligible for social security disability; when social security is approved, the insurance contribution will be reduced.

Disability insurance is essential. Don't try to do without it, but be sure to examine the policy carefully. Shop around for this insurance, and talk to different agencies to find out about their policies. When a company and a policy meet the needs, a lawyer should review the policy before the practitioner signs up; if problems crop up afterwards, it's too late to check the policy. Both the practitioner and the attorney should understand and agree about all the clauses in the policy. Find out whether the insurance company makes any medical stipulations. If there is any need for clarification, have the attorney make an addendum to the policy. Most attorneys who deal in litigation will know what to look for in a policy and will ensure that the practitioner is adequately covered.

Umbrella Coverage

Finally, the practitioner should apply for an umbrella policy, which is designed to come into effect after all other policies have been exhausted. Coverage is usually for one half million to one million dollars.

For example, a client trips on a waiting-room rug, sues the counselor for one million dollars, and is awarded the full amount by the court. The counselor's bodily liability policy is for $300,000.

After the bodily liability policy has paid $300,000, the umbrella policy would come into effect, providing the remaining $700,000 of the award. A policy of this sort is usually purchased in the form of a rider to a homeowner's policy, and is currently a fairly inexpensive policy to buy.

Insurance should be an integral part of a private practice for both the financial and emotional security it offers. Practitioners should make sure they are not underinsured or lack the proper type of insurance. Putting the package together will usually involve a number of insurance companies and various agents. The key to making this work is a good consultation relationship with an attorney and an accountant to ensure that the practice is covered by the best possible insurance package with the most coverage for the best price.

SUMMARY

In summary, when setting up a practice, decisions must be made about location, equipment, how the telephone is answered, and fees. These decisions should be made with careful consideration of the therapist's own personal and financial responsibilities to the long-term projection of the practice and should take into account the economics of the geographic area. Locating a practice in a home may be the best decision, or it could prove to be a financial and clinical disaster.

The choice to either sublet from someone or to lease space directly has many long-term implications and should be done only after consultation with an accountant and a lawyer as to what is in the best interest for the practice in the long run. Selecting office equipment and ensuring professional visibility are the first steps in the marketing process. Choice of a telephone answering service or an answering machine should not be made on the basis of cost, but on the basis of building a sound practice. Answering machines should be avoided if at all possible.

The need for a wide variety of income sources to a practice to guarantee stability is extremely important. Therefore, a thorough analysis of the best utilization of the therapist's time with regard to income generation is vital. Setting a clinical fee is a decision that has long-term implications for the health of the practice. Consequently, it should be made after a thorough analysis of income needs, the fee range in the community, and the therapeutic effect on clients. Protection of the practice by proper insurance beyond malpractice insurance should always be a priority in setting up private practice. The only time insurance is needed is when there is a problem, and at that point, the lack of proper insurance coverage is a moot point. Time and energy spent in solid planning in these areas will increase the chances of success significantly.

Opening the Practice

WHAT'S IN A NAME?

The first decision that will affect marketing and name recognition of the new business is determining what the practice will be called. In all marketing endeavors, the idea of a name with which people can identify is vitally important. Usually people refer clients to a specific individual, yet many private practitioners began their training in an agency or school setting in which referrals were made to the agency or school. The temptation may be great to consider calling the private practice by some name other than the therapist's own. If private practitioners decide not to use their own names, an attorney for the practice should be consulted and a rationale behind the choice of name should be thoroughly explored and understood. In a private practice setting, most referrals will be made to therapists by their names, not to the name of the organizations they have created.

Once the name is settled, the next criterion is the legality of the name. Many states require a fee for granting a separate license to practice as a business, which differs from the license to practice therapy, psychology, social work, or any other discipline. This license is to protect the business name. If the therapists use their own personal name, there will be no problem with that state license. But if the practice will be opened under some other name, there is a need to verify that the name is not already being used. It is also important not to give a wrong impression. If the name chosen, for example, is similar to "Counseling Center" or "Associates," it is important to have an attorney check the state laws to make sure that it is not illegal for a one-person practice to be called a "Center." It may be that the sole practitioner who calls the practice "Joe Smith and Associates" may legally need to have some associates in reality. Implying that a solo practice has associates could be termed fraud or deception and may be in violation of state laws. An attorney will know what is permissible. It is important to remember that whatever name is used, an attorney can help ensure the investment in the practice, and the marketing efforts and name recognition efforts will not be in vain.

FOUNDATION FOR MARKETING

The name of the practice becomes the foundation for all marketing efforts. If the therapist's own name is not used as the name of the practice, try out the proposed name on friends. Sometimes the initials of the name spell something unethical or contradictory, for example, North Orange Testing (NOT), or Educational Assessment and Testing Service (EATS). It's also important to remember that people will have different feelings about the name chosen. A sex therapist may want to include the term "sexual" as part of the practice name to help clients who are searching for a sex therapist, but it also may be detrimental to general clients who might like to work with that therapist but don't want anyone to think they have a sexual problem. The same holds true for people working with problems of addiction who choose to use terms such as "Recovery, Inc.," or "Addiction Resources." They may find themselves receiving few referrals from those who do not have an addiction. Taking time to think through carefully the choice of name and the overall image the name will present, making sure it is legal and all proper licenses are obtained, are two important steps in opening a new private practice.

TIME LINE

Opening a practice requires a time line because certain tasks have to be accomplished in sequence. People come to my own workshops after starting a new practice but without having made the necessary decisions to maximize its effectiveness. It is always interesting to compare those who have already opened their practice and those who come to the workshops prior to opening their practice. One of the goals of my workshops on private practice is that people leave with a specific time line and goals for their practice. It is important to set up a specific time line for decisions that need to be made regarding printed material and advertising.

WHAT TO CONSIDER BEFORE PRINTING

There are basically four steps to the printing process: idea, layout, proofing, and printing. A common mistake therapists make is underestimating the time necessary and the decisions to be made at each step in the process. The most time-consuming part of the process is developing the idea that will be presented in the printed material. Printers are not usually idea people, or layout people either. The initial decision about anything that will appear in print is two-fold, and must be made by the practitioner. The two key questions to ask are, "What do I want to say?" and "To whom do I want to say it?" Taking the time to research and develop an idea thoroughly will save untold hours and dollars after the printing process begins.

Layout

The traditional way to handle layout is to take a rough draft of the material to a printer and ask the printer to lay it out, giving some basic idea of the format.

The next step is for the printer either to typeset the material in-house, if the equipment and personnel are available, or to send it to a subcontractor to have it typeset. In typesetting the difficulty is cost. In most cases, the printer does not do the typesetting in-house and usually sends it out to a typesetting company, receives a galley proof back, and has the customer proof that galley. Whenever the author makes a correction or change in the galley proof, there will usually be an additional cost to the original estimate. This process can be very costly, especially if the material is lengthy or complicated.

The other way of doing layout is by computer, either on the customer's own computer with special software for design and layout, or by subcontracting with a company that specializes in computer layouts. The advantage to using a computer system is that it is possible to observe the layout instantaneously, correcting most errors and confusions immediately, this saving both time and money. The computer cost may be higher initially than the typesetting cost, but if the layout material needs any graphic designing, or if it is fairly lengthy, the computer cost will be negligible compared to typesetting cost. Whether the layout is done with typesetting or by computer, it is important to make an initial decision regarding the finished size of paper and whether it will have any folds. It is important to consider the finished appearance and size that are desired.

Proofing

Proof printed material is an important step usually hurried through or overlooked. Often people simply review the proofs at the printer or at the computer company. Typeset material, whether done by the printer or by a computer, should be read by at least two people in addition to the author. A grammatical, punctuation, or spelling error may be overlooked repeatedly by the person who wrote it because the content is familiar, but someone who does not know the content and is reading it for the first time will be able to pick up errors the author has missed. Material longer than 200 words should be proofread by one person reading it aloud and the other person following it on the page. The person reading aloud should also mention all punctuation aloud, as well as spelling out any words that have an unusual spelling. This allows to check both for the word flow as well as grammatical or punctuation errors. If the typesetting is done by the printer, the author needs to acknowledge his or her approval of it on the proof and understand fully that the printer will take no responsibility for content or errors once the proof has been returned.

Printing

Printing costs vary greatly. The printing market is very competitive. Shop around for costs and estimates. Printers give pricing based on volume of work and on the content itself. The following criteria should be kept in mind before going to the printer:

- size of finished piece;
- quality of paper;
- folds in finished piece;
- photographs or other artwork;
- color of ink or multiple colors; and
- quantity.

Size

Depending on the size of the material to be printed, there can be a significant difference in the price. If the finished printed piece will be on an 11 × 17 sheet or an 8 1/2 × 11 sheet, the cost may be less because those two sizes are standard and may require no cutting. Anything smaller or larger may incur a cutting charge. In fact it may be cheaper to use a standard size paper than a slightly smaller or slightly larger size. Sometimes the printer can buy standard sizes in bulk and doesn't have to pass a cutting charge on to the customer. It is important to remember that not all printers have the same restrictions, so the client should check for the most economical way to handle the size requirements desired.

Quality

Paper quality varies widely, as well as the criteria for selection. Most people depend on a printer to choose the quality of paper, but printers do not know individual needs. The best way to choose the quality of the paper is to ask the printer for sample swatches of the different weights, colors, and textures available. Rag content and weight are two considerations. Weight is the thickness of the paper. Rag content is the amount of fibrous material in the paper. It is important to understand the intended use of the printed material before choosing weight and rag content. In the case of weight, the heavier the weight, the more professional the image will be, except that the heavier weight material is also more difficult to fold. If there are several folds in the finished printed piece, a lighter weight would be better. The rag content is important to consider. If, for example, the finished product will be stationery and a laser printer or a photocopier will be used to print form letters on the stationery, the rag content should be 25% or less. Textured papers such as a linen finish will not work as well with a laser printer or photocopier as a satin finish will. The toner doesn't adhere to the hills and valleys in the paper too well, causing the finished product to look splotchy. These factors should be considered when choosing stationery and other paper material to be used in marketing.

Folds

Ask the printer ahead of time what the folding cost is. In some cases a local franchise printer may be able to do only one fold of material. That may not be divulged, but the customer will be charged an extremely high price for something folded three times because the piece will have to be sent to a larger printer for folding. Special machinery is needed for more than one fold. Discussing the folding needs with the printer may save an additional cost.

Color

Most printers use certain stock colors of ink on a daily or weekly basis. Knowing ahead of time what color will be used on a certain day reduces printing costs. Blue ink might be used on Mondays and brown on Tuesdays, for example. My office works with a printer who uses stock blue ink on Mondays, so we really scramble to get our camera-ready copy prepared by Fridays to take advantage of the free blue ink on Mondays. The decision to use the standard color the printer is using that day will reduce the ink-wash charge and set-up charge. Some printers charge the customer every time they have to change ink becaue the press has to be cleaned, and the customer is charged for the time involved in washing the machine and setting up the new ink color. Not all printers do this because many have presses that can handle two colors with one pass-through. It is wise to discuss set-up charges with the printer before agreeing to do business.

Multiple Colors

Multiple coloring in printing requires material to be run through the printing presses more than once unless the printer has a four-color press. A change-of-ink-charge is incurred for each color. Sometimes the effect of having more than one color can be achieved by printing with green ink on blue paper, or brown ink on yellow paper, and so forth. Multiple colors also require one "separation" for each color of ink. A separation is a separate plate the printer makes for each color: red, blue, yellow, black. A separate charge is added for making the separation and for washing the press and changing the ink. This is why four-color printing is so expensive. Many printers do not have four-color presses and have to subcontract those jobs, thus the costs are passed on to the customer.

Quantity

Paper sold at retail usually comes in lots of 500 sheets called a ream. If the quantity is less than 500, the printer still may charge the customer for a full ream of paper. (Some printers use paper by the roll, however, and this would not be an issue.) Price per piece is more expensive when printing a lesser quantity. For example, 800 pieces may be what is needed, but an additional few dollars would give 1000 pieces. Printing can be very expensive, but if these suggestions are followed, the private practitioner should find the printing budget manageable.

THE YELLOW PAGES

Clients increasingly are using the yellow pages as a referral source. I did a survey and learned that approximately 80% of my clients had used the phone book, either choosing my name or that of one of my associates directly from the yellow pages. If they were referred from another source, they had used the phone book to validate the existence of Southern Maine Counseling Center, to check for the phone number or address of the therapist, or to look for the name of the therapist. These figures convinced me that the telephone book is the most essential part of a private practitioner's marketing approach. I have asked other therapists across the country to validate my results and they have reported similar results when using a display ad versus a single listing.

When I first started advertising in the phone book, only single listings appeared under the headings of marriage and family therapists, psychologists, or substance abuse counselors. Few were advertising extensively in the phone book. When I took out a double-line ad, I noticed an immediate increase in telephone referrals. As my practice grew, I increased the size of the ad until Southern Maine Counseling Center was running a half-page ad in the yellow pages.

Getting the Most for Your Money

In an area where there is little or no telephone book advertising by therapists, the new private practitioner has a distinct advantage. One new counselor who opened his practice in northern Maine was able to get a four-line ad for the price of the two-line ad he had asked for because the telephone company knew that his advertising would lead other therapists in the area to enlarge their own ads. The ad has had a definite effect on the development of his practice. He has received a number of referrals from it, and discussions with colleagues indicate that his phone book rate referral is higher than theirs. This implies that because his ad stands out so clearly among the other listings under marriage and family therapists, people are more apt to call him. This is, of course, the purpose of a yellow pages listing; the more prospective clients respond to the listing, the greater the therapist's chances of attracting clients.

In developing an effective ad for the yellow pages there are eight fundamental issues to be aware of: size, name, service, phone number, and color, clarity, simplicity, and competitiveness.

Size

Before structuring an ad, check the size of the competition's ads, and determine how much money can be spent for advertising. Because ads placed in the yellow pages mean a monthly charge added to the phone bill, new practitioners should not take out ads that are too big for their budgets. However, cost must be balanced against impact. The difference in impact between a $60.00 ad and a $100.00 ad can be significant. If it is a solo practice, two to four lines should suffice to give the necessary information; with a two to four person group practice, four to six lines would be appropriate; in a highly competitive area, with more than six people in the practice, the therapist should consider a quarter-page ad to ensure maximum visibility and exposure.

The deciding factors for the size of the ad are competition and cost. If the competition is keen and referrals are needed, money should be spent on a good-sized ad. If it is a solo practice and the budget won't allow spending enough to compare with competitors' ads, a reasonable alternative is half the size of the competitor's ad, but with a special flair such as color, a logo, or a brief message. Make it easy for a prospective client to find the listing. In a group practice, all members of the group do extensive market development. Prospective clients use the phone book to see if they recognize a name and to validate names they are given. If an ad is too small, they may not see the name quickly enough.

Name

The placement of the name is critical. Make the type style and size of the name appropriate to the space available in the ad because the name will draw the reader's attention to the ad. If it is a solo practice, the name should be in clear, bold print. For an agency, association, partnership, or corporation, make the name of the group larger than the names of the individuals; the group name should be the heading for the ad, followed by the name of each individual counselor along with the appropriate degrees and certifications or licenses. Prospective clients want to have that information, and locating it strategically in the ad lets them know the therapists and their qualifications right away.

Service

The telephone company will usually print the information the customer supplies. The customer is responsible for the accuracy of the information as well as for its compliance with the law. Many states have licensing laws or regulations governing the terms an individual can use to describe a service. For example, in one state, only certified marriage and family therapists, psychologists, and psychiatrists are allowed to indicate in an ad that they do marriage and family work. Including such a statement without the mandated qualifications is illegal.

Then again, the licensing terms in many states stipulate only whether therapists can call themselves social workers, psychologists, or psychiatrists. Keep these legalities in mind when choosing terms for the ad. In addition, make sure the terms used will be understood by the people reading the ad, for example, "divorce counseling" or "marriage counseling," versus "men in transition." The ad should not list services the therapist is not qualified to perform. A therapist who advertises counseling services for children, adolescents, and adults as well as for marriage, family, and geriatric issues should be able to defend the qualifications in each individual area to the client, insurance companies, peers, and licensing boards. Listing services helps the prospective client and draws attention to an ad, but state clearly and specifically what services can be performed. Clarity is the key; lots of yellow space and a listing of a few key services works best.

Phone Number

The phone number is a vital part of the ad and should be placed to make it easy for a prospective client to see it. It should be set in a clear type style and be large enough to stand out in the ad. Remember, the purpose of the ad is to draw the attention of a prospective client and make him or her call. Make sure the telephone number is easy for a caller to find. The phone number should be the second largest item in the ad—the name of the practice should be the largest.

Logo

The logo is an essential part of name recognition. Too many therapists miss the opportunity to identify themselves or their practice by an effective professional logo. If the private practitioner has one, it is important to use it in the ad. Anything with good graphic design is eye-catching, especially on a page full of names and numbers. Another advantage of using the logo in advertising is that people often forget names but not visual symbols. Every time they see the logo, they are reminded of the practitioner. (For further information, see the discussion on logos later in this section.)

Color

If the marketplace is extremely competitive and most ads are run in black and white (really, black on yellow), consider adding color to the ad. Many phone companies offer the use of red ink for a nominal fee. Their marketing studies indicate that the addition of red to a yellow page with black lettering is a definite attention-getter, and, in a highly competitive marketplace, might give the edge needed. Consider using red ink first for the name or logo, then for the phone number, and third, for the generic term used to define the services. Many therapists in group practice now indicate that they offer a full range of mental health services. Using bold red lettering will often draw the attention of the reader.

Clarity

The wording of the ad is important, but so is blank space—space with no lettering, symbols, or printed material. Enough empty space in an ad enhances readability; if the ad looks clear on the page, it is easier for an individual to identify with it and read it. Often, when I'm travelling around the country, I'll look at the yellow pages of the city I'm in to get an idea of what the marketplace is like for mental health professionals. I'm keenly aware of ads that try to carry too much information in too small a space. Be sure to allow sufficient empty space in the ad to draw readers' attention to the specific information they need to know. Don't overuse the space.

Simplicity

A general rule of thumb for any marketing is: Don't tire readers by giving them too much material to digest. The person who turns to the listing in the yellow pages is likely to be in a hurry, or looking for something eye-catching. Prospective clients are unlikely to sift through each individual ad, looking for the specific words that match their needs. It is important to keep the ad simple, with as few words as possible, but words that will draw the reader's attention.

Competitiveness

An ad needs to be reevaluated each year to be sure it remains competitive. I've found this an interesting process as I've worked on my ads over the years. When I first began advertising in the yellow pages, a two-line ad was large for our area. Over the years, as I increased the number of associates in my practice or wanted to market more extensively through the phone book, I increased the size of my ad, and I have watched my competitors become equally concerned with their ads. The purpose of any ad is to induce prospective clients to call about the availability of services, fee structure, types of clinicians, and other information. It is the practitioner's job to book the appointments and to supply the best service possible, but that can't be done if the client doesn't make the initial call.

The phone book ad is a vital link in the overall marketing picture. Do not underestimate the importance of advertising in the phone book, and always remember that competitors will be using the phone book as a way to attract clients. Most people in business are sophisticated and aware of phone book advertising. They know the cost of advertising, and they know which ads draw the most interest. Consequently, when marketing to that population, advertising in the yellow pages is a must.

Many other prospective client groups have been taught successfully that the yellow pages are the best resource when they need a service. Many people who do not know how to contact a counselor or therapist find themselves turning to the yellow pages, looking for someone to help them during a difficult period. Others may have been given the therapist's name but have forgotten it or lost the telephone number. They want to see a certain therapist and use the yellow pages to refresh their memories or to find the missing information. The attention therapists pay to the yellow pages ad is critical in ensuring that some of these individuals come to them for help.

Because the yellow pages are so well known and trusted, people turn to them for validation that an individual is a legitimate businessperson offering a service. When a practitioner is not listed, a potential client may get the impression that the therapist is not in business, or that he or she is not a professional. Remember, clients have odd ideas at times, and the telephone directory has successfully marketed the image that all legitimate businesses are listed in the yellow pages. Counselors in private practice run a business. No private practitioner can afford not to be listed in such an essential market resource.

One last point needs to be made about using the yellow pages as a central part of a practice's marketing. If the practitioner is using an answering machine, I recommend that yellow pages ads should be name listings only. Repeatedly I hear stories of therapists who invested a great deal of money each month in an ad and received minimal results. In all of these cases, the therapists had an answering machine. The key to yellow pages ads is to get the prospective client to book an appointment. When clients take the time to call and find they are talking to a machine, they call the next number until they find someone—therapist, secretary, or answering service—that helps them set up an appointment. Consequently, yellow pages ads are an effective way of marketing a practice if time is taken to design a good ad and there is someone at the office to answer the phone.

NEWSPAPER ADS

Over the years, I have purchased a variety of newspaper and other advertising. I cannot say that it has had a direct dollar-spent/dollar-received benefit, for that is not the purpose of such paid advertising. What it does do is bring the name of the practice to the attention of a vast array of potential clients. When an ad is placed, it will be seen by thousands of people. Attention then needs to be paid to the details of the ad and the message. Placing an ad to announce a change in the practice (adding new partners, announcing a location change) is an effective way of showing that the practice is successful and growing. Holiday ads are a nice, professional way of telling the public that the practice exists and give an image of success, especially if the practice focuses on the business community, such as a career practice, or one that does stress management or business consultation. Businesses know the cost and value of advertising in the print media and therefore tend to see the practice that advertises in this way as successful. Over the years I have placed a wide variety of advertising and have always been told by my clients that they noticed it.

This medium can also be used to advertise seminars and workshops. Generally I've found that if there's a fee, the response will not be large unless the practice is sponsoring a nationally known speaker. When I'm doing my lecture on recovery out-of-state, I develop the ad at the office and have it placed in the local paper a week before I'm lecturing. This usually brings a good response from the public. I do the same thing for anyone I'm bringing into Maine. Usually the response pays for the ad.

Consequently, local paid advertising for a lecture or presentation by the practitioner draws an audience if the lecture is free. The cost of paid advertising in printed material such as newspapers or local magazines is high; it's excellent for name recognition, but not for immediate short-term gain to the practice.

LOGOS

Marketing studies continually show that people are drawn to a catchy name, phrase, or symbol. The type of marketing companies do today indicates a trend to market the identification of a product by continually drawing attention to a symbol or name with which people can identify. Think of Coca-Cola, McDonald's,

GE, or Ford Motors. Each name brings to mind a product or service.

The development of a logo is similar to marketing a name. McDonald's has capitalized on its golden arches symbol so that the symbol is now recognized as quickly as the name. A logo is extremely important in the consumer's quick recognition of a product. Putting a marketing strategy together and looking for ways of keeping a name in front of referral sources or potential clients require an awareness of how much a logo can help.

Developing a Logo

The development of a logo does not need to be an expensive or time-consuming task. A logo should have a clear symbolism of the specialty of the practice. For example, a pastoral counseling group I am aware of uses a shepherd's staff as a logo. Some people have a creative side that allows them to come up with a symbol representing the nature of the practice; for others, the creativity just isn't developed enough to spark the creation of a logo. That may be why so few counselors use a logo in their practice. For those who haven't developed a logo and would like some help and ideas, here are some ways to get that help.

Using Students

I have had great success in the past by going to an art school or public high school and asking the art instructor to run a contest for me. I will usually go into the class, explain that I want to have a logo designed for my practice or business, tell the students a little about what I do, and ask the instructor to run a contest for the best logo. When the students finish their work, there is usually some type of public showing where I select the logo I feel best represents my practice or business. Not only is this an inexpensive way for me to develop my logos, but it also gives the students a chance to compete and to see their work being used. My work in education taught me that being in competition always brings out the best in students, and for those who plan to continue in art as a career, the selection of their logo designs gives them another item to use in their portfolios.

Commercial Development

Sometimes student talent is not available and the help of a professional designer is necessary. Finding one need not take long because there are several immediate sources to check. The first source is the printer and the second is an advertising company. Most printers use a graphic designer on either a full-time or part-time basis; after an initial conference with the customer, they should be able to develop a logo. If the printer does not use someone for graphic design, he or she should be able to suggest the names of several free-lance professionals in the community.

If the practice is adding professionals or expanding in any way, the practitioner may want to talk with an advertising company. Such firms always employ design professionals, and will design not only a logo but all the printed material as well. This is the most expensive way to handle the need but it produces professional results. Before talking with an advertising agency the practitioner should have a well-thought-out, comprehensive plan for advertising in order to save time and money. Only the practitioner can tell the advertising agency what the goals are. The agency can help to reach them.

Don't miss out on the eye-catching appeal of a logo for the practice, whether it is a solo or a group practice. A good, clear logo draws attention to the organization or the individual practice. Use the logo on business cards, stationery, letterhead, envelopes, and any other promotional material. The logo should always be used in conjunction with the name of the practice when developing name recognition. It takes years of using a logo before the public recognizes it apart from the name. The more often the logo is seen as an identification piece, the more the marketing image and marketing approach are enhanced. The development of a logo need not be a complicated undertaking, but competing in a highly competitive marketplace requires this basic component of developing an image for the practice. A logo represents the business; therefore, the logo should be meaningful and descriptive, not just decorative.

BUSINESS CARDS

The first requirement of a business card is fairly simple: It should provide the name of the practitioner, the practice name (if different from the practitioner's own name), the address, and the telephone number. Attractive graphics or color on the card may be pleasing to the eye, but they are secondary in importance to the information. The most important item on the card is the name. The next most important item is the telephone number, then the address. Therefore, the name should be set in the largest print size, with the telephone number in the next largest, and the address in the smallest print.

Keeping the Card

It is important that the card not be thrown away. It should be handed out and either used for reference or passed on to someone else. If the object is to have people keep the card and not throw it away, the therapist shouldn't list the services offered on the card. Listing the services will fill up the card with too much information, presenting a cluttered appearance and obscuring the name and address. Many clients don't want to advertise the fact that they consult a therapist. If a specialty in sexual counseling is listed on the business card, how many clients would be willing to pass that card on to a friend, risking the friend's assumption that the client had a sexual problem? Many of the issues confronted in therapy carry a stigma.

Privacy

By the same token, the client's next appointment should not be listed on the back of the card. This invades the client's privacy and ensures that the card may never be given to anyone else. It announces that the client is seeing someone for therapy. To maintain a professional image, the practitioner would need a duplicate set of cards, one with the appointments, and the other blank to give to potential referral sources. It is better to use a receipt system with appointment slips or a separate card to indicate the next appointment. Some practitioners use the back of their business card to list various service organizations and their phone numbers, including AA (Alcoholics Anonymous), AL-ANON, (Family Groups), ACoA (Adult Children of Alcoholics), hospital emergency numbers, hotline numbers, and the department of human services number. These emergency numbers are convenient without being compromising, so the recipient of the card is likely to keep it.

Another technique is to print a calendar on the back of the card. This transforms the business card into a pocket calendar for quick reference—and ensure that the card will be kept and referred to often.

A third clever technique is printing the word "Note" on the back, followed by the line, "Why I kept this card." This encourages the recipient to do what many of us do anyway—make a quick note about the person who gave us the card and the reason we were interested in it.

One of the latest types of business cards on the market is the photo business card. Several companies produce these, using a photo of the person on card-size photograph paper and overlaying the printing. The marketing value is obvious for the private practitioner: The prospective client can look at the photo business card and see how caring and friendly the therapist looks! It is hoped that the client will decide that therapy wouldn't be so scary after all and will call to make that first appointment. These cards are not overly expensive and can even be produced in post-card size.

Location

Placement of the information on the card should be effective. Visualization studies have shown that eye movement goes from left to right, top to bottom. If a logo is on the card, it should be placed in the upper left-hand corner. The name should be placed in the middle of the card, with the phone number in the lower right-hand corner. Sometimes the phone number, in small print, is placed with the address. It is better to put the phone number in the right-hand corner, and the address in the left-hand corner. It is important to remember that the business card is designed to get people to telephone the practitioner, so the phone number must be easy to locate on the card.

Some practitioners like to include the phrase, "By appointment only" on their cards. If this is used, it should be set in small type and placed above the telephone number.

If therapists maintain more than one office, or have more than one phone number, it is advisable to use two separate business cards. If they wish to have all the information on one card, they should include some kind of notation to indicate which phone number should be used, and which address to use for correspondence.

Color

The basic cost of printing business cards usually includes one ink color. Adding another color for variety or as an accent can be effective, but the practitioner should be aware that it may add substantially to the cost if the cards have to go through the printing press a second time for the second color. Using colored card stock can add interest to business cards at a lower cost. Effective combinations for single-color printing include black ink on white stock, brown ink on tan, dark green on light green, or dark blue on grey. Keep in mind that although yellow, red, and orange are eye-catching, the desired effect is a professional appearance. After all, clowns are eye-catching too.

Texture

The business card is one item where the feel of a printed piece is as important as the look. People tend to finger the card absent-mindedly while talking to the person who gave them the card. Raised printing on quality card stock reinforces the message of quality and professionalism. If extra money is available, raised type goes a long way to presenting a professional image.

Using the Card

Once the card is printed, the only way to reap the benefits of having business cards is to use them. After a business lunch, a thank-you note with a business card enclosed is a nice touch. Another good idea is to attach the card to articles or announcements sent to the local newspapers. The cards should also be passed out at presentations. When personal introductions are made, the therapist should offer a card. I use my business card when I am carrying on personal business, too: talking to car sales people, insurance brokers, or others who might refer to my practice, or anyone from whom I might expect a return call. I have actually received referrals from business people who referred to me because they remembered that I was a therapist.

I also never give out my home phone number. I prefer to have all business calls made to my office, which is a subtle way of marketing and a clear way to protect my privacy. People with whom the practitioner has any individual contact are potential referral sources. If they have one of the therapist's business cards, it can be given to the potential client with a personal endorsement. Business cards should be kept in the waiting area and on the tables in the office. Often clients take cards to share with friends they want to refer to the practice. Whenever the therapist sends a referral source a thank-you or requests information about a client, a business card should be included with the letter. Often professional referral sources will to give a therapist's card to a prospective client.

In short, a well-designed business card is an inexpensive and effective marketing tool. But it will work only if it is in circulation, not in the bottom drawer of the practitioner's desk.

Stationery

The kind of stationery selected can often be a very expensive, showy part of the practice with no real value. The important thing to remember in selecting stationery is that it should pres-

ent a professional image to correspondents. The practice stationery can be used to correspond with anyone, not only
professionals. That is why stationery should present a clean,
professional image with the practice name, address, phone number, logo, and license numbers if the state requires them. I have
received many examples of stationery over the years in which
individuals have also indicated the type of services they perform.
I recommend strongly that the new practitioner begin using stationery from the practice for all correspondence, professional or
personal, so that a professional image is always projected. Listing services compromises that image. The type of paper, match-
ing envelopes, and ink selected are all cost factors. Far more
money is spent on stationery and envelopes than is needed. A
very expensive envelope and piece of stationery do not convey a
professional image. They only convey expensive taste. Appropriate stationery, preferably with raised printing, that conveys
a clear, professional image is the best choice.

SELF-DISCLOSURE BROCHURES

When I first opened my practice, I looked for a way to introduce
myself to prospective clients. I wanted to tell them who I was,
what I believed about counseling, and what I expected from the
client/counselor relationship. I decided the easiest and most
straightforward way to do this was by putting the information
in brochure form. I was, and am, proud to be a counselor. I
worked hard to get my degrees and certificates, and I felt that
clients should know about them. I also wanted to tell clients
about my personal way of looking at counseling. In addition, I
had a few policies about the process that I wanted clients to be
aware of before they started counseling with me.

But when I looked for samples of self-disclosure brochures, I
couldn't find any. It seemed that either other counselors had not
discovered the idea, that they didn't feel it would be useful, or
that they did not want to give clients information about themselves and the therapeutic process. This made me ask myself
why I was a counselor and what I believed about the process. As
a professional, I felt I had a responsibility to educate the public
about counseling and counselors, so I began writing my first
self-disclosure brochure. Since then I have found this brochure
to be one of my best marketing tools—it has even solved some
sticky issues between clients and myself.

Marketing Tool

How does a self-disclosure brochure act as a marketing tool? The brochure speaks for the practitioner, even when he or she is not present. Whenever the practitioner gives a talk for a group or organization, brochures and business cards should be taken along. At the end of the talk, the therapist can invite people to help themselves to the information. Reading the self-disclosure brochure could give potential clients the confidence needed to pick up the phone and call for an appointment. (I've had people call on the strength of a 5-year old brochure.) By using the information in the self-disclosure brochure, a potential client can ask informed questions and compare different counselors and the services offered. This educational aspect of the brochure works.

Self-disclosure brochures left in waiting areas disappear. That's good. Clients are doing the marketing for their counselors by taking their brochures and handing them out to friends. A group practice should have two types of brochures: one for the collective group as a whole, and one for each individual counselor in the group.

Self-disclosure brochures also help when a referring professional or organization calls for information. When those requests come, set up a formal meeting and send a brochure and business card for review prior to the meeting. It makes a good first impression to know the credentials and policies in advance. This professional openness often leads to the establishment of a positive relationship from the beginning, and is crucial in establishing a referral source.

Contract Between Counselor and Client

The brochure introduces the business contract between counselor and client. Sending the brochure to the client at the time the appointment is booked allows the client time to rethink the commitment to see the counselor in light of the office policy, specified fee, client responsibility, and cancellation policy.

The first session is an opportunity to review the business and professional commitments being made. Taking a few minutes at the beginning of the first session to go over the brochure with the client is also a good way to make an evaluation of the client's preparation for the session. Because it is important to a proper assessment that everything said and done at the first session be analyzed and understood, the practitioner should ask the following questions:

- Did you read the brochure?
- Do you have any questions about the counseling process?
- Do you have any questions about using insurance?
- Is my fee structure clear?
- Do you understand my cancellation policy?

Content of the Brochure

The brochure should be clear, well written, and concise. The therapist should try to stay clear of terms and phrases clients are unlikely to understand, such as *holistic* or *eclectic*. A better way to convey the idea would be to say that a wide variety of approaches is used to help people understand themselves better. The general public is not always sophisticated when it comes to counseling. Use clear, comprehensible terms. Many people will be baffled by terms like "men and women in transition," but will understand "divorce counseling."

Use clarity when describing training, certification, licensing, and professional affiliation. Avoid "alphabet soup"; write out American Association for Counseling and Development, rather than AACD; American Psychological Association, rather than APA; National Association of Social Workers, rather than NASW; or American Association of Marriage and Family Therapists, rather than AMFT. Although clients often like to know what educational training their counselor has received, they are confused by too much professional breast-beating.

A little personal information is often welcome, but the practitioner must consider the type of client before giving such information. Adults and couples appreciate knowing that the practitioner is married and has children, for example. If the client is a sexual offender, however, revealing facts about the practitioner's personal life might interfere with the therapeutic process. Base the decision on whether knowing such information would be helpful to the client.

If the practitioner requires anything special from the client for the counseling process, it is best to mention it in advance. I have always encouraged my clients to tape-record their sessions with me. I have many therapeutic and ethical reasons for doing this, so I indicate in my brochure that I see this as valuable. This is a personal decision, of course, but knowing they can tape the sessions may help some clients decide to see that particular counselor. It has definitely helped in my practice.

What are the financial requirements? If the fee charged is equitable, there is no reason not to state the fee and explain the policy on insurance reimbursement. This helps the prospective client to compare one practitioner with another, and relieves any potential discomfort when the fee is discussed at the initial session. If explanations are needed, they can be given at the start of the session, not at the end, when time might not allow adequate discussion to clear up any problems or concerns.

The brochure is an opportunity to explain the cancellation policy to the client. Most counselors have a policy that clients pay for missed, cancelled, or late appointments. There are various reasons for this policy, including the therapeutic aspect of paying for the appointment. If a client understands this policy before the process begins, later problems may be avoided. Asking a client, "Have you read my brochure and do you understand my policies?" not only helps to clarify the business relationship, but can also reveal some issues that should be dealt with therapeutically. In some states the brochure also fills the requirement of the licensing law to clarify the clients' rights and counselors' responsibilities. Many states are developing procedures to advise all clients of their rights, and this information can be comfortably worked into the procedure.

A brochure is a tool to use in developing the practice and client relationships. A well-thought-out, visually appealing, clearly written presentation describing the practitioner and the practice can be a valuable part of the marketing plan. The more the community hears about the new practice, the greater the name recognition will be in the area. With the potential for misunderstanding between client and counselor over the financial aspects of the relationship, a clearly written explanation of policies is helpful (see appendix A, form 10).

HIRING A SECRETARY

When I first began my practice on a limited basis in my home, I used my secretary from my school job to do the limited typing that I needed in my practice. When I made the decision to open a full-time practice and left my school job, I hired her that summer to work for me, giving her the responsibility of purchasing the office equipment and setting up my office. She worked 32 hours a week—Monday, Tuesday, Thursday, and Friday—and basically took full responsibility for managing my office and scheduling. It was by far the best decision I had made, for in my community most private practitioners had answering machines or answering services. Few had secretaries. I credit my first year of unexpected growth to the fact that when anyone called my office, they had a person to talk to who could answer their questions and book their appointments. Many clients indicated that the reason they had come to me was because of the secretary—first, because she had been there to answer their questions and confirm their appointments in writing, and second, because they did not have to wait for a return phone call or wonder about the cost. I took Wednesdays as my day to generate paperwork, planning, and marketing, and gave my secretary that day off. So my office was really covered 5 days a week. With that in mind, I am an advocate of hiring a secretary in a private practice setting from the beginning.

In considering a secretary for a practice, there are basically three forms of help to choose: consultant, out-of-house, or in-house. A consultant secretary is an individual who is hired to perform a clearly defined set of services and is paid a gross wage with no deductions taken. The practitioner is not required to pay any insurance. The consultant secretary may or may not work in the practitioner's office space, but works as an independent contractor. For some, this can be a beneficial arrangement, especially if the work is less than 40 hours a week. It is a contractual arrangement with clearly defined services but no requirements of physical space or time parameters.

An out-of-house secretary is an individual who is in the practitioner's employment, but simply does not work in the practitioner's office. This may be an individual who does typing or bookkeeping services and is an employee; consequently, the practitioner must deduct all necessary taxes and carry all necessary insurance. Many find this effective, especially in being able to hire individuals who have some type of injury or disability. Due to the tax breaks available in this type of situation, it may be advantageous for a person to explore this alternative. A wheelchair-bound individual or visually impaired individual may not be able physically to get to the office, but may be able to perform many of the services required, even to the extent that the phone may ring where the secretary is located instead of in the therapist's office. This may be a cost-effective way of employing a secretary without having to supply the physical space required.

An in-house secretary is someone who works in the practitioner's office and is paid as an employee, requiring all proper insurance to be carried and taxes to be deducted and paid. The in-house secretary is directly responsible to the practitioner.

In selecting any of the three types of secretarial help discussed, the first thing to decide is what days of the week coverage will be needed and what services will need to be performed. It is recommended that the first two primary days be Mondays and Fridays. Studies I have done have indicated that the primary

days for new referrals are Mondays and Friday afternoons. So it
is important that a secretary who is also going to book appointments be available on those two days. The next two busiest days
are Tuesdays and Thursdays, with the least busy day being
Wednesday. Therapists, like many other professionals, take
Wednesdays off. Also the psychological issues people face around
the weekend cause Mondays and Fridays to be the two busiest
days.

How to Find a Secretary

There are a number ways to look for a secretary. Unless the
practitioner needs on a secretary 5 days a week, using an agency
will probably not be worth the fee and effort. If the practitioner
needs a part-time secretary, placing ads in a local newspaper,
contacting local churches, or contacting the local chamber of
commerce or professional businesswomen's association may prove
effective. Often individuals do not want full-time employment for
one reason or another, but would enjoy a professional position
on a limited basis.

Criteria

First and most important are good voice skills, for the secretary
is the primary link to the community. If you intend to have the
secretary answer the phone, make sure the person has good voice
and enunciation skills as well as patience and sensitivity. Typing
and grammatical skills can only be proven. If the plan is to have
the secretary do correspondence, giving him or her a sample of
written work and asking that the sample be edited and prepared
in a letter form or other form is effective in ascertaining skills
and typing level. If a computer will be used in the practice, making sure the prospective secretary understands computers and
how to use them will save valuable time and energy.

Professional Appearance

Setting a professional image and tone in dress and appearance
is of vital importance to the practice's image. The saying goes,
"You get what you pay for," so pay your secretary well. Do not
assume that a competent, professional person who is organized,
self-motivated, and willing to work alone for long periods of time
with minimal direction can be hired for the minimum wage.

Due to the solitary nature of a secretary's work in a private
practice, it is important that he or she be kept involved and
stimulated. Giving projects and ideas that challenge and prevent

boredom is important. The secretary should be made to feel a part of the team. One of the greatest faults of private practitioners who have secretaries is that they fail to keep them involved in the workings of the practice. Secretaries need to know when little successes happen, when clients are stressed out, what projects lie ahead, and what changes are anticipated in the practice. This helps the secretary handle situations professionally. Don't let the secretary be the last to know; it's inconsiderate on the part of the practitioner and embarrassing to the secretary.

It has been my style of working with secretaries to keep them involved, especially if they might need to make decisions for me while I was seeing clients. Often a secretary who feels involved and committed to the practice can point out areas of improvement the practitioner might not see. A secretary can make or break a practice by virtue of the fact that he or she is the link to the public when the practitioner is not available. Treat secretaries as part of the team, pay them what they are worth, ask their opinions, and listen to their feedback. The secretary can also be an excellent referral source. Taking the time to find a good secretary will speed the success of the private practice. In today's competitive marketplace it is extremely difficult to keep ahead of the paperwork, insurance forms, and marketing efforts without some type of organized help, whether it be a consultant, an out-of-house secretary, or an in-house secretary.

SUMMARY

In this section the specifics involving the opening of a practice were explained. The need for a clear plan with time lines and expected outcomes is critical as a practice develops. The choice of a name for the practice becomes the central aspect of all marketing. The practitioner's own name is always the best choice when it is a solo practice, but if more therapists are involved, the name should reflect the expanded scope of the practice.

With the large amount of money being spent on printing, which for many practitioners is an area of little or no expertise, the explanations about layout, proofing, costs, size, quality of paper, folds, colors, and quantity will make this section a reference guide. A busy, diversified practice has a wide variety of printing needs, and a proper understanding of the printing process can keep the costs down and the quality up. The presentation of the printed message is critical.

Yellow pages advertising can be an effective way of bringing a consistent flow of clients to the practice. It may seem strange, but people do use the telephone book to find therapists. Attention paid to the details of the advertisement such as size, name, services offered, phone number, logo, color, and simplicity will help maximize effectiveness, but if there's no one at the office to answer the phone, only an answering machine, don't spend the money on a display ad. Yellow pages clients don't wait for return calls. Newspaper advertisements are helpful for name recognition, but being aware of cost and effectiveness is critical. Logo design can be a tedious process, especially for someone who doesn't have an artistic eye. A good logo has been shown to be a wonderful marketing tool.The choice of student help or commercial development should be considered for the struggling new practice.

The many suggestions this section contains about business cards will be helpful as a reference guide. A card is an important part of reminding people of the practice. Self-disclosure brochures are both an excellent way to educate clients about the practitioner's services and a way to make a clear statement about the business requirements of the practice. The examples and explanations should provide help in developing a brochure.

A brochure doesn't have to be complicated. Clarity and simplicity are vital. A well-thought-out message will go a long way in building the image of the practice. As the paperwork increases and possible expansion becomes a reality, a secretary should be hired. I've often said that had I not hired a secretary in the beginning, I would not have experienced the rapid success I enjoyed in my first year of practice. A secretary is not only a time-saving partner in the practice, but a front-line person for the practitioner's clients and referral sources. The cost may seem questionable to someone who has never used a secretary, but the long-term advantage of better utilization of the therapist's time as well as efficient response to clients, insurance companies, and referral sources will far outweigh the cost involved.

Marketing: The Key to Success

OVERVIEW OF MARKETING

A clearly delineated marketing campaign is necessary to start a successful private practice. Marketing is often one of the areas about which private practitioners are most confused, for nothing in their training ever covered the necessary information about marketing. Very few private practitioners have had any undergraduate courses in business administration or public relations. My first degree was in business administration, and I often draw upon the concepts and ideas I learned in the courses I took in my early undergraduate years.

This section will not be a complete analysis of marketing, for there are many facets of the marketing game that cannot be covered in a book of this length. Therefore I will attempt to offer only an overview with some specific examples. It must be emphasized in the beginning that people's own sense of self is what will determine success in their marketing efforts. There are no quick answers to marketing, but there are some specific guidelines.

THE ABILITY TO SELL ONESELF

Individual therapists are the foundation of their practice and their marketing efforts. They must be able to sell themselves. The product is an elusive one; it cannot be statistically reviewed, tabulated, or compared to another product, as consumers often do with the products they buy. Therapists offer a service that is very hard to qualify. To convince the client that the service is worthwhile, therapists must be able to sell themselves because they are the deliverers of the product. Here is a self-test to help examine skills in this area:

- Do I like people?
- Do I get along well with people?

- Have I maintained relationships over long periods of time?
- Do I feel comfortable with most people?
- Do I feel comfortable speaking to strangers about myself?
- Do I feel comfortable talking about my profession in front of a large audience?
- Do I see myself as able to project a confident image over the phone?
- Can I think quickly on my feet and respond to questions easily?
- Do I like to go to meetings where there are large numbers of people I do not know?
- Am I able to approach strangers easily and comfortably, introduce myself, and establish a conversation?
- Do I feel comfortable with my own physical appearance?
- Can I explain what I do in terms that the average nontherapist would understand?
- Am I able to deal with argumentative people?

Even if the therapist's services are excellent, they still must be sold to the community. If the answer was "no" to some of these questions, consider some of the following suggestions to improve skills in these areas:

- Take a course in public speaking.
- Sign up for a course on sales.
- Become involved in the local or state professional organization where it will be necessary to talk about yourself and the purpose of the organization.
- Attend a professional development seminar on clothes or business style.
- Engage in an active weight training or exercise program.

In short, therapists should look to themselves first, making sure they feel good about themselves and are prepared to start marketing.

A MARKETING PLAN

The successes and failures of a private practice often hinge on the effort that the private practitioner makes in marketing. The difficulty for most private practitioners is that they've never had any experience in marketing. They've never taken any courses in it, nor do they understand its basic issues. It helps to look at marketing as an organized body of information that contains specific goals and objectives.

The sample market analysis (see appendix A, form 11) will help private practitioners to analyze their own marketing plan, develop new strategies, and assess the outcome of their efforts. A few premises must be accepted at the outset.

The first is that marketing costs money. Without designating a specific amount of the private practice budget to marketing, the marketing efforts will be doomed to failure. Without a particular plan in mind and a measurable way of assessing the outcome, a private practitioner would do better to not market at all. Marketing always begins by understanding the identified population, developing specific strategies to reach that population, and assessing the outcome of those strategies. In the highly competitive marketplace that most private practitioners face today, they need a multifaceted marketing program—a variety of approaches to the marketplace. These approaches fall under two general categories: name recognition and target marketing.

Name Recognition

Name recognition is marketing with the specific goal of establishing the name of the practice in the eyes of the community and referral sources. Name recognition will occur over time; it is not an instant way of establishing clients. Name recognition is designed to give a long-term effect and positive flow to the practice. Tactics such as billboard advertising or constant newspaper advertising are good name recognition methods because by their very nature they provide an awareness of the practice to the public, but they are not practical for private practitioners. In private practice, effective and practical name recognition methods are yellow pages ads, business cards, stationery, signs outside the office, listings in community resources—any effort that continually makes the public aware of the practice name.

Target Marketing

Target marketing, on the other hand, is marketing with a specific goal in mind, a specific way of directly generating clients for the practice. Target marketing methods include advertisements or columns in local newspapers, announcements, flyers, open houses, workshops, speaking engagements—specific time-oriented efforts designed to have a measurable, immediate response. A good marketing effort throughout a 12-month period will involve both types of marketing: name recognition and target marketing.

A marketing analysis should be completed each year, and may need to be revised every 6 months as a way of assessing present marketing efforts as well as planning strategies for future marketing. This plan does not include all the factors that should be considered for any local area. Depending on the specifics of the practice and considerations regarding state regulations, licensing laws, and ethical standards, the marketing plan may need to be slightly modified. But it is designed to give structure to understanding marketing for private practice.

Marketing Takes a Positive Attitude

To be successful in private practice therapists must develop a positive attitude, a commitment, and a strategy to market their services. Many therapists seem to view marketing as self-promotion and often feel it is self-serving and inappropriate. This may be due to family upbringing or professional training. Therapists who feel this way need to explore their reasons for not marketing because in private practice marketing is essential for success. Marketing can be defined as anything a therapist does that makes clients or referral sources aware of the type and quality of service they offer. Marketing has to become a way of life. Each day is filled with potential opportunities to market the services of the practice. Recognizing and utilizing the opportunities begins with the counselor's attitude that must be based on confidence, assuredness, and stability in personal beliefs, because the foundation of any marketing is the practitioner. When the therapist has a positive attitude about the practice, it is projected in all verbal, written, and visual forms of communication. The attitude of "Why should I market?" has to be replaced with "I owe it to myself and my clients to market."

The reason a private practitioner opens a practice is to offer quality service to the public in exchange for a fee. If the counselor believes that the service is ethically and morally sound, assuring clients of that is an obligation. In fact, marketing protects the client. The counselor who neglects to market is not only minimizing him- or herself, but also is avoiding the responsibility to help inform the public of what good therapy is and what the standards of competence are. Consequently, lack of marketing might prevent clients' needs for therapy from being met simply due to ignorance about what is available. When practitioners actively market various approaches, techniques, and methods, the public learns that there are choices. When practitioners are willing to market, they are willing to open themselves and their practice to public appraisal. It's important to remember that the hallmark of a successful practice is satisfied clients, and satisfied clients will market their therapists most effectively.

Marketing Takes Commitment

It takes time and money to tell people about the therapist's values, approaches, techniques, and training. This commitment is time-consuming. It is not something done one day and then left for a week or a month; marketing is continuous. Each day marketing takes place either directly or indirectly: directly, by something that is said or done (talking on the phone to a prospective client, providing therapy for a client, or giving a talk to a local church or civic organization), or indirectly (by a yellow pages ad, flier left at someone's office or a newsletter sent from the practice office). When I first started my practice, I learned painfully that my practice would not be successful unless I was willing to put time into it. I have often reminded myself that what made my practice so successful so quickly was that I started each day considering it as a full day of work and planned to work a full 40-hour week, even though I didn't see that many clients. In the beginning, I simply went into the office each day, sat at my desk, and planned ways to market—made calls to set up meetings, developed workshop proposals, and wrote letters. All this became the foundation for a sound marketing commitment.

Marketing Takes Money

A wise saying states, "You can't make an omelet without breaking an egg, and you can't make money without spending money." In the beginning the expense will be more than the income. This expenditure is designed to do five things:

1. **Increase the Appointments in the Book.** It is important to remember that clients do not come to a practice by chance; they come because in some way they were made aware of the existence of the practice. To increase the appointments in the book, the practitioner must keep in mind that a consistent marketing effort will maximize chances for a full appointment book.

2. **Improve the Quality of Clients.** Consistent marketing will attract a higher grade of client. New practitioners usually get clients who terminate prematurely, who are often unable to pay the full fee, or who may not be motivated to accept the particular techniques the therapist wants to use. But with a consistent marketing effort, the practice will begin to attract clients who will come specifically for the service offered, knowing the cost and willing to make the commitment.

3. **Expand the Types of Services.** By a continual marketing effort, the therapist becomes aware of other needs within

the community and can plan how the practice may be able to meet those needs. As a result, the practitioner can start offering other services to the general public such as workshops, lectures, and speeches that will improve and expand the base of the practice.

4. **Maintain Existing Referral Sources.** The marketing effort is expanded by keeping contact with good referral sources. One of the greatest mistakes established private practitioners make is failing to keep an active commitment to their referral sources. With the high level of competition among practitioners that exists in many communities, referral sources pay the most attention to the therapists who stay in constant touch with them. A diligent marketing effort reminds those referral sources of changes in the practice and of the need for a flow of quality clients.

5. **Keeping Ahead of the Competition.** With a consistent marketing effort, the practitioner is able to evaluate the competition and what needs to be done to meet new trends. Our culture is one that always creates trends. Some of these trends are short-lived and some become established changes in society. The practitioners who market their services will also be aware of what other colleagues are offering and be better able to match or offer better services.

Marketing Takes Concern

The rationale for marketing is to let the public know what practitioners do and why that is of value to the public. Everyone goes into private practice for a purpose. If the purpose is shallow or morally or ethically wrong, that will manifest itself in the marketing. The marketing reflects the practitioner's beliefs. Hundreds of fliers and newsletters from therapists come across my desk every year. I always look to see what the real message is for me, the potential consumer. Does it reflect a warm openness and caring? One of the most important elements in any marketing piece is the reflection of a warm concern for the public and for the potential client.

Does It Reflect the Need of the Public?

Putting together a workshop flier, yellow pages ad, or any other type of marketing that does not tap into the needs of the public gives the impression that the therapist is isolated from the public, and not fully aware of its needs. Any marketing effort must reflect the current needs of the community. Each community is unique; each community has its own needs. I'm reminded of an example in a local community where there was a very high incidence of drug abuse. Some therapists in that community began to offer drug awareness workshops for parents when this crisis was reported in the local newspaper. These therapists were, in fact, reflecting the needs of the community.

Does It Reflect a Sense of Values?

In a society in which values are often confused and misunderstood, therapists should be willing to put their own values into their marketing effort. Practitioners who invite the public to judge them and their practice often find themselves in an enviable position. Not everyone may like what the therapist has to offer, but by clearly stating what the services are, clients who need these services will be attracted. An example would be therapists clearly stating they work from a certain religious orientation and are offering services to the community. Their statements reflect their value systems in their marketing.

Does It Reflect the Person?

Anyone who considers coming to a workshop or training session wants to have some sense of who the leader or trainer is. A picture or a biography personalizes the marketing so the public can feel they have some idea of who this person is and that he or she can be trusted. More and more yellow pages advertisements for professionals use pictures. The effectiveness of this marketing technique has been proven. People do select professionals on the basis on their comfort level with them, and seeing a photograph of the professional in an ad conveys a sense of the professional's willingness to stand behind the service.

Marketing Takes Strategy

Practitioners must know themselves, the community, and the competition to launch a successful marketing effort. The strategy should be based on a marketing plan that involves personal, mass, and passive exposure. **Personal exposure** is accomplished through personal contact such as calls, lunches, meetings, and open houses where the therapist has the opportunity to sell him- or herself in a one-to-one situation. **Mass strategies** are workshops, seminars, lectures, teaching experiences, talk shows, television appearances, and membership in various community organizations in which the therapist presents an overall image of him- or herself to a large group of people. Mass marketing strategy is based on name recognition and involvement. People will learn about a therapist through the mass presentations where the seed has been planted. When the opportunity arises to seek the services the therapist has to offer, the therapist's name will surface as the appropriate person to deliver those services. **Passive marketing strategies** involve yellow-pages advertisements, practice newsletters, and advertisements in local papers, publications, or professional newsletters where the intent is to place the practice's and therapist's names in front of a large body of potential referrals or clients. The consistency of this name recognition effort without the therapist's having any direct involvement is why it is considered a passive strategy.

A private practice is successful when the public is satisfied with the service. The satisfaction of the public is, in fact, successful marketing.

Demographics

To plan a successful marketing approach, private practitioners must understand where their clients come from and the type of clients they have. This demographic information can usually be obtained if there is an intake form used as part of the practice. (The use of an intake form will be discussed in greater detail in a later section.) The market analysis also includes specific information about the types of client problems. This often gives a clue for developing a marketing strategy based on the type of client problems presented. Another item to consider is the type of problem worked on in therapy. The importance of this is to find a contrast between what a client may give as the presenting problem and what the problem worked on in therapy actually is.

The other two aspects of demographic information deal with the average number of sessions. This can often reveal whether the practice is the type that attracts long-term clients or clients with short-term problems. An analysis of the number of intake sessions and return visits each month helps to form a picture of what is going on in the practice. Keeping these specific numbers month to month and year to year often helps in understanding what kind of marketing effort needs to be developed during specific months of the year.

Referral Sources

In analyzing a practice, it is important to understand the sources of clients. Within the professional community there are a wide variety of professional sources. Everyone may be trying to attract clients from physicians and chiropractors, not realizing the number of clients that may be available if one markets to ministers, youth-aid officers, police, or lawyers. Private practitioners need to know whether they are missing a segment of potential referrals. This knowledge comes from continually analyzing referral sources. This analysis will help in understanding what additional marketing efforts may be needed, especially in seeking new clients. Many referral sources have only a limited number of professionals to refer to simply because no one has ever asked them to refer clients. Local police departments and social agencies are prime examples. Many therapists who work with youth or family problems fail to realize that police departments and social agencies would often be excellent referral sources. Many therapists who work with substance and chemical abuse fail to realize that attorneys are often excellent sources of clients in that area.

Another analysis that needs to be made in regard to referral sources is personal referrals to the practice. What percentage of clients are coming from present clients, past clients, and personal friends? The analysis of this information often gives a sense of how strong the practice is for present and past clients. When present and past clients refer to a practice, it builds a strong foundation for a referral pyramid. The broader the base of referrals, the stronger the practice will become. Depending on a narrow group of referral sources can be detrimental to a practice. For example, I have kept all my past clients on my mailing list along with neighbors, friends, and other colleagues. Often I receive referrals from those individuals for workshops, seminars, and in some cases, personal therapy, simply because they are on my newsletter list and constantly receive information about changes in my practice.

Assessing Techniques

After analyzing types of clients and referral sources, the practitioner's self-analysis is extremely important because self-marketing is the foundation on which the marketing campaign is built. Therapists should analyze their own personal assessments as therapists on a regular basis so that they do not miss areas that could lead to marketing strategies. Examples: What makes you qualified to do what you do? What makes your approach different from others'? These questions will help the therapist understand specific treatment methods, techniques, or experiences that can be offered to the public that will be different from other therapists' who are competing for the same marketplace. Understanding specifically what type of clients respond best to the practitioner's methods will also help narrow the marketing campaign to its particular target clients. Analyzing the types of clients whom the practitioner refers to other therapists will help to shape marketing efforts so that the wrong type of clients are not attracted to the practice. Analysis of specific strengths and weaknesses will help the ongoing change in the practice. Identification of a weakness can help bolster the overall effectiveness of the practice by analyzing what to do about that weakness. The importance of keeping new awards, degrees, certifications, or recognitions in the media through free public advertising cannot be overestimated.

Competition Analysis

To plan a successful marketing strategy one must be aware of the competition's activity. Listing four specific competitors will help the practitioner understand what is happening in the marketplace, who the major competitors are, what types of marketing they are doing, and what strengths are evident in their marketing. When the phone book comes out each year, the first thing I do is compare my ad with the ads in the book of my major competitors. Often I've found crucial points they have emphasized that I have not, or areas that I have emphasized that they have not. Knowing the competitors allows the therapist to tailor the marketing. Assuming that the competition's marketing efforts do not need to be analyzed is failing to realize that often the same referral sources or potential clients will be trying to choose a therapist based on the information contained in the marketing efforts. Taking time to analyze the competition will often reveal methods to improve marketing.

Marketable Strengths

In analyzing marketing, it is important to understand that specific words or concepts are critical. Using specific words or concepts to which the public is most sensitive provides a way to analyze each piece of promotional material or marketing. Examples follow:

Specific Certifications. If a therapist is certified to do certain kinds of work such as sex counseling, rehabilitation counseling, rational emotive therapy, or biofeedback, these particular terms should be noted.

Types of Population. Specifying the types of clients the therapist works with is important in marketing. Knowing what type of clients to gear the marketing to, and using words that would attract those clients, ensures that the marketing will be successful. Examples of words or phrases are children, adolescents, adults, recovery, adult children of alcoholics, pain, or spiritual development.

Hours. In some cases it is important to indicate if evening hours or weekend sessions are available. I am reminded of one therapist who built a very successful family counseling practice by offering Saturdays and Sundays as primary office days. He chose to take days off in the middle of the week, knowing that more families could come on weekends. By advertising that in the yellow pages and in the newspaper, he found that his practice flourished within the first 6 months. He has been able to cut some of the weekend work back now that he has developed a strong referral base, but in the beginning, knowing that he could market those the hours was extremely valuable to him.

Types of Therapy. Marketing group work, individual work, couples' work, or marriage, family, and specific types of counseling or approaches should be included in any marketing literature.

Insurance Reimbursement. Insurance reimbursement is part of the payment system. Noting that reimbursement is approved and accepted may be an important drawing card.

Use of Picture. More and more professionals are including a picture as part of the marketing effort. People easily identify with a face.

Promotional Activities

Analyzing specific promotional activities with attention to type, cost, and usage will help to break down the variety of materials and approaches a practice is using to promote itself. It bears repeating that yellow pages advertisements consistently attract clients. Promotional activities can be divided into internal and external types. Internal promotional activities include promotional materials available in the office or mailed that specifically deal with name recognition.

Business Cards

Business cards should always be made available in the waiting area of a practice. Often clients will take a business card with them to give to a friend when they leave the waiting area. Business cards also should be passed out at workshops, presentations, or lectures. Keeping a record of how many cards were purchased each year and how many were passed out will often give an idea of the success of the marketing effort in name recognition. Practice brochures fall into the category of internal promotional materials because they are often made available in the waiting area, handed to referral sources directly, and passed out at workshops.

Handout Materials

Handout material in a waiting area is another often-missed opportunity. This is material prepared and made available to clients on specific community resources, such as a listing of community churches, meetings, support groups, hospitals, and dietary centers. Any information made available to clients should have an imprint stamp or some other notation indicating it is "compliments of the practice." Clients often take these internal promotional materials and pass them on to others. This clearly works as a name recognition method.

Purchased Materials

These consist of booklets, pamphlets, and newsletters purchased by the practice to provide helpful information to its clients. I purchase a number of 2- to 4-page booklets that focus on the problems my clients face. Examples would be booklets on stress, drinking, or family communication. All purchased materials are clearly marked as coming from the practice.

Practitioner-Developed Materials

Often practitioners write their own material for handouts at workshops, write columns for newspapers, develop practice newsletters, or have articles published in professional journals or general public magazines. All these materials serve as marketing tools when made available to clients.

External Promotional Activities

If a practice newsletter is developed, notation should be made of the cost of production, the number sent out each time, and whether the newsletters are made available in the waiting area for clients to take. Promotional fliers are target marketing tools designed for a specific workshop, lecture, speech, or program that involves the practitioner. Listing each one with cost, number used, and frequency will help in analyzing the effectiveness of this material. Paid advertisements include ads placed in a specific targeted newsletter, school yearbook, or other source.

Promotional Budget

In doing the monthly analysis, it is important to break out the figures to know that in certain months there are standard recurring costs, such as yellow pages advertising, and specific costs, such as the printing of cards, brochures, or fliers that will be used throughout the year, but the cost may be incurred only in one particular month. In breaking down monthly costs it is best to have two columns, one for fixed costs and one for specific costs, with a notation as to what those items were. Then it is important to look at the projection for the following year. Again, certain items are known to be fixed, and other items may be planned as the budget is projected into the following year.

In conclusion, having a specific marketing plan and evaluating it every 6 months allows a therapist to apply effective techniques for increasing the business market share. The plan that has been proposed is designed to allow modifications and changes for individual needs. Marketing without a plan is a waste of time and money. Not evaluating the marketing to know whether it is effective is also a waste of time and money. Running a business requires a good business plan. Running a good marketing effort requires a good marketing plan. Repeatedly, a strong marketing effort has been shown to be the reason for success in private practice.

GETTING YOUR NAME IN PRINT

Most small private practices with one or two therapists have a limited budget for advertising and marketing. Because of this, advertising tends to be restricted to word of mouth, with some use of printed materials. And yet, advertising is essential to the growth of the practice, to bring the therapist's name and services to the attention of prospective clients and referral sources.

One solution to the budget problem is to take full advantage of the possibilities for free advertising in the mass media. A well-planned, consistent effort to market in this way can double or triple public exposure, thus increasing the share of the market.

I learned a long time ago that getting my name and services mentioned in the paper translated into more clients. As my practice has grown, I have maintained my commitment to using this kind of publicity. The continued marketing of the group as a whole, and of the individual therapists, increases public awareness of services. Having the practice's name appear in the newspaper has an added advantage: Because newspapers carry a great deal of weight, and are perceived as printing only provable facts, having the name in print can establish the practitioner in the public eye as an authority.

There are essentially three ways to get a name in the paper: sending a press release, sending a PSA (public service announcement), or convincing the editor to do an article on the practice and its services. Most newspaper articles result from a suggestion made to a writer. The services the practice provides could easily form the basis for such an article. To take advantage of these opportunities, there are a few key rules to follow.

It's up to the individual practitioners to let the press know what they do. Often a therapist feels that he or she is doing great things with clients, or is engaged in exciting new research, but no one else seems to know about it or to be interested. The only way to get them interested is to tell them. Newspapers are always looking for material and will print an article about anything they think would interest their readers.

Look at things from the newspaper's point of view. The media want subjects that will capture readers' attention. The therapist may be fascinated by new developments in diagnosis, but most lay people really aren't. Facts are great, but there's a human interest side to therapy, and that's the side to present to the press. Don't send in long, dry copy that requires a lot of work for media employees; they probably won't do it. Give it to them in a form that makes it easy for them to rewrite or edit the information.

Be familiar with the media in the local area. Most communities are served by more than one newspaper, and these will vary in format and focus. For example, in this area we have three newspapers, two dailies and a weekly paper. The daily papers give a blend of national and local news, but each weekend they publish a statewide edition with a section on human interest stories about people in Maine. This is the edition in which I would try to get an article printed. The daily papers are strictly local and serve a small population. Working with this type of paper usually requires a personal contact with the editor. A thorough discussion of the type of stories the editor is looking for will increase the chances of being printed.

Public Service Announcements

Occasionally it may be possible to get an article featuring the services offered by the practice into the paper. However, most papers print PSAs and press releases regularly. A public service announcement (PSA) does just what the title suggests: It lets people know about a public service. If the therapist is giving a talk, presentation, or workshop that is open to the public, the paper may be interested in a PSA. To qualify for this, the event being announced usually has to be free to the public, but check with the local newspaper for guidelines. The information in the PSA should include the answers to: who, what, where, and when, and the name and telephone number of a contact person if the newspaper or readers want more information.

A Sample PSA

Here is an example of the kind of PSA I send. Once or twice a year, I speak at a support group called Divorce Perspectives. This organization was formed about 10 years ago to help individuals who are separated, going through a divorce, or divorced. They meet every week and have either a speaker or an open discussion meeting; I have spoken to them on sexual issues at least once a year for the past 10 years. Because they have no money to pay speakers, I volunteer my time to them, and then try to take advantage of the publicity this community service can bring.

First, I prepare the press release myself, even if the group I am speaking to offers to do it. Because I'm not getting paid for my services, I want to be sure that I receive some benefit, and writing and sending the release myself ensures this. At the top of the sheet I put the name and telephone number of the person at my office to contact for more information. The body of the release goes as follows:

NEWS

Release Date:	Oct 28, 1999
Contact Person:	Sam Smith
Phone:	555-0000

There will be a free presentation sponsored by Divorce Perspectives, a support and informational group for individuals going through a divorce, or already divorced, on Wed. Nov 4, 1999, at 7:30 p.m. at the Woodfords Congregational Church. The speaker will be Dr. Daniel L. Richards, PhD, NCC, a sex educator and counselor certified by the American Association of Sex Educators, Counselors and Therapists. His topic will be "Divorce, How to Maintain a Healthy Sexual Outlook."

Dr. Richards has said that "divorce is a devastating experience for one's sexuality. Both parties often feel exploited during their marriage and divorce only heightens these angers and insecurities. With today's fears about the singles' life, a thorough understanding of one's sexual needs and desires will often go a long way in eliminating the fears of seeking a new relationship and sexual partner. Sex does not need to be taboo, but communication is a must."

Dr. Richards has a private practice in sex counseling in Portland, Maine. He has spoken on the topic of sexuality throughout Maine and New England. He has published a number of articles, and is on the editorial board of the *Journal of Sex Education and Therapy*. Dr. Richards will share his frank and honest comments about sexuality and sexual expression with the public at this free presentation. For more information about Divorce Perspectives, contact Sam Smith at 555-0000.

●   ●   ●

As you can see, this release contains all the essential information in a few brief paragraphs, with the facts about who, what, where, and when in the first two sentences. Editors are busy people and don't have time to read pages of information. Long, wordy descriptions tend to end up in "circular filing." If editors don't have to hunt to find the information, they're more likely to use it.

Receiving free publicity from the press is not hard to arrange, and it will definitely increase the exposure in the community and expand the practice. To get the exposure, the practitioner must be willing to do a little homework on how the press works in the local area and then prepare the material for them. The press generally won't seek out the practitioner, but if they are offered a story they think is relevant to their readers, they will often print it.

Press Releases

A press release is simply a way of giving information to the press. Suitable topics for press releases can include: a new practice, a new associate or partner, a book or article that has been published, or a report of a presentation given at a national professional association convention. Most things that affect a practice are of potential interest to the public. As with PSAs, press releases should be brief and to the point. Include the practice's name and telephone number and a short biography.

Here are some tips to help ensure that a PSA or press release will be used by the newspaper:

Who is it about? Be clear and concise, but state all the qualifications relevant to the topic. Include only those certifications and licenses that apply to the current subject.

Where is the therapist speaking? If the talk is to a group or association, be sure to include this information.

Provide quotes. Supplying direct quotes from a sample talk or article means the paper can quote without having to take the time to call personally. Also, an interesting quote can catch the eye of an editor or writer and prompt them to follow up later for a feature or story.

Include a photograph. If a professionally taken photograph is available, send it with the release. Generally speaking, newspapers like to include photographs, and this makes the public familiar with a face as well as a name.

Send it to the relevant editor. Call the newspaper to obtain the name, so that the announcement doesn't get lost in the interoffice shuffle. If a cover letter is sent with the release, make it short, and emphasize the importance of letting the public know about the presentation. Thank the editor in advance for publishing the release. After the release has appeared and the presentation has been made, a note of thanks is a nice gesture. The editor handling this kind of material often doesn't get much recognition, and this may bring a positive reaction next time a release is sent.

GETTING FREE RADIO EXPOSURE

Radio is an excellent way to reach a large population because almost everyone listens to one radio station or another sometime during the day. The diversity of listeners' needs has caused radio stations to become extremely specialized. One growing area is that of talk radio—news and public interest programming. As a professional skilled in the area of human growth and development, the private practitioner is an excellent candidate for an interview or presentation on these programs. Such a presentation will enhance the practitioner's image in the community as a professional, even as an expert, on a given topic.

The first step to being heard on the radio is to choose a program or talk show, and let the program manager or talk show host or hostess know about the product, specialty, or service. The best way to do this is to write a letter and follow up by a telephone call. Using a letter as an introduction means that the message is more likely to be seen directly by the person it is intended for and not screened out by someone else, as often happens with telephone calls. To ensure this, the letter should be short and specific. Letters that take more than 45 seconds to read will often remain unread, or will be put in a pile of letters to be read "when there's a little more time." In most cases, three paragraphs suffice. An example might read as follows:

Dear (name of manager or host):

On a recent show I heard you (or your news commentator) discuss the issue of sexual abuse and the growing concern nationally, and specifically in our local area. Sexual abuse is of major concern to all of us and I commend you on your comments. I would like to offer my expertise in this area if you (or your station) would like to cover this topic further.

I am in private practice and am certified as a sex counselor by the American Association of Sex Educators, Counselors and Therapists. Within the scope of my practice I have worked with a number of individuals who have been sexually abused as children.

I am enclosing a copy of my self-disclosure brochure and my practice newsletter, as well as copies of articles I have written on this subject. I realize your schedule is busy and I appreciate the time you have taken to read this letter. I will be calling your office on (list a day about a week from the date of your letter) to discuss my interests further.

Sincerely,

(Your Name)

On the date stated in the letter, telephone the station manager as arranged. Because people seek therapy for many reasons that are likely to be of interest to a radio audience, there should be little difficulty in convincing the news staff of the value to be featured on a talk show, or to be interviewed by one of the news staff.

People tend to be apprehensive about being on a radio talk program, so here are a few suggestions. To begin with, speaking on the radio is best thought of as "powerful speaking"; that is, radio speakers won't be able to see and respond to the people listening, so they must present themselves as powerful and knowledgeable without that feedback. Some easy rules to follow for giving a powerful presentation follow.

Be Yourself

First and foremost, when talking on the radio, be yourself! As an individual in the helping professions, a therapist's personal style is to deal with people. Let that come through to the listeners. Don't be stuffy, tight, or controlled. Speakers will be judged by their voices; ensure that the judgment is positive. A good way to conduct a self-test is to tape a conversation with a friend, then replay the tape and see how confident your voice sounds. Does it seem to communicate energy to the audience? They can't see the speaker, so the voice must excite, engage, and hold their attention. If the speaker doesn't seem to be excited, even passionate at times, the audience will quickly lose interest.

Be Aware

Be aware of the listeners. Speakers must never speak to themselves. Have a dialogue with the commentator and imagine that he or she represents hundreds of others. Keep good eye contact and read the host's facial expressions. The host's responsibility is to bring out the best in the guest, and a guest can help make that job easier.

Project Self-Esteem

Project self-esteem by sounding strong, definite, and resolute. Listeners respect assertive speakers. They want to sense that the speaker is comfortable with him- or herself and the topic. The speaker is the expert and listeners want what he or she has to offer.

Radio is a wonderful way to reach a large, diverse population of potential clients. Getting on the air may take a little effort on the practitioner's part but, with persistence, it can provide a great deal of free advertising. Don't be afraid to use the media. They are an excellent way to increase name recognition in the community.

USING FREE PRESENTATIONS TO ATTRACT PROSPECTIVE CLIENTS

Every private practitioner has a unique skill or way of working with clients; in some way, however small, each therapist is an expert. As an expert, the practitioner could put together a workshop, speech, or talk about his or her area of expertise. Because private practitioners depend on the income generated by seeing clients, consulting, and training, they often develop the attitude that whenever they do something, they should be paid. This idea is valid enough on the whole, but if carried to extremes, it can strangle practice growth by limiting the activities to those that generate a fee. A workshop or talk given to the public free of charge will increase public exposure, enhance the therapist's name as an expert, broaden the referral base, and increase the opportunities to give talks and workshops for a fee, ultimately resulting in more clients.

Planning the Presentation

When planning a free presentation, start by choosing a topic, keeping in mind that the audience will consist of lay people. Because presentations are usually geared to the professional community, it is important to remember that most lay people are not familiar with professional terminology and "jargon." Choosing a topic that is likely to appeal to the general public, and one with which the therapist feels competent, is a sure formula for attracting people. Describe the topic in simple terms, for example, "Helping Children Improve Their Self-Esteem," "Ways for Single Parents to Deal with Teenagers" or "Food: How I Wish I Could Control Myself!"

Duration

Any of the topics suggested above could provide material for a day-long workshop, but for the purposes of a free presentation, a briefer format is better. Most people will pay attention for 1½ hours at the most. Plan to present for this length of time, and break the topic down to its simplest level. To help with this, use something called the 50–25 rule. To use this technique, write the talk out either in a concise written outline or a complete draft of the entire talk. Leave it for a day or so. Then come back to it and cut out 50% of the content. Leave it again for a few days, then return and cut 25% more. Doing this will reduce the subject matter to its simplest form and leave the essential substance of the topic. It may also help to remember that, although 1½ hours are available, the talk should be half that length, leaving 45 minutes for questions. The audience will come with more questions than can possibly be answered.

Handouts

The essence of good marketing is getting the name out to people. Whenever a workshop or presentation is given, participants should leave with the name, address, and telephone number of the speaker. The easiest way to do this is by preparing material for them to take along at the end of the presentation. A simple outline of the talk with the major points, no more than a single side of a page in length, with the imprint of the practice at the top makes a good handout.

The handout should be prepared carefully. Use good quality paper, and either have it duplicated on a good photocopy machine or have it printed. If the talk will be given often, or to a large number of people, it may be worthwhile to spend a little extra to have it typeset, which adds a great deal to the appearance of the handout. A typeset page can be either printed or photocopied. The emphasis here is on professional quality; a poorly typed outline produced on a smudgy photocopier conveys the message that quality isn't important to the speaker, and may keep people from seeking that practitioner's advice.

Make sure the name, address, and telephone number are clearly displayed on the page. I have often received handouts at professional presentations that lacked the presenter's name. This defeats much of the purpose of giving a free presentation. The purpose of a handout is for people to use it and keep it, whether for themselves or to give to a friend. Make it easy for people to contact the practice by imprinting the name and telephone number on all material handed out.

Location

Where should the presentation be held? In my experience, if I feel that I'm going to use my talk to enhance my client base, I hold it in my office. This can present a problem for those who have home offices because it might not be a good idea for the general public to come to the speaker's home. It might be better to hold the talk in a colleague's office, or in a church, school, or other public place. Doing this may have a negative effect on the marketing, however, because the office reflects the practitioner, and when the office can't be shown, some potential clients will judge the therapist based on someone else's surroundings.

For those who lease space or own their own offices, holding a talk in the office space allows participants to see the practitioner in his or her work surroundings. It also means that if they decide to become clients, or if they refer someone else, they know just how to find the office or provide directions for friends.

Time

Two points are important in setting the date and time of a presentation: The date should not be too close to a holiday, and these should be enough time to prepare a marketing approach and the relevant marketing material. Tuesday through Thursday evenings seem to be the best times for talks and workshops, with Tuesdays and Wednesdays drawing the greatest response. Because people generally don't like to be out after 8:30 p.m., starting times of 6:00 p.m. or 7:00 p.m. are best. Marketing studies repeatedly show that if people are going to shop or go out in the evening, most do so after supper, returning by a reasonable hour.

Marketing the Presentation

The purpose of giving a free presentation is to make the practitioner's name better known, therefore marketing the presentation is important. Target three main groups: the press, radio, and TV; professional referral sources; and former clients. Because the presentation will be free of charge, most media will respond favorably to a request for exposure as long as their requirements are met.

To announce the presentation in the press, a PSA should be sent to the appropriate editor, with a cover letter stating that the workshop is free of charge to the public, and thanking the editor for publishing it. It is also a good idea to include a photograph with the PSA.

Because this announcement will generate most of the calls received, the PSA should state that space will be limited and reservations are required. This allows the practitioner to control the size of the group; 25 is the optimum number. Not only does this keep the group size manageable, but it also helps to determine how much material to prepare for handouts. Usually after 20 people have made reservations, I tell callers that they will be added to a waiting list, and if someone cancels we will let them know. Otherwise, the talk will be given again on the following Tuesday because of the interest shown, and we will add them to that list if that is acceptable. This gives the practitioner a certain amount of flexibility. If a total of 27 calls are received, the choice is between giving the presentation to all 27 people, or to present to 20 this week and 7 the following week. With good press coverage, a free presentation will often generate 75 or more calls, so be sure to have backup dates in mind.

Like the press, TV and radio have a commitment to PSAs, but some stations will do more than others. To let the local TV and radio stations know about the presentation, send a letter to the station manager with a brief PSA. An example would be:

"Drugs—What to Do to Help Your Child" will be the topic
of a free lecture by (the practitioner's name or the name
of the group) on Tuesday, October 5th at 7:00 p.m. For
more information call (telephone number).

Most stations devote a certain amount of time to PSAs. If the
station is given sufficient notice, the practitioner may be allotted
some of that time. Stations often receive more PSAs than time
allows, but a professional presentation often stands a better chance
of being aired than a fund-raising yard sale or public supper.

The other two target groups for marketing are professional
referral sources and former clients. If the practice has a newsletter, use it to announce the upcoming presentation, making
sure the referral sources and clients will receive the issue with
the announcement well in advance of the presentation date. An
alternative is to use a brief letter with a flier-type insert that can
be posted on a wall or bulletin board. Referral sources may post
this in their offices, and former clients may have access to a
bulletin board at work where they could post the announcement.

The Actual Presentation

Make coffee, tea, and light snacks (fruit, crackers, donuts)
available before the presentation so that when people arrive, they
can mill around and get comfortable. Use charts, a blackboard,
or overheads, but prepare the material so that everyone will be
able to read and see it clearly. At the end of the presentation,
give participants a 3 × 5 index card with a space for their name,
address, telephone number, and comments on the presentation.
Should you plan to hold a group session on the presentation
topic, this kind of presentation can be a good way to recruit
members to a group. The comment section on the card gives
people the opportunity to say that they would like to see the
therapist without having to reveal that publicly in front of the
group. When the cards are passed out, let people know that if
they would fill out the card and leave it in a box on the table at
the back of the room, they could also pick up materials available
such as business cards, self-disclosure brochures, practice
newsletters, a bibliography on the topic of the presentation, and
other items of interest. Asking participants to put the cards in
a box versus leaving them on a table, or signing up on a sheet,
will increase the chances that participants will give their name,
possibly revealing an interest to join a group or see the practitioner on an individual basis. Emphasize the fact that the cards
are confidential and any information received will not be made

public. Displaying the practice material means it doesn't have to be discussed during the talk when time is limited. Most people will pick it up if it's available.

A free seminar, talk, or workshop with a good title, relevant materials, and efficient marketing will enhance the practitioner's visibility in the community and broaden the client base. Giving something for nothing, if properly done, will always bring clients. Private practitioners shouldn't be afraid to give their expertise away because it always comes back to pay dividends.

WHEN PROFESSIONALS ARE HARD TO REACH

Working effectively with other professionals is an area that practitioners should be aware of in marketing the practice. Everyone who has had experience with professionals knows that they are sometimes hard to reach. The following guidlines should help.

When calling a doctor, lawyer, or other professional, the call usually will be screened by a secretary. The attitude the caller shows toward the person answering the phone will affect whether or not the desired contact with the professional will be made.

Be personable. The person answering the phone often has a stressful job, with most callers wanting their needs taken care of yesterday. The secretary will appreciate it if the caller is not aggressive.

Be respectful. Many callers treat secretaries or receptionists as unimportant people, as obstacles to be overcome in reaching the employer. A point to remember is that the employer trusts that person's judgment; the caller should trust it as well.

Develop rapport with the screener. Find out the screener's name and use it. Rapport begins when the names of both the screener and the caller are used.

Be brief and concise. A receptionist often has to answer a number of telephone lines, and time is important. A short message is easy to write on a message pad. Too many words means writing on the back of the pad or editing the message.

Be polite. Callers must remember to keep their temper if they have to be put on hold while another call is answered. No one likes to put a call on hold, so don't take it personally.

Leave a message that matters. The receptionist will want to write a message to record the call. Don't say, "Just tell him I called." Try instead: "Need to talk with you about referral," or

"Have information on a client you referred." This prepares the person being called regarding the subject the caller wants to discuss when they finally do get to talk.

Say thank-you. If the caller telephones frequently and the messages do get through, consider sending a thank-you note to the secretary or receptionist. Everyone likes to be appreciated. When sending the thank-you note, remember to include a couple of business cards. Referrals come from many sources.

Ask about time. Find out at what time the practitioner is most likely to return the call. Tell the receptionist if that is not a convenient time to receive calls and work out a different time. Take the responsibility for clearing the way for the return call. Many busy people try to return a call once, but then give up.

Answering machine etiquette. If the caller has an answering machine, he or she should tell the receptionist that, and indicate the times the phone will be answered personally. If the caller will not be available to answer the phone personally, he or she should ask about a time the call can be made again. Busy professionals don't enjoy talking to machines and may be put off by having to leave a message on an answering machine.

When the call comes. When the call is returned, thank the person for calling back. Showing respect and appreciation of their situation will go a long way in increasing the success of the call. Callers should imagine themselves in the other person's place and consider their convenience. People who are hard to reach are busy, but that need not deter the caller from getting in touch with them.

THE BUSINESS LUNCH

Almost everyone has heard and read about the advantages of taking prospective referral sources out to lunch, or sharing a business lunch with a colleague. It's tax-deductible, and 80% of the cost of such a meal can be used as a business write-off, based on the present tax law. Unfortunately, many private practitioners have never learned the procedures for making a business lunch effective. These are the kind of procedures in which large companies train employees, but which the private practitioner must discover personally. Over the years I've been in practice, I've taken many people to business lunches—and been taken out by others. Here are some the things I've learned to make the most of the meeting.

Setting It Up

Setting up a business lunch involves engaging the guest (a prospective referral source or colleague) at a time and location convenient for both parties for the purpose of sharing business information. The host or hostess must defer to the convenience of the guest. When calling to invite someone to lunch, have a couple of dates in mind and let the guest choose the date as well as the location. This not only conveys the message to the guest that he or she is worth extra effort, but usually also results in the guest's being able to give more time to the luncheon itself. For example, I have often found that busy physicians are almost impossible to meet, unless I meet them at the hospital cafeteria while they are on rounds or on call and have some free time. Being flexible and willing to defer to the other person's convenience creates a good impression from the beginning, which can be improved upon at the meeting to make the meeting as productive as possible.

The Luncheon

The first priority on the day of the business luncheon is to arrive before the guest. This gives an opportunity to alert the restaurant staff that one party has arrived (if you have a reservation), or to place the name on a waiting list. If the restaurant is extremely busy during lunchtime, reservations are advisable. If the guest has only an hour available, spending 20 minutes waiting for a table is not a good idea. Be sensitive to the guest's preferences regarding smoking or nonsmoking seating. Again, leave the choice up to the guest.

Once seated, allow the guest to make the selection from the menu first. This will give some idea of the tone and direction of the meal; if the guest orders a four-course meal, conversation will be limited, but if he or she is eating light, more time will be available to talk. The host or hostess should make a choice appropriate to the guest's; if the guest orders an appetizer followed by a large sirloin steak and baked potatoes, don't order a small cottage cheese with lettuce on the side, and don't order something that will take a lot of time and effort to consume. Remember that the primary purpose of this meeting is to discuss business, with culinary appreciation a definite second on the list.

Alcohol

One of the *don'ts* in a business lunch is the use of alcohol. People may talk about the three-martini lunch as an industry standard, but the mental health professional is aware of the effects of alcohol and substance abuse. Consuming alcoholic beverages at a business lunch may give the impression that what is preached is not practiced, or that the practitioner is uninformed. Even if the guest orders wine or another alcoholic beverage, it is inadvisable for the practitioner to order alcohol. This meeting has been arranged to develop a professional relationship with the guest, not to have that relationship judged by whether or not the host or hostess drinks.

Discussion

As the meal progresses, the host or hostess should begin the discussion and get to know the guest. It is important to talk with the referral source first about the type of practice or business being run, what the needs are, and how an effective working relationship might benefit both parties. Business lunches often go sour because the host or hostess starts right in with a sales pitch. Instead, begin the lunch by attempting to draw out the guest with the following four questions:

1. **What is your practice like?** By attempting to get an understanding of the type of client or patient the guest works with, the host or hostess will get an insight into the issues of the practice and information about potential ways for working together.

2. **What changes have you seen in your practice?** This question will give an opportunity to assess the historical background of the guest's practice, as well as the background of others in that professional field. For example, if I am meeting a gynecologist, I may ask him or her how developments in PMS and endometriosis over the last 10 years have affected the practice. This is usually an interesting subject for the gynecologist, and the treatment of it gives a good indication of how he or she looks at depression and anxiety in patients, which often are side effects of PMS and endometriosis.

3. **What do you feel are your needs for mental health practitioners?** This question is to find out what the guest sees as the role the mental health counselor, therapist, psychologist, or social worker plays in the professional field. This will often give some idea of the rate at which the guest refers clients, and the overall relationship desired with professionals referred to.

4. **How do you make referrals? Who actually makes the referral?** Is it the individual sitting across the luncheon ta-

ble, or is making the referral delegated to a secretary, nurse, or other person in the practice? This is important for follow-up. When communicating with the office, knowing the name of the person who should be called or added to the mailing list, along with the guest's name, is a wise move. For example, if physicians say that they only make the recommendations and that a nurse-practitioner actually selects the therapist, be sure that communication from the practice goes to both the physician and the nurse-practitioner.

The Host's Information

Because the host or hostess asks questions about the guest, the guest will eventually turn the focus to the host or hostess and will begin to ask questions about **his or her** practice. The guest will want to know what the host or hostess does, and how he or she might be helpful. Be ready to answer these questions in a clear and straightforward manner. Being able to express what you do and what makes you qualified will help project the image of a confident professional.

What do you do?

When answering this question, try to confine the answer to those areas of the practice that are strengths. If practitioners present themselves as generalists, it can be confusing to the referral source. Most referral sources want to think of the practitioner in one or two areas of expertise, so being able to point out those areas where the host or hostess is most comfortable helps in referral. This doesn't mean that the practitioner can't suggest, as conversation continues, that he or she is also competent in other areas, just that these are specialty areas.

What makes you qualified?

Be ready and willing to discuss qualifications. Mental health professionals often seem unwilling to explain the type of training and experience they have had in the areas where they claim specialties. Just telling a physician that you are a licensed psychologist, social worker, or counselor does not let the physician know that you have the skills and training to work in the area of need. Practitioners should formulate in their own mind what makes them qualified to work in their area and be ready to articulate it clearly to their guests.

Why should they refer to you?

Be careful: This question is loaded. The guest, a potential referral source, may say that he or she is presently using another individual or group for referrals; why should the guest use the luncheon host or hostess instead of the other individual? Under no circumstances discuss the competence, professional integrity, or professional credentials of another individual or group. Enhancing your own image by tarnishing someone else's doesn't work. If you put the other professional down, you may end up sounding frustrated, small-minded, or jealous, but never like an unbiased professional. Take a look at these two exchanges:

> **Dr. X**: I have always used Mary Smith as my primary person to deal with postpartum depression. I find that she has the understanding I am often looking for, so why should I refer to you instead?
>
> **Hungry Professional**: Mary Smith? You really refer to Mary Smith? Oh, no, she's nowhere near as qualified as I am; I'd do a much better job. I'm really good at working with postpartum depression, and I've heard that she isn't great in this area. Besides, look at her degree—it's from Podunk U. Who ever heard of a good therapist from there?
>
> **OR**
>
> **Hungry Professional**: I don't know why you should choose me over Mary Smith. All I can say is that what I do in the area of postpartum depression is based on my training, expertise, and years of work in that area. I don't know Mary Smith's work and can't compare what she does to what I do. It sounds as if you are pleased with her. I only hope that you would consider me if you ever feel you would like to have another therapist to whom to refer clients.

Even if the host practitioner does not believe that the other professional is well qualified, it is never wise to put down the other person's credentials or ability. The guest may know the individual in question and may have been referring to this person for years, or may have some other relationship with him or her, which could put the host practitioner in an awkward position. Belittling someone else will make the practitioner look childish, and the purpose of a business lunch is to make a favorable impression.

The Host's Paperwork

At some time during the meal, the guest will indicate that he or she would like to have some of the host's material, such as a self-disclosure brochure or some business cards. Although many professionals take this opportunity to load the guest down with papers, I don't. The way I see it, I would prefer to have my guests look at my papers when they are back in the office, in the setting where they usually think about referrals. Giving them the paperwork at the end of the meal doesn't ensure this. My cards could get stuck in a pocket, disappearing until that coat is worn again, or they could end up in the bottom of a full briefcase. Instead of complying then and there, I tell my guest that I would like to forward some business cards and my self-disclosure brochure, as well as a copy of my practice newsletter, either the current issue, or a back issue relevant to the subjects we discussed over lunch. I also tell my guests that I will add them to my mailing list, and that they will receive my practice newsletter every month. When I return to my office, I write a personal note to my guest, enclosing the promised material. In this note, I begin by summarizing what my guest said to me about the practice, the changes seen over time, the use made of mental health professionals, and the individual in the office I should communicate with directly. I then indicate that I have enclosed some business cards and other written material on my practice, and that I have added the guest to my mailing list. In this way, I reinforce my image as a professional who follows through, as well as putting my material in front of them when they are at the office and have the time to review the material comfortably.

The End of the Meal

The final step in the business lunch is paying for the meal and deciding on the tip. The host practitioner is responsible for paying the whole cost of the meal. Unless you are in a restaurant that accepts only cash, try to pay with a business credit card. This gives a receipt for claiming the deduction, and also avoids the problems of using cash, such as miscalculating how much would be needed and being short, or having to fuss over getting the right change.

No matter what the service was like, tip generously. Treating staff badly or tipping poorly can ruin the good impression the practitioner has worked so hard to create. A tip of 20% will recompense the staff adequately and the practitioner won't look like someone who tries to skimp and cut corners.

If the guest wants to split the bill, I have always found it helpful to respond: "I invited you to join me for lunch. I appreciate the idea that you would like to split this with me, but I would prefer to pay for this one, and let you pay for the next lunch we have together." This puts the other person at ease, and will often reveal whether the meal went well and whether the guest would like to have another opportunity to meet.

The Follow-Through

The meal is over, and the follow-up letter has been sent. Stopping now would lose a considerable part of the benefit of the business lunch. This benefit involves recontacting the referral sources within a month of the lunch to see if they received the material, and to ask whether they read the practice newsletter and if they would like additional copies for patients or clients. That second contact is often the one that will reveal whether the meeting was successful and whether they are in fact considering the host practitioner for referrals.

Taking a colleague or potential referral source out for a business lunch can be an effective way of developing referrals, but only if it is handled in a professional manner and the legwork is done before and after the lunch. Don't be afraid to set up business lunches. They are an excellent way to develop the professional network a practice needs, but remember that the purpose of the lunch is business, not eating or socializing. Furthermore, the follow-through after the lunch will reveal the impact of the time spent with the guest.

THANK-YOUs GO A LONG WAY

Some years ago I was having lunch with a doctor who refers a number of clients to me. After lunch he said, "You know, Dan, I want you to know that I send a lot of people to you because I appreciate the follow-up you give me about them. I value the level of professionalism you show in your contact with me." This man has a very busy medical practice, and his referrals have been the foundation of my practice over the years. I've taken his comment to heart, and have increased my efforts to thank and inform referral sources.

The Backlog

For years I wrote personal letters to thank professionals for referrals. Unfortunately, as my practice grew and I got busier, it became harder and harder to find the time to write these letters. I began to develop a backlog of responses to write. The worst thing about having a stack of notes to write is that I never have enough time to write them all at once, so the letters don't get written. This was despite the fact that I was saying essentially the same thing in every letter.

Around this time, a chiropractor friend sent me a card to thank me for a referral I had made to him. I was struck by the simplicity and effectiveness of the idea, and by the professional image the card presented. Although I knew that the card was a stock card he had purchased, I appreciated the fact that my friend had remembered, and acknowledged, the referral I made.

Acknowledgment Cards

I have since used these referral acknowledgment cards myself, and have ultimately moved to developing them myself and having them printed. The advantage to using these cards is that they are a simple, cost-effective way to convey a message of thanks.

I have developed and now use four formats of acknowledgement cards:

The Friends' Card

The highest compliment I can receive about my work is when a person like you recommends someone to me. I appreciate the trust and confidence you have in me, and I will do my best to help your friend.

This card was designed to use in thanking friends who refer to a practice, such as neighbors, personal friends, and former clients. As many as a third of my referrals come from former clients, and although some therapists question whether a former client should be thanked for a referral, I believe that within the limits and structure of the professional relationship, my clients and I become friends. When they decide to give my name to someone and that person contacts my office, I appreciate the reaffirmation of trust, and I use this card to get back in touch with them.

The only thing I write on the card is my name. I do not put the name of the new client on the card in order to preserve confidentiality. I realize that the person giving the referral is usually aware of whether or not the friend contacts me, but just in case, I do not mention the new client by name. I do indicate to the client that I would like to send such a card and receive the client's permission to do so, and have never had a client object to this.

Client Card

> Referrals are a vital part of my practice. Your recent referral is appreciated and I will do my best to assist your client.

This card was developed as a way to communicate with professionals, such as other therapists, lawyers, and accountants, who refer to the people who use their services as "clients." Again, this card makes no reference to the name of the person referred; it simply acknowledges that someone to whom they gave my name has in fact contacted my office, and that I appreciate the referral. The card is always sent after the first session and, like the first card, only with the client's permission.

Patient Card

> Referrals are a vital part of my practice. Your recent referral is appreciated and I will do my best to assist your patient.

The only difference between this card and the preceding one is the substitution of the word "patient" for "client." I use this card with physicians, chiropractors, dentists—any professionals who consider people "patients." I send this card after the first session to indicate my appreciation of their giving my name.

I use this card only when I feel that the referring professional does not have an ongoing professional interest in or relationship with the client. If clients tell me that they phoned the physician's office and were given my name, or that they are not ongoing patients of the physician, I use this card.

Client-Named Card

> _____has been seen in my office and indicates that you are the referral source. Referrals are a vital part of my practice. I want to thank you for your trust and confidence. I expect that your patient will keep you informed of the progress of our work, but if you should have any questions, please feel free to call me.
>
> Sincerely,

On this card, with a release from the client, I use the client's name. I use this card with physicians who need follow-up from me regarding a client, but who do not need to receive a detailed letter from me at this point. The card lets the physician or other referral source know that the client has in fact come to see me, and I follow this up in a few weeks with a more detailed report. I have received an excellent response from using this card. The physician's office often calls me to thank me for the card and for the information that the patient has come to me. They value the fact that I communicate with them in a professional manner.

Time

Referral acknowledgment cards work because they are easy to use. I see clients back to back and put off paperwork until I have a large block of time. Thanking people often falls by the wayside when I have to fill out insurance forms and to do billings and other correspondence.

These cards are always at my desk, ready to be used. When I have finished seeing the client, I simply take out the appropriate card, address it, and sign and send it. That way the referral source receives an immediate response, but I have not had to tie up valuable time trying to compose a letter or make a telephone call. Timing is important; waiting until a personal phone call can be made or a letter can be written may cause delay in getting back to the referral source, thus hampering the relationship with that person.

Professional Image

Some people have questioned the professional image these cards present. After using these and similar cards in my own practice for a number of years, I have found that referral acknowledgment cards enhance my image and show a strong commitment to professionalism. The clear copy and raised printing show that I care enough to send quality pieces, and the fact that I personally hand-address and sign the cards reiterates my personal interest in both the client and the person who referred to me.

It is extremely important to get back in touch with referral sources immediately after a referral is received. The need to do that in a timely and cost-effective way is a high priority in the private practice.

I would encourage every private practitioner to use some type of acknowledgment form or card. Remember, acknowledging referrals is essential in producing a thriving private practice.

PLANNING A SUCCESSFUL OPEN HOUSE

An most often overlooked yet highly effective marketing tool is the open house. An open house, correctly done, can give excellent exposure to the private practice. From a cost-effectiveness standpoint, it represents the highest return for the investment. Open houses can be done to inaugurate a new office space, celebrate a new partnership or associate who has joined the practice, to show off a new service, or to target a potential referral group.

New Office Space

With the time and expenses involved in selecting a new or different office, most practitioners don't realize that professional referral sources, former clients, colleagues from a former group, and friends who are potential referral sources all would like to see and be a part of the excitement involved in the new venture. Inviting them to see the new space is not only good for public relations, but also for the professional image. People have a natural curiosity about seeing something new or redone. A professional office is no different. Often people want to know where the practice is located. Seeing the therapist's space also reveals a sense of the openness, warmth, and style of the service the practitioner will offer.

Celebrating a New Partner or Associate

People commonly consider that expansion of a business is a sign of its health and success. When a practice grows, an open house provides an opportunity to demonstrate the success of the service the practice offers. It also gives an opportunity to introduce the new members to supporters of the practice. Often those who come to such a gathering are already using or referring to the practice. Consequently, they already have an interest in its success. The opportunity to meet face-to-face and briefly discuss the advantages the professional offers is an excellent way to increase the chances of success.

Showing Off a New Service

With technology playing a bigger role in mental health services, the addition of a new computer, new screening services, or testing services or equipment for biofeedback provide an excellent chance to expose referral sources to the advantages these services hold for them. Many practices that use technology in their delivery base find this an excellent way to promote those services. People are naturally curious, and the best way to get referral sources to support a practice is to have them speak with confidence about the service. Many practitioners never think to invite people over to see a demonstration of the service. Instead, they simply send a letter or flier indicating that the service is available and why it is effective. For example, a practice has purchased a new computer for use in administering and scoring career tests, or biofeedback equipment for the treatment of stress. Inviting professionals to an open house and a demonstration is likely to increase the referral base from these people because they will have had an opportunity to view and even try the equipment first-hand, consequently making them more knowledgeable as a referral source.

Targeting New Referral Sources

Over the years I have used open houses to increase my referral base by targeting specific populations and inviting them to attend an open house. Often therapists don't realize how effective an open house can be in gaining exposure. Some examples of such targeted open houses are:

School Personnel

Consider inviting counselors, social workers, psychologists, special education staff, principals, nurses, or assistant principals (especially those handling discipline problems). In every school there are specific personnel who work closely with troubled students and families. These personnel are often frustrated by the lack of appropriate referral sources, especially in the private arena. Inviting them to an open house can open a whole new base for referrals.

Community Support Services

Headstart or day-care directors, public health nurses, social workers, community agency program directors, ministers, priests, rabbis—all are faced with the daily problems within the family and with individual family members. Very seldom are these people invited to an open house by a therapist in private practice.

Medical Community

Doctors are often too busy to come and their nurses or receptiontists are often the ones who handle referrals. If they like the therapist, the doctor will often refer to the practice. Consequently, inviting either specific medical personnel such as obstetricians/gynecologists or urologists and their staffs, or the greater medical community to an open house will pay off in referrals later.

Hospital Staff

Social workers, emergency room social workers, psychiatrists, and in-patient and out-patient staff are often looking for outside referral sources for clients or patients released from the hospital.

Business and Industry

Employee Assistance Program coordinators, placement coordinators, industrial nurses, and owners and managers of companies are all potential users of the service. These people are not typically invited to a private practice's open house and usually will respond favorably to being included.

College and University

Teaching staffs in the health and counseling or psychology fields, college counseling center staff, placement office staff, and school medical staff should also be a targeted group to invite to an open house.

The Actual Open House

The success of the open house will be based on proper structuring and timing. Invitations should be sent within 2 to 3 weeks of the event, with an RSVP request, preferably a printed RSVP card rather than a phone number to call. The card, especially if there is a self-addressed, stamped envelope, will encourage acceptance of the invitation.

Open houses should be held on Tuesdays, Wednesdays, or Thursdays from 4:30 p.m. to 5:30 p.m., except in the case of school personnel, when the time should be from 3:00 p.m. to 4:00 p.m. Mondays and Fridays are poor days to hold open houses in general. When people arrive at the open house, there should be someone there other than yourself to greet them and ask them to sign a guest book. This can be handled by a member of the family or a good friend. It is important that each guest sign so that a personal thank-you can be written to each person who made the effort to attend. This maximizes the effect of the open house. The thank-you should include a copy of the therapist's business card or information about the aspect of the service that was the reason for holding the open house.

Handout material such as business cards, brochures, abstracts of talks, information about services, or newsletters should be made readily available throughout the office space so that as people are milling around, they can select materials they wish to take along. The practitioner should avoid passing out material and should only refer people to locations where the material is available.

Keeping the open house informal and comfortable with soft background music and light snacks such as peanuts, crackers, and finger-foods is a must. If food is going to be served, it is important that someone other than the practitioner serve it so the practitioner is free to mingle with the guests. Guests tend to leave cups and napkins around the room, so the person serving should also pick up these used items and throw them away. Alcoholic beverages should not be served at an open house. With the conflicts in society over alcohol use and with more and more mental health practitioners being seen as crucial to the drug-alcohol recovery process, alcoholic beverages should be avoided.

Open houses can be valuable and important marketing tools. Holding one or two a year can bring excellent exposure for the practice, but proper planning and selection of target groups is critical for success.

KEEPING AHEAD OF THE COMPETITION

Keeping ahead of the competition means that practitioners must continually market their services. Too often practitioners fail to realize that a consistent, constant marketing effort is needed if growth, expansion, and ability to select clients for the practice is going to continue. This continual advertisement of the practitioner's services is what will determine whether the practice is running ahead of the competition or running to keep up with it. I have observed many practitioners who have allowed their marketing efforts to slip and their community involvement to wane. Then they become concerned and blame others for lack of referrals. Often they indicate that the lack of referrals is caused by the influx of new professionals in the marketplace. In fact, their referral bases are drying up simply because they are not keeping ahead of the competition by continually improving their marketing efforts. Reviewing the marketing plan on a systematic basis and offering some unique services in the practice will go far toward the continuing exposure of the practice.

PROFESSIONAL INVOLVEMENT

Practitioners do not always realize that being involved in their local, state, and national professional organizations is both an active and a passive way to market their practice. Many feel that the time required to become involved is lost money to their practice, when in reality the time involved often boosts the referral base and the long-term financial health of the practice. This professional involvement serves two different purposes: exposure of the practice and making known the needs of individuals in private practice.

Exposure of the Practice

As practitioners become involved in their organizations and choose to serve in some type of leadership role, they will receive the benefits of passive marketing of their practice. Often the professional organization will list the practitioner's work setting for members and leaders of the organization. Being able to indicate after the therapist's name that he or she is in private practice provides positive exposure. Colleagues also begin to learn what services the therapist has to offer. Involvement in professional organizations develops potential referral sources, that is, colleagues who are knowledgeable about the trends and changes in a practice.

Opportunities to Present at Conferences

Professional involvement increases the opportunity for the practitioner to present at local, state, or national meetings. All of these can be parlayed into successful marketing. I would like to explain how this method has been an effective marketing tool for me. I began my professional involvement in my local organization and have had a number of opportunities to present workshops and talks at local meetings on different concerns about private practice or about patients or clients. Subsequently, I was elected state president, which put me in an advantageous position to coordinate the state conferences. This increased my exposure as well as my knowledge on how to present workshops and presentations at the state level. Through that exposure from presentations and leadership, I went on to become chairperson of a regional conference, and subsequently presented on various occasions. I also attended the regional leadership program of my professional organization and subsequently was chosen to serve as chairperson. The exposure as chairperson led me to involvement with a national organization, and when the national organization made a decision to offer a workshop on a national basis on running a successful private practice, I was asked to lead that workshop. That was many years ago, and since then I have had many opportunities to present my thoughts and ideas about private practice, culminating with this book. I can look back now and realize that had I not become involved in the local professional organization, I would never have arrived at this point, nor have trained well over 1,000 therapists in my ideas and techniques of private practice.

Making Known the Needs of Individuals in Private Practice

The other advantage of professional development is that private practitioners are constantly reminding colleagues, as well as local, state, and national organizations of the needs and interests of individuals in private practice. It does take time to serve in a leadership capacity in organizations, but it should be noted that the professional involvement brings significant exposure to one's practice and is an excellent marketing tool.

HOLIDAY ACKNOWLEDGMENTS FOR REFERRAL SOURCES

With the approach of a holiday season, many practitioners begin to ask about the appropriateness of sending some kind of acknowledgment to referral sources. For years, I have used the holiday season to contact the people who have referred to me during the year to acknowledge their confidence in me and to wish them a successful new year. My rationale is that I am a business person, and they are sources of continued business growth for my practice. After all, the vast majority of a practice's clients come because someone tells them about the practice's services, indicating that they can receive help. That person then becomes a referral source. The more confidence the referral source has in the practitioner's work and professionalism, the more potential clients will be referred.

The purpose of sending this acknowledgment is twofold: to thank referral sources for their support during the year, and to remind them of both the therapist and the practice. People appreciate being recognized and thanked for their efforts; sending something that indicates appreciation of a referral source will go a long way in furthering a relationship. This is especially important when considering the number of requests for referrals professional colleagues receive. Let them know at holiday time that their support is remembered and appreciated.

What Is a Referral Source?

A private practice receives referrals from two sources: professional and personal. Professional referral sources are individuals who know the therapist on a professional basis and are professionals themselves. This category of referral sources includes doctors, lawyers, dentists, chiropractors, personnel directors, bankers, accountants, administrators, school counselors, and mental health colleagues. These individuals refer clients, patients, employees, or friends to the practice. In most cases, a professional acknowledgment is sent to these sources at the time of the referral. Personal referral sources are individuals whose relationship with the therapist is as an individual, not as a professional. They may be clients, former clients, friends, or people who have heard the therapist speak at a group function. Depending on the relationship with the individual, the therapist may or may not acknowledge referrals.

At the end of the year, I find that some of these sources, both professional and personal, deserve further acknowledgment.

What Kind of Acknowledgment?

The type of acknowledgment sent is a personal choice, determined by a number of factors.

> *Cost.* The cost of the acknowledgment can be as little as the cost of a piece of personal stationery or as much a specific gift.

> *Appropriateness.* It is extremely important to select the form of acknowledgment that is appropriate. Each referral source does not warrant the same acknowledgment. The form of acknowledgement reflects the person sending it.

> *Type of relationship.* Different referral sources have different types of relationships with the practitioner. There may be a wide variety of referral sources, all of who refer for different purposes and all of who see the practitioner differently.

> *Purpose.* The last factor to consider is the purpose of the acknowledgment. What does the therapist hope to convey with the acknowledgment and what is expected as an outcome?

Types of Acknowledgment

Here are some of the wide variety of acknowledgments I have either used or received from others.

Personal letter. A personally written, specific letter to the individual thanking him or her or extending wishes for success in the new year.

A card. A holiday greeting card or a specially designed card with a tasteful message.

Calendar. A calendar imprinted with the practitioner's name, accompanied by a personal note.

Gift. For a specific referral source, a thoughtful gift appropriate to the job position and the relationship is often well received. The gift may have the practitioner's name or the name of the practice on it, depending on the nature of the gift. Select a gift that the receiver will feel is personal.

FOLLOW-THROUGH TO PROFESSIONALS

Private practitioners often neglect to follow through to other professionals. The basic concept of "Your client or patient is important; thank you for your trust" is central to the process of developing a smooth, working relationship with referral sources. Too often, practitioners use confidentiality as a an excuse to avoid the tedious process of acknowledging referrals and offering feedback to the professionals who made them. Following through with professionals does not have to be a complicated process. It simply requires a little forethought and commitment to the process of ongoing dialogue between professionals. From a marketing standpoint, it only makes sense. Each time material crosses the doctor's or lawyer's desk, the more often that individual will be reminded of the services available from the private practitioner. A simple acknowledgment or thank-you will go a long way in keeping that door open.

Over the years I have developed and used a three-part process with medical practitioners who refer to my practice. It should be noted that no communication is made without the client's having signed a release form. The process involves a simple acknowledgment that an appointment has been made or kept. After three to four sessions, when a client has made a commitment to work with me, I complete and send the summation form to the physician. The third part of the process involves the ongoing work with the physician. This ongoing work usually occurs because a medical referral often involves some type of medication or medical condition, and it has been my general policy to send a brief note of the progress the client is making in therapy to the physician prior to the client's next appointment with the doctor. All written communication is shown to the client for approval prior to being sent. What it does from the physician's standpoint is maintain a flow of communication and remind the physician of my appreciation for the referral. In the case of lawyers or dentists, a simple acknowledgment of the referral is usually sufficient. If lawyers wish to have additional information, they will often request it.

The Feedback Process

Professional feedback is best accomplished by using a pre-designed form. The following form is a good example and will facilitate the discussion. Some of the key elements of the form are basic biographical information about the client, specifically age and date of birth. In many medical practices, files are kept by name and date of birth. The form begins with an initial thank-you and the heading "History" (see appendix A, form 12).

History. The history should be brief and relevant to the medical needs of the client and provide information for the physician. It is not important nor even practical to discuss psychological problems such as child abuse or sexual, mental, or physical abuse that are significantly affecting the client's psychological condition, but only that information relevant to the medical condition, such as any history gleaned about prior medical conditions that lead to the referral to the private practitioner. This will indicate to the physician whether the therapist has an accurate medical history of the patient or whether additional information should be supplied.

Diagnostic Impression. This is usually a listing from the *Diagnostic and Statistical Manual of Mental Disorders, Third Edition, Revised*, DSM-IIIR (American Psychiatric Association, 1987), or the *Manual of the International Statistical Classification of Diseases, Injuries and Causes of Death* (ICD-9) (World Health Organization, 1978), with a brief explanation of particular characteristics of the code that applies to the patient.

Treatment or Disposition. This is the opportunity to indicate to the physician whether the patient has been accepted for ongoing long-term treatment or short, brief therapy; whether this will be done on a weekly or bi-weekly basis; whether the patient will be involved in any ongoing group; or whether a referral is being made to another individual for treatment based on issues that have come up in the therapy sessions.

Remarks. This is often the opportunity to note concerns that the physician may be able to address with the patient, or make brief one- or two-line statements indicating the progress the patient is making in therapy.

In using this form, it is important that all information be clear, typed if possible, and not be longer than one page. The reason for this is that most information a physician receives will be filed in a patient's folder, and due to filing space limitations, it is always appreciated when material can be limited to one page. The form should always be forwarded to the physician with a signed release from the patient and a notation that a copy has been given to the patient. This intake findings process will go a long way toward instilling confidence in the physican about the therapist's clinical work, and it provides the therapist the opportunity to create a synopsis of the findings from working with the client.

MARKETING A SUCCESSFUL WORKSHOP

Over the years I've done hundreds of workshops, most of them sponsored by someone else. I've also spent thousands of dollars on trying to market groups, workshops, and presentations that never went beyond the marketing stage. I've produced brochures with expensive typesetting and printing and sent them to prospective attendees and referral sources. In most cases I sat waiting for the phone call that never came. Great idea, but nobody wanted it. Then I got smart.

I had been sending out a monthly newsletter that shared information about the practice and other ideas and activities in which I was involved. I wanted to do a 12-hour, Friday-night-all-day-Saturday workshop on "The Child Within." How could I market it? What would make it work? I decided to use a technique I had learned through my national training activities.

Be committed. I became truly committed to doing these workshops. I spent time thinking about them, planning them, talking about them, and setting up a schedule to do them. I realized I needed both to plant the seed and to help it grow. The seed to plant was letting people know that this workshop would help those in recovery who wanted to understand the concept of the child within. Helping the seed grow was an active marketing campaign and a schedule of not just one date, but a list of dates.

Don't "one-shot." In the past I had given one date to whatever I had tried to market. If enough people signed up, it was a "go" and a good idea. If not, I shelved it. I didn't do that with these workshops. Instead I set up dates for November, January, February, and March. It worked. People started signing up for the dates that worked for them.

Market the idea not the content. In my previous attempts I had gone into great detail about the workshop and what would be covered, along with the expected outline. This time I remembered the saying, "Keep it simple." I gave only the title and a brief two lines about what would be covered in the workshop. That's right. Tease people to want to know more. When people called or wrote, I answered their questions and gave a rationale for the workshop, but no structural content. Structural content seemed to scare people. They didn't want to know what would happen, only why they should come and what they could learn.

Don't give the cost. I had always put the cost out front in big letters standing out on the page. This time I didn't. I decided that I wanted people to become interested in the idea first, then deal with the cost. I'm reminded of that sales technique I heard, "If the customer asks the price first, they won't buy it. They're looking for an excuse not to buy. Sell them on the need first, then deal with the price." Consequently I didn't list any price in the announcement for the workshop, and it worked.

Offer a payment plan. When I tell people the price, I ask for a deposit and allow them to pay the rest before the workshop begins. It works. They sign up more readily knowing they can budget the payment. We are a payment-plan society.

Market It

I simply used my newsletter. No fancy brochure, no expensive printing. I just added a statement that I was offering a 12-hour workshop entitled "Working With the Child Within You—Pathways to Your Recovery," listed the dates, and said to call for more information. I limited the enrollment (that really makes people want to sign up) and I stated "for women only" or "for men only."

I incurred no cost in marketing these workshops because I used the regular mailer that goes to my mailing list on a monthly basis. After the first workshop, I told my readers about how successful it was and not to miss out on the next date (build their interest in what they missed). It also is important to note that I mailed information only to the people on my mailing list. These people are present clients, former clients, referral sources, and friends.

It worked. Every workshop has been full. I had to add more dates, and soon those were full also. I added an advanced 2½-day weekend retreat for those who had taken the 12-hour workshop. That was full also. The word is out and people not on the mailing list call to sign up for the workshop. If I had not made the commitment in time, if the marketing had not been cost-effective, and if I had not used sound sales techniques, the workshops would never have become an integral part of my practice.

Maintain Contact With Practice Newsletters

A practice newsletter is also an excellent way to maintain contact with professional referral sources. Most professionals, once they have been in practice a few years, find it impossible to keep in touch on a personal level with all referral sources. The best way to keep in touch, of course, is through personal contacts like meetings, business lunches, telephone calls, and personal letters. With a busy practice, however, it is not always easy to find time for personal contact. Using a practice newsletter helps maintain regular contact with referral sources in a professional manner, reminding them on a monthly or quarterly basis that the therapist is available, and educating them regarding the benefits of using the therapist's service. The fact that the newsletter is sent enhances the practitioner's image as a knowledgeable and competent professional who provides valuable services to the community—including the educational service of sending out a newsletter.

Workshop Handout

A practice newsletter is also a perfect piece to use as a handout at speeches, workshops, and presentations. For example, if one newsletter issue covers anger and the practitioner plans to do a workshop on anger, offering the newsletter at the workshop is a convenient way of giving people the therapist's name, address, and telephone number, and serves to remind them when they go home of how informative and helpful the speaker was on this subject. It is also a handy piece for them to give neighbors, friends, relatives, or coworkers who did not attend the presentation but might be interested in the topic.

Who Should Receive It?

The practice newsletter is an ideal vehicle to multiply the impact and effectiveness of every marketing contact made, and if a newsletter is purchased rather than the practitioner's writing it him- or herself, little extra effort is required. In the case of a purchased newsletter, either an additional page is developed about the practice, or the newsletter is personalized at the time of purchase. The nucleus of a mailing list already exists in each practice. Start with the names of all current and former clients. They will appreciate receiving the newsletter and feel that the therapist cares enough to maintain contact with them.

Community Contacts

Add the names of contacts in the community to the mailing list. These include contacts resulting from speeches, presentations, and workshops given in the community, social service agencies, or mental health clinics. Remember to add lawyers, accountants, bankers, and any other professionals seen in the course of doing business. Sending these professionals the newsletter shows them that the practice is being conducted in a businesslike way. These people are also ideal potential referral sources because they have regular contact with a number of people who might need the therapist's services.

Referral Sources

Finally, add the name of anyone who has referred clients in the past, who refers now, or who might refer in the future. For example, if a therapist specializes in women's issues, send a newsletter to all the gynecologists and family planning clinics in the area. Receiving the newsletter on a regular basis may be just the reminder needed to start referring. Be sure to let professional referral sources know that they can receive multiple copies to place in their waiting areas. A brief newsletter is the kind of material people are likely to read while waiting to see their dentist, doctor, or chiropractor.

How Often?

The most important thing to keep in mind when deciding how often to send a newsletter is to be sure to set a schedule you can keep. When people receive a newsletter on a hit-or-miss basis, maybe every couple of months, maybe less often, they never get in the habit of expecting and waiting for the newsletter. It may be a pleasant surprise when it comes, but its arrival is not part of the individual's routine. The newsletter should become important to and be so valued that recipients will wonder where it is if it arrives late. Whether sending a newsletter monthly, bi-monthly, or quarterly, it should go out at the same time of the month each time.

What to Send

Once a decision has been made regarding recipients and frequency, the actual newsletter must be finalized. Essentially, there are two choices: buy one already written, or write one. If the decision is made to produce a newsletter, how should it be approached?

Style

The style and content of the newsletter are of paramount importance. The information should be presented so that it is both interesting and easy to read. The subject matter should be relevant but be handled in such a way that people would not be embarrassed to be seen reading the newsletter. People want information on some touchy subjects (sexuality, substance abuse, AIDS) but they are afraid to ask. They are afraid others will think they are either impotent, alcoholics, or gay if they do ask.

Lay Public

Remember that the newsletter is being written primarily for the lay public. The referral sources who receive the newsletter will look at it in the light of its usefulness to their clients, the lay public. Studies have found that use of technical terms and long sentences limits understanding. Try to write at the eighth- or ninth-grade level. This will be clear to most readers without being too basic for those with more education.

Subject Matter

People are interested in a wide variety of mental health-related topics. A successful approach is to divide the issues between the areas of "mental health" and "personal wellness." For example, one month the subject might be intimacy or decision making, and the next month, codependency or problem drinking versus alcoholism. If the subject is always "serious," people whose lives are basically healthy but could use improvement will lose interest. If only "light" subjects are treated, people with more serious problems may not feel that the practice could help them. A regular mix from month to month will interest both groups.

Of course, if choosing subject matter is put off until it is time to write the newsletter, writer's block will probably make its presence felt. To prevent this, keep a file folder labeled "newsletter articles" to provide ideas for future articles. Keep an eye on all paperwork (memos, mail, media stories, and other sources) for possible newsletter articles. Whenever an idea for an article pops up, write it down and add it to the file. When the time comes to do the actual writing, the ideas folder will have plenty of starting points for articles, and all that needs to be done is to decide which one to use.

Newsletter Design

To be effective as a promotional piece, the newsletter must project a professional image. Typing articles on the practice stationery and running them off on the office photocopier will not create a quality piece. The newsletter should be professionally typeset and printed on quality stock. When choosing a typeface, opt for a *serif* face rather than a *sans serif* face. (*Serifs* are the little "feet" on the letters that help draw the reader's eye along the line, making the copy easier to read; *sans serif* typefaces have no "feet.") A printer can help to choose typefaces and paper.

Color

Another point to consider is the use of color in the newsletter. Black ink on white paper is readable but not very distinctive. A printer can produce the newsletter using two colors of ink, one for the body of the text and one to call attention to the logo, name, and address (or anything else that needs to be highlighted). However, two-color printing may be considerably more expensive than one-color printing if each sheet must go through the printer twice. Another option is to use colored paper, possibly with a different color ink; for example, gray paper with dark green ink, or tan paper with navy ink. Such combinations can add distinction at less cost than two-color printing.

How Many?

The printer will have to know how many pieces to print. Consider all the uses for the piece before deciding this. If the mailing list includes 200 names, but the newsletter will also be used as a handout at presentations, enough copies for both uses should be printed at one time. Each printing job includes a charge for setting up the job; the more pieces printed at one time, the less each piece costs because the setup cost is spread out among more pieces. If the amount of copies needed is underestimated, the setup charge will have to paid once more on the second run, so it it is better to be generous in the estimate on the first run.

Both referral sources and other individuals appreciate receiving a regular newsletter that educates them about what therapists do and reminds them of the practice's services. One survey reported that more than one third of all consultants making $70,000 or more annually send a newsletter to their clients, and the vast majority of them (almost 90%) rank it as their first or second most important marketing tool.

CUTTING POSTAL COSTS

With the increased cost of postage rates and the need to do a lot of mailing in a successful practice, it is necessary to be aware of the cost and save whenever possible. It is important not to cut back on the mailing when times get hard and competition increases because continued name recognition is vital. Here are some options:

> *Replace letters with postcards.* Often it is necessary to send a short note to someone, thanking him or her, confirming a meeting, or requesting a response. Consider using postcards. One of my colleagues often sets up his luncheon dates with me by sending a postcard and attaching another postcard for my response. When I've had room left in a workshop or wanted to remind people of a meeting, I've used a postcard. It's simple, easy, and doesn't cost as much as a first-class letter.
> *Use bulk mail.* Why pay 25 cents to send something if you are going to be mailing 200 or more pieces that could be sent bulk rate for 18½ cents each?
> *Consider an electronic scale and postage meter.* If the practice is large and requires a lot of mailing, and there is a quantity of mail that is over one ounce, the

savings with an electronic scale and meter can be significant. I mailed my practice newsletter and a holiday calendar in December to my mailing list, knowing that December mail is always busy and wanting people to receive my greetings at the end of the year. I sent it first class, but due to its weight (it was more than one ounce) I needed to eliminate one piece of paper. I didn't want to do that, so by using the electronic scale I knew that I had to pay only 20 cents more, not 25 cents. By metering, I saved time and cost (450 times 45 versus 450 times 50). A number of companies rent electronic scales and meters.

Use address corrections on all bulk mailing. There is a fee to be paid to the post office for the service, but if a lot of mailing is going out from the practice, it's worth it to keep the file current and know that the information is getting to the people on the list.

Use certified, not registered, mail. If it is necessary to know that a piece of mail has been received by a person or company, send it certified. The rate is cheaper and the result is the same as with registered mail. The post office will be glad to explain the difference between the two.

Watch the weight of packages. When sending packages, an electronic scale is a great help. Ounces cost money. Use light cushioning material and light-weight boxing. If a lot of packages are sent, see a consultant at a boxing or shipping company. They can demonstrate ways to save money.

END-OF-YEAR STATEMENT FOR THE CLIENT

Some years ago, I was reading a tax book and realized that counseling/therapy was a tax deduction under the medical section of itemized deductions. This gave me the idea for a service I have used successfully with my clients ever since. I send them a "tax letter" at the end of the year.

At the end of each year I balance the books for my practice. This is a laborious job that involves tabulating the amount billed and paid for each client, and cross-checking that with the receipt ledger and bank deposits. However, when I have finished this necessary part of closing the business year, I have also computed information about each of my clients.

In January, I prepare a statement letter for each client seen during the previous year, whether that client was seen once or 50 times (see appendix A, form 13).

I enclose a copy of the latest IRS ruling regarding medical deductions as well as the number of sessions attended and the amount paid. Knowing the number of sessions allows the client to multiply that number by the average miles to and from my office by the allotment per mile (a per-mile deduction established by the IRS, highlighted in the copy of the IRS ruling I send them). They are also entitled to parking fees if relevant.

I send these letters for a variety of reasons. First, it is a service that helps the client. Private practitioners are in the service business, and by sending this statement, it is easier for clients to complete their tax forms. Like most of us, my clients are always looking for legitimate deductions, but they are often unaware that the amount they paid for counseling could be deducted. Also, if clients have paid in cash but lost the receipt, they might not be able to take the deduction without further documentation; this letter serves to document the year's expenses.

This letter also helps to reinforce the client's perception of the therapist as a business person, showing that records of each visit and each payment are kept. Because the therapist's hourly fee is considerably higher than the hourly wage most clients earn, it is good for them to be aware that their money is being accounted for on a businesslike basis.

Another function of the letter is to remind clients who still have an outstanding balance that payment would be appreciated. In such cases, I always note the outstanding balance and ask for payment, enclosing a return envelope for the client's use.

The letter acts to jog the memory of a client not seen for a while that the therapist is still there and cares enough about him or her to send the letter. This statement also reminds clients of the professional and business relationship. I'm always surprised at the number of referrals I receive just after I send out these letters, and how many of them come from former clients. I've always found that former satisfied clients are the best sources for new clients, and reminding them professionally of my name doesn't hurt.

Another reason for sending this letter is that it takes care of that part of the record keeping responsibility for clients. I have had a number of clients who have been audited for medical expenses, but when they have produced my letters, no further documentation has been requested. (The IRS did check a client's claim with me once, to see if the letter was correct!)

Finally, sending this letter acts as another item in the "paper trail" if I should ever be audited myself. I can document my cash flow with my appointment book, receipts, ledger card, bank deposits, and this letter.

One last point: I'm not a big user of insurance and I try to arrange for reimbursement to be sent to the client, so I usually type a brief note indicating that a client should subtract the amount received from the insurance company from the amount paid to me when figuring the allowable deductions. If a therapist receives reimbursement directly from the insurance company and the client pays a set amount of 50% or 20% for example, the therapist will have to indicate in the letter what was billed and what amount the client paid. Only what the client paid is deductible.

This letter is both a service to clients and a good business practice for the therapist. Good record keeping and good business practices go hand in hand with offering a professional business service. The end of the year is an ideal time to touch base with clients and to remind them of the practice's services, of any outstanding balance they may owe, and of the professional nature of the practice.

SUMMARY

Marketing is critical to the practice and there just isn't enough material available on how to do it properly. As more and more therapists open their practice they will need a thorough understanding of marketing because the practitioner will have to market to stay competitive. The step-by-step process and many examples I've offered should become invaluable over time. Taking the time to do a marketing plan and analysis will prove a wise move. Using open houses can become a most effective way of getting an excellent response rate from potential and present referral sources. Free advertising is available and is discussed in detail as an excellent way of keeping the advertising costs down while maximizing the exposure of the practice. Well-planned, free presentations have proven to be an excellent way of developing an interest in the product or service. Knowing how to get through to a busy referral source is always a problem, but the process can be simplified by knowing the screener and developing a professional first-name relationship with that person over the phone.

The business lunch is a good way to impress a new referral source or thank an existing one, but the do's and don'ts are critical. The tips in this regard will help the practitioner to obtain the desired results. Referral sources are vital and the impression given at a properly conducted business lunch will go a long way in establishing or maintaining a referral source.

Keeping ahead of the competition is a necessity. There is always a new group of practitioners opening up practice. Consequently, proper use of thank-you's, holiday acknowledgments, and practice newsletters all keep the practice in the eye of referral sources as well as cultivating new contacts. Marketing is a must. The practitioner shouldn't take it lightly, but should make the most of marketing efforts by being prepared with a well-thought-out plan and a diversity of activities.

SECTION SIX

Running the Practice

GETTING THE MOST OUT OF THE INTAKE PROCESS

The intake process begins with the client's first contact with the office. This contact is the first impression a client has of the practice, and is the beginning of the counselor/client relationship. The therapist should immediately begin to establish the client's confidence in the service offered, whether that service is counseling or consultation. The way incoming clients are handled is a critical part of both the business and therapeutic aspects of a practice. The intake process will have a direct effect on the success of the first session with the client, and can also affect referrals from other sources in the future. Many practitioners overlook the importance and potential that first contact represents.

Purpose

The intake process serves two purposes: to establish the contract for services, and to introduce the client to those services. From a marketing standpoint the intake form and the process of the first session can also be structured to gather information about who referred the client, to gain information about other possible referral sources, and to maintain further positive contact with these sources, which can result in more referrals in the future. The intake is a client's first contact with the therapist and the service; maximizing the effectiveness of this contact will ultimately enhance the practice.

Structure

When a client contacts my office, the receptionist sets up an appointment and sends a confirmation letter and a package of information. It is important to ask the client whether a letter can be sent, and what address is appropriate. Most clients have no objection to receiving this information but may not want it sent to their homes; therefore, they may give a different address. I have found that sending a confirmation letter cuts down considerably on the number of clients who simply don't show up for the initial appointment. Also, from the client's point of view, it helps establish an excellent business and professional tone for the first meeting.

Confirmation Letter

Each item in the package of information serves a purpose for the client and for the therapist. The first purpose of the confirmation letter itself is to review the details agreed upon over the phone, such as the time, date, and location of the appointment. Other pertinent information such as fee agreements, insurance issues, or whether the session is for an individual, a couple, or whether a child is involved, and whether the child will be brought to that session may also be included if necessary. When discussing the appointment over the phone with a client who has been referred by a professional colleague, my receptionist tells the client that we will send some material to review prior to the appointment and that, if there is no objection, I would like to send a copy of the confirmation letter to the referring doctor. The advantage of sending a copy of the confirmation letter to a professional source is that, in addition to telling that source that the client has booked an appointment, it lets the source know that the therapist is responding to the referrals in a professional manner, and that this referral is appreciated. A professional referral source who receives this kind of feedback is likely to keep sending referrals. Moreover, having a piece of paper with the therapist's name on it come across the desk is another way to make the name stick in the memory for a future occasion (see appendix A, form 14).

Self-Disclosure Brochure

The second item to include in the information package is a copy of the self-disclosure brochure. This gives the client information about the process of counseling, the fee, and other details of how the practice is run. The client is asked to review this information before the first session. This ensures that there are no nasty surprises for either the client or therapist.

Intake Form

The third essential component in this package is an intake form, which the client is asked to complete and bring to the first session. Again, this has a dual purpose. Besides obtaining information that will help the therapist work with the client, using an intake form ensures that the client will get an impression of professionalism about the office and how the therapist works. Other professionals use some sort of intake form; why should a counselor be different? Using such a form engenders the client's confidence in the therapist and the service (see appendix A, form 15).

Basic Areas Addressed

Over the years, I have used different versions of the intake form, and have finally developed one with which I am comfortable and that works well for me. This form is a two-sided document. The first side addresses four basic areas: biographical information, employment and marital information, medical and psychological history, and referral source.

Biographical information includes name, address, age, social security number, and insurance carrier and number. This gives the information needed to set up a file on the new client and to complete any necessary documentation.

Employment and marital information includes where a person is employed, for how long, and the type of job; marital status, name of spouse or ex-spouse if divorced, spouse's age and employment data, children's names and ages, and whether they are living in the home. This gives a picture of the client's personal and work life.

Medical and psychological history includes names and addresses of physicians and therapists, history of hospitalization, and any medication presently used.

Referral source. It is extremely important to get the name of the referral source and the reason for referring the client, or, if the client is a self-referral, why the therapist has been chosen.

These questions are similar to the basic questions that would be asked in any other professional's office, and they give the information needed to set up a folder for the client.

Potential Problem Areas

On the other side of the form, the emphasis is a little different. Here the client is introduced to the counseling process by questions pertinent to the type of client I usually see in my practice. Included are questions about the parents' names and ages, siblings' names and ages, any history of drug or alcohol abuse within the family, any history of physical or sexual abuse, any medical problems the client has now or has had in the past, and any sexual problems present or past. By requesting this information, I hope the client will start thinking about the counseling process before coming in to see me. Then in our first session I am able to review quickly some information that I find valuable in making an initial assessment.

An intake form for a different specialty would require answers to questions appropriate to the client's history. For example, a career specialist might ask about a client's past and present work situations and history; a consultant might want to know about the type of company that is considering hiring the consultant and what use the company has made of consultants in the past. No matter what the specialty, a one- or two-page form eliciting basic information from the client helps to prepare for the session, and saves time by having certain information available at the first session.

There are two key questions I would encourage any therapist to ask before doing any diagnosis and treatment planning. On the first side of the form I ask specifically for any names of prescription drugs, and on the other side I ask about alcohol and drug use. I ask both questions again in the session and note the client's answers. I do this to protect myself from any legal responsibility if a client should hurt himself or herself (overdose) or others (drunk driving). While under my care, I want to know from the beginning if a client is using drugs either legally or illegally, in case I am held accountable later.

Expanding the Contact

During the first session, I ask the client to sign a release form. This is to obtain permission to contact various individuals named on the intake form who may have information relevant to the client's situation. If the client was referred by another professional, I get a signed release from the client and contact the referral source, asking for any information that might help me in working with the client. If I know the referral source, I may just call to discuss the information; if not, or if I realize the referral source is too busy for a telephone discussion, I usually send a form letter with a copy of the signed release, asking for information relevant to the client. I may also ask the client for permission to contact the other physicians listed if there is any hint that the client's problem may have a medical basis, or if the client is taking medication prescribed by any of the physicians listed (see appendix A, form 16).

Purpose of Contacts

Medical contacts are made for two reasons: They give me information about the client that furthers the development of a treatment plan, and they also enhance my practice by letting physicians know that I am in business, and that, professionally, I would value any information they might have relevant to the patient. I have often found that I end up receiving a complete medical picture of my client, and later receive more referrals from that source once the physician is aware that I work with that type of client.

The intake process is important in establishing a good professional relationship with the client and developing an appropriate treatment plan from the beginning. It also helps to establish a good business relationship with the client and to collect information that will be helpful in developing or responding to referrals. A well-developed intake form filled out by the client becomes a sound mechanism to perform all this. A well-prepared, planned response to the client's first contact will bring a greater first-visit response, cut down on no-shows, supply the therapist with valuable information for assessing the client's needs, and give direct information about referral sources. A private practitioner's business and professional relationship begins with the client's first phone call; following up on this in writing helps develop the relationship and can avert many questions later.

Fee Collection and Billing

A positive cash flow is the basis for a strong, healthy practice, and a fee need not be extremely high to establish a successful practice. Working out a fee that will have a positive effect on the practice and will not deter clients from using the service is essential to the long-term success of the practice.

In determining the fee, there are two major points to consider. First, the fee multiplied by the clients seen must pay the bills over the long term; second, to be effective, the fee must be an amount that can be collected from the clients.

Make the Fee Affordable

To qualify as collectible, a fee should be affordable for the target market. If wages in the target population average $150 weekly, a fee of $100 per hour will price the service right out of the market. A survey of the income level of the clients in the community the practice hopes to attract is a wise idea.

The therapist should also survey the fees that colleagues charge. In performing this survey, here are some points to consider:

Limited versus full time. Clinicians in a limited practice are risking less by going into practice and usually have a lower overhead than do full-time practitioners. Thus, their fee is more likely to be decided less by costs than by choice.

Length of time in practice. Experienced clinicians are likely to have higher fees because they are in a position to limit clients. These clinicians tend to have strong referral bases, which means they can insist on seeing only clients willing to pay the fee.

Insurance-dependent clinicians. Clinicians who rely heavily on insurance often have inflated fees to cover insurance overhead cost, billing delays in reimbursement, and rejected claims.

Type of client population. Short-term, high-volume practices may have high fees to cover "down time" months, as opposed to long-term selective practices that have a more consistent volume of sessions per month.

It is important to remember that the combination of a high fee and low client volume leads to practice failure. Too many clinicians make the mistake of expecting to get premier fees from the time they first open their practice, and then are forced to make the practice dependent on insurance reimbursement to support their fees.

The next step in a collectibility survey is understanding the target population. It is not possible for every clinician to serve the top 10% of the economic and social structure of the community. What are the specific demographic features of the community? What is the average income, family size, and type of household? What are the working conditions, education level, types of community counseling or health agencies, and types of private and public hospitals and psychiatric institutes?

The reason for gathering this information is that the private practitioner will need a fundamental marketing plan for the community, and determining a fee is an essential part of this plan. Fifty percent of the population could use mental health, consultation, vocational, or rehabilitation services, but that same 50% percent often can't afford the escalating fees common today.

The key to collectibility is to charge a fee that can be collected at each session—a fee that doesn't depend on insurance reimbursement, gives the clients a choice about using insurance, and enhances the volume of clients. Past and present satisfied clients are the best source of referrals. The greater the volume, the more the referral base expands, thus increasing the volume.

The Gray Area of Fees

Missed Appointments

It is standard practice for mental health practitioners to indicate that they require a 24-hour notice, or else a fee will be
charged for the missed appointment. It's important to understand that it will be difficult to convince a judge that a fee is due
when the service was not performed. Indicating to clients that
a 24-hour notice is required or they will be billed is a nice way
to attempt to deal with a resistant client. It is also a way to
manage the appointment book. In reality, if a client chooses not
to come for a session, entitlement to the fee is an issue between
the therapist and the client. A quick poll of attorneys yielded the
opinion that without providing the service, the therapist is not
entitled to the funds.

Late Sessions

If a client does not arrive on time, the therapist is free to charge
for the full hour. The important thing to remember is that the
client is entitled to 50 minutes, or whatever time has been indicated as the length of the session, not one minute more, nor
one minute less. If the therapist is running late and does not
start the session on time, the therapist is still obligated to supply
the allotted time for the client. The client has entered into a
contractual agreement with the therapist for service, and the
therapist needs to fulfill that agreement. Many issues will arise
over the manipulation of time, but it has always been my policy
that when a session begins, it begins on the hour, and the client
is fully entitled to 50 minutes of my time. If for any reason I am
unable to start on time, the client is still entitled to a full 50
minutes, and I take the responsibility of making sure that clients
who follow will be given their full 50 minutes also.

Phone Consultations

This is definitely a gray area and many therapists have asked,
"How should I handle phone consultations?" It has been my own
policy not to do therapy or consultation over the phone. Prolonged discussions over the phone do not facilitate the counseling or therapeutic process. There are always exceptions to all
rules, of course. There are times when it is impossible for a client
to see a therapist, and a phone consultation is warranted. If that
is the case, the client should fully understand the terms of that
consultation and the cost that will be incurred. Some therapists,

due to circumstances beyond their control, have chosen to consult with clients over the phone and have charged them for that time, but that was clearly understood by both the client and the therapist.

Late Charges

This is always a difficult area for therapists. Once a client is allowed to run a tab, charging late fees will not increase the chances of the client's paying the bill. The best way to receive payment for that past-due bill is by a constant billing process. A number of legal experts have noted that allowing a bill to accumulate increases the likelihood of a client's choosing to sue for some type of malpractice. Attorneys involved in defense or litigation have indicated that within the medical community in general, psychotherapy being no exception, when a patient or client incurs a large financial debt to the supplier of a service, that patient or client is more likely to question the quality of the service out of guilt, shame, or anger about his or her financial situation. As a general rule, therefore, it would enhance the financial base of the practice's stability simply to ask that all bills be paid at each session, thus avoiding finance charges or large balances, and helping the practice become much more stable.

Insurance Forms

Many therapists consider that collecting for the time spent in filling out insurance forms or mental health status reports is a "gray area." The reality of the situation is that when a therapist charges a fee for the service, there are some implied assumptions about the support work that needs to be done for the client. Fees are generally high across the nation, and it is questionable and potentially unprofessional to charge clients for time spent in filling out forms. The assumption clients make is that the fee involves both the work with the therapist and any other support work the therapist may be required to do.

Collection Procedures

When a client has run up a substantial balance, what options does a therapist have when the client has terminated therapy? It is possible to take the client to small-claims court to seek remuneration? The difficulty is the time involved in the small-claims court process and the potential for the judge to rule against the practitioner. Many judges do not understand the cost incurred by practitioners and often view the client as the victim of those costs. The alternative may be to look to a collection agency for help. Due to the ethical considerations of the counseling profession, turning to a collection agency to harass a client who has chosen not to pay the bill is a futile endeavor and may cause the client to question the integrity of the practitioner. The best procedure for collection is that of an ongoing monthly billing that reminds clients of the balance due. Calling the client after two or three billings to try to resolve the problem will often reveal whether the client intends to pay the bill. When I have found that a client simply does not intend to pay, I stop billing, call it a business loss, and move on.

WHY USE A BUSINESS RECEIPT SYSTEM?

When I started my practice more than a dozen years ago, I set up a system I thought would meet my needs. When I collected fees from my clients, I recorded the fee on the client's folder and gave the client a receipt from an inexpensive receipt book. Because my practice was fairly small, I saw no reason for a more elaborate system.

After being in practice for a few years, I switched from doing my own taxes to having them done by an accountant, and received a rude awakening. My accountant told me that I was potentially in violation of state laws, and would definitely find myself in a difficult situation if an audit were ever done. He told me that the laws of the state were very specific. As a cash business, I needed to have documentation of each cash transaction I performed. If the state were to audit my business, they would want to know about each occasion on which I had taken in cash, and what had happened to it. He also told me that the receipt system I was using would not be much help to me in the case of a tax audit. I would find myself going through an expensive process to defend what I was doing in my business.

When I asked him what I should have, he told me about receipt and general ledger systems. He explained that I needed a system with consecutively numbered receipts so that each cash transaction could be shown and documented as a receipt given to the client. I also needed some kind of posting procedure that would allow my receipts to be tallied and cross-checked against my bank deposits.

He further explained that there were business systems designed for this purpose and reminded me that most medical and dental practitioners used them. A number of such companies are usually listed in the phone book under "business systems." These systems are called "one-write" and are readily available.

How a System Works

The purpose of a one-write system or a receipt system of any kind is to accomplish three things:

Give a client a receipt for payment made, whether the payment is cash, check, or credit card. When a client pays by check, it is easy to assume that the cancelled check will be sufficient receipt, but that is not the case, especially if the client is seeking reimbursement. With any other type of business a receipt is always given. A mental health practice should be the same.

Provide some type of posting that indicates what each client has paid for therapy and gives a listing of the date of each of those services. Most states require that some type of posting be made each time a cash transaction is performed.

Act as a general ledger system to track the cash flow of the practice and to match the appointment book (sessions held) and the bank deposits (money received). The system will usually consist of client ledger cards, receipts, and ledger pages.

Client Ledger Cards

This card serves three purposes:

It is the permanent record of each cash and service transaction with each client seen. The ledger card allows completion of all the necessary personal data on the client, including the client's name, address, city, work telephone number, home telephone number, referral source, date of birth, date of the first appointment, the therapist's file number, and the diagnosis being used.

It serves as a billing form for the insurance company. My experience with insurance companies has been that the company requires an initial form once a year, but after that, it will process a statement of account as long as it contains all the necessary information. This receipt card gives all that information in such a form that the therapist need only photocopy the card onto his or her stationery and give the copy to the client, or send it directly to the insurance company.

It acts as a billing form for the client. If a client is allowed to run up a balance, and there is a need to bill the client, a photocopy of the card will give the client the necessary information about payments made and current balance. Each transaction in a practice regarding the client is noted on that card.

Receipts

The receipts come in sheets of 25, and are designed expressly for the individual private practice. A receipt carries the practice's name and address, the office number, the therapist's social security number or business ID number, a place for the diagnostic code used, and a description of up to 11 services performed and billed. This allows a client to have a receipt with the date of the appointment, a description of the services performed, the fee charged, the payment received, and an indication of any present or previous balance owed. There is also a space to indicate the client's name and file number. This file number enables client confidentiality to be maintained in the case of a tax audit. I use only the client's first name and last initial, then a file number. So client number 42 and client number 67 may both be listed as "Mike R.," but I know which is which based on the file number.

At the end of each session, I simply complete the receipt form and schedule the next appointment, which I indicate on the receipt. The tear-off part of the receipt allows me either to keep a note of the next appointment for my own records, or to give it to my receptionist. I then give the client the rest of the receipt, which gives the client a permanent record of the transaction with me.

Some of my clients are directly reimbursed by their employer for sessions with me. In such cases, the client only needs to give the receipt to the employer because it contains all the information needed.

Ledger Page

Each ledger page has 25 entry slots that correspond to the 25 receipts. This page serves three functions. First, it gives an ongoing, complete picture of all financial transactions in the practice. It also gives an accurate system for tracking all cash, both in a general ledger and with an individualized posting for each client. Finally, by using the coding system, there is a way to compare, month by month or year by year, exactly what is happening in the practice in terms of billing hours, the types of clients seen, and the types of problems handled.

As each receipt is written out, a carbon copy of the receipt is made on the client ledger page. When all 25 receipts have been used, the carbon paper strip on the left hand side of the ledger page is removed, producing a record of each session, with the coded description of the session, and a notation of each fee charged, money collected, and any balances due. Tabulating these four columns gives a clear picture of what happened financially with each of those 25 transactions. By adding that to the totals from previous ledger pages, a running total can be kept of what has been done in the practice to date, that is, how many sessions have been held, how much has been charged, how much has been received, and how much is currently owed. This can be tabulated on a monthly basis so that, at the end of the year, the therapist just needs to bring the final page of the receipt system to the accountant. This will provide the accountant with all the necessary information about cash transactions in the practice.

THIRD-PARTY REIMBURSEMENT

To begin with, how does third-party reimbursement work? Essentially, a client purchases an insurance policy, either as an individual or through an employer, to cover specific medical and/ or psychiatric conditions. The insurance company is based on a medical model in that a medical advisory board establishes the criteria under which the company will pay for an illness or injury. Within the company actuarial managers determine the rate at which these illnesses will occur within a certain population and, based on the best information available, the average cost expected for these illnesses or injuries. The company then establishes a fee to be charged for this coverage. Each company determines its own set of guidelines for claim, payment, and the responsibilities for the subscriber, the employer, and the care provider. Although the rules covering reimbursement for medical payments are usually fairly straightforward, the rules governing psychiatric illness are not always as clear.

Who Is Eligible?

Most companies use the following categories:

- Payment only to psychiatrists;
- Payment only to psychiatrists, licensed psychologists;
- Payment only to psychiatrists, licensed psychologists, licensed social workers;
- Payment only to psychiatrists, licensed psychologists, licensed social workers, licensed mental health counselors;
- Payment only to psychiatrists, licensed psychologists, licensed social workers, licensed mental health counselors, licensed marriage and family counselors;
- Payment only to approved participating professionals based solely on guidelines established by the company (may or may not have license);

- Payment to any MD, PhD, EdD, MSW with or without license;
- Payment to anyone who is co-signed by a state licensed professional; and
- Payment to anyone who is co-signed by a MD or DO, whether licensed or not.

Basis for Payment

- Only with a diagnosis from the *Diagnostic and Statistical Manual of Mental Disorders, Third Edition* (DSM-III-R) or the *Manual of the International Statistical Classification of Diseases, Injuries and Causes of Death* (ICD-9);
- A statement of reason for seeing client; and
- A bill with no stated condition but referral from MD or DO.

Types of Payment

- Set amount per visit with no cap;
- Set amount per visit with preestablished annual cap;
- Set amount per visit with pre-established cap for life;
- Percentage of fee (80%, 50%, 25%) with annual cap; and
- Percentage of fee (80%, 50%, 25%) with no annual cap.

Required Documentation

- Completion of company's specific form;
- Completion of Health Insurance Uniform Claim form;
- Submission of bill indicating diagnosis, number of sessions, and cost per session; and
- Mental Health Status report every 3 months, 6 months, or once a year.

As can be seen from this partial listing, a great number of combinations of these requirements are possible, and each company is free to establish its own regulations. Where does all this leave the private practitioner? Can it be assumed that:

- if there is a state license the practitioner is eligible?
- if there is no state license the practitioner is not eligible?
- the practitioner can charge whatever fee is desired?
- the practitioner can charge whatever fee is desired to insurance clients and noninsurance clients?
- if the practitioner writes a diagnosis on a claim form it will be covered?

- the practitioner must keep the fee the same during the total time the client is seen?

If the therapist assumes anything about the reimbursement process, there could be difficulty ahead. Involvement with the reimbursement system carries certain responsibilities of which the practitioner should be aware. Each company is different and policies within a company may be different. The best way is not to assume. If in doubt, call the company.

What Is the Law?

Prior to getting involved with third-party reimbursement, the therapist should consult a lawyer about any state or national statutes regarding fraud, and theft by deception. These are the legal dangers of accidental or intentional misrepresentation to an insurance company, and it should be remembered that ignorance of the law is no defense in court. A lawyer should be able to explain specifically what is involved and how the case law in that state has been applied. It is also important to note that when dealing with a company that processes claims outside of the therapist's home state, mistakes or violations then constitute interstate trade and are under the jurisdiction of the federal government and FBI.

Bearing this in mind, here are some guidelines for approaching reimbursement. The private practitioner should discuss all of this with a lawyer because a few minutes of discussion in advance could save hours of work if a problem does arise. Discussions with insurance companies and representatives of Medicaid and Champus indicate that due to the rising costs of psychiatric claims, they will be taking a harder look at reimbursement.

Eligibility

This determination is made by the company; the therapist does not need to check with each company regarding eligibility. The company has the right to refuse eligibility to anyone it feels does not meet the guidelines of the subscriber's policy. This can cause problems for the mental health professional because it is not known in advance whether or not a particular company will approve eligibility, and if the practitioenr begins accepting partial payments from a client on the assumption that reimbursement will follow, it may be difficult to collect the remainder from the client if the claim is refused. A written statement can help, informing the client of the hourly rate and stating that partial payment will be accepted as long as the insurance company pays, but that the client is responsible for the full fee. The insurance company is not obligated to the therapist; it can accept or reject a claim based on its interpretation of its policy.

The other area of eligibility where problems can arise is that of co-signing. A therapist should not assume that eligibility for reimbursement from a particular company automatically grants eligibility to any co-signer, based on the power of the practitioner's signature, license or contract. In certain situations, co-signing can be seen as fraudulent by the insurance company.

Determination of Payment

The rules in this area seem to be clear: No reimbursement will be received unless the therapist uses either one of the accepted diagnostic codes, or an approved statement or description. The one thing to be aware of is that in some states only certain individuals have the right to make a diagnosis. In such a state, the therapist might comply with the insurance company by making the diagnosis, but run into trouble with state law. This is one of the areas a lawyer should be able to clarify.

Use Caution

Sometimes mental health professionals make a diagnosis of a client only so the client can receive insurance reimbursement, for example, using a reimbursable diagnosis for a client who is in fact receiving marriage counseling. The insurance company is not the only one who may have legal grounds for complaint in this case. If the therapist does not inform the client of the diagnosis that becomes part of a permanent record, that client may later have a case against the therapist for defamation of character. If the therapist is seeing a child and diagnosing the child but does not inform the parents, the family could file suit against the therapist.. If the therapist sees the child only in family counseling because the therapist feels that the child is treatable only within the dysfunctional family, the claim could be disallowed by the insurance company.

A Diagnosis for Life

Once a diagnosis is made, it becomes part of the client's permanent medical record, available to anyone authorized to look at that record. As clients become more aware of the implications of psychiatric labeling, the private practitioner needs to be perfectly clear with proper documentation regarding the diagnosis.

Many clinicians recommend that informing the client of the diagnosis in the beginning is protection from possible suits later. Because all diagnoses have certain actuarial ramifications, as do smoking, age, weight, sex, and other past medical conditions, the therapist may want to inform the client of this fact. Many clients are not aware that seeing a therapist and using insurance for reimbursement requires psychiatric labeling, and that if they are ever asked whether they have been treated for a psychiatric problem they will have to answer "Yes," because their medical records will show that they have been so treated. Using a diagnosis only so a client can get reimbursement when that is not what the client is being seen for can put the therapist in jeopardy with the client as well as with the insurance company. For this reason, I have a policy that if I am going to accept insurance and give a diagnosis, I give a copy of that diagnosis to the client before submitting the form. This is to avoid misunderstanding regarding diagnosis and its purpose.

What Happens When the Claim is Made?

When a therapist makes a diagnosis and requests reimbursement, the company has the right to request whatever documentation it deems necessary to determine the legitimacy of the claim. Once the claim has been approved, it can request whatever additional ongoing information it feels is appropriate, ranging from periodical reports to reviews of the therapist's case notes and appointment and billing records. If the insurance company determines that the therapist is in error either in treatment or in billing, it can disallow the claim, seek retroactive reimbursement, or notify legal authorities of possible fraud or theft by deception. Does this happen? Yes! Insurance companies are becoming more aware of what they need in the area of reimbursement, and they are becoming more aggressive in protecting their rights and the rights of the client for proper treatment for the diagnosed condition.

Red Flag

The internal auditing process insurance companies use is a well-kept secret. Companies are beginning to follow the example of Medicaid and Champus in that they are able to track a therapist's billing rate and diagnosis classification through the computer, and will become suspicious if they see a practitioner using the same diagnosis for every client whose claim is submitted for reimbursement. That doesn't necessarily mean that the diagnosis is inappropriate, but if the therapist always makes the same diagnosis, it may draw the insurance company's attention.

The Hazards of Co-Signing

When I travel, I have wonderful opportunities to listen to and learn from my colleagues. As part of the workshop I present on setting up and developing a private practice, I go into depth about the issues involved in insurance reimbursement and fee setting, and I often hear horror stories from workshop participants about dealing with insurance companies.

One area that abounds with these horror stories is the area of "co-signing" or "sign-off." This practice involves having a state-licensed professional sign off or co-sign for another professional, who may or may not be licensed. This may mean a psychiatrist's signing for a psychologist, social worker, or mental health counselor; a social worker's signing for a mental health counselor; or, in states with licensure for mental health counselors, a licensed mental health counselor's signing for a nonlicensed counselor. The purpose of signing off or co-signing is to obtain insurance reimbursement for a client. Although the motive is admirable, the therapist should be aware that when co-signing, or accepting co-signing, the therapist may be committing insurance fraud.

The following stories are among the many I have heard, and they have been chosen to illustrate some of the different pitfalls of co-signing.

The first story involves a psychiatrist and a social worker who shared office space. The social worker took a referral and made an initial assessment, then had the psychiatrist see the client for an assessment. The psychiatrist concurred with the social worker as to diagnosis and treatment, and the social worker began therapy. The insurance company was billed for services performed by the social worker, but co-signed by the psychiatrist.

After a year of therapy the insurance company requested an audit of the psychiatrist's and social worker's records on the client. As a result of this audit, the social worker was charged with theft by deception and the psychiatrist was charged with fraud, in that he had never delivered the services for which the insurance company believed they were paying, because he had signed at the top and the social worker had signed below. It was the insurance company's contention that he was the primary therapist and the social worker was the secondary therapist, which was not the case. The case was eventually settled out of court, with heavy legal costs charged to the psychiatrist and the social worker, and an even heavier cost in emotional distress.

In another case, a psychiatrist and a mental health worker were working jointly with a client, with the psychiatrist doing the signing of all insurance claims. However, the client's insurance policy had a clause indicating that direct treatment could be performed only by a psychiatrist. The insurance company audited the patient records and accounts of both the psychiatrist and the mental health worker. After months of frustration and heavy legal costs, the two mental health professionals agreed to pay back to the insurance company all monies collected for this patient.

Another case involved a psychologist and a social worker who was renting from him. The psychologist was co-signing on all claims submitted by the social worker without seeing the clients directly, only meeting with the social worker to review client cases. Because of the excessive number of claims submitted under the psychologist's license number, the insurance company demanded an audit. When they found that the psychologist did not see the clients, they charged him with deception and fraud, and only by an out-of-court settlement was he able to avoid criminal prosecution. He was required to refund to the insurance company all fees collected by him and the social worker, and to agree not to submit any further claims to the insurance company. This process so disturbed him that he closed up his practice and has left the profession.

One last case involved a psychiatrist who was co-signing for a mental health counselor. In this case the insurance company noticed that the mental health status reports submitted by both were not consistent and that triggered an audit. The audit revealed that the psychiatrist did not have direct contact with the client other than "med checks" but no direct treatment. The insurance company took the provider status away from the psychiatrist and required the counselor to refund all fees to the client and the insurance company.

These examples should serve to remind the therapist who is a co-signer, or uses a co-signer, that there are certain responsibilities to the client and to the insurance company.

What does the individual policy say regarding who must deliver the service?

If the co-signer is not the direct deliverer of service, what are the responsibilities to the insurance company?

If the therapist is the direct deliverer of service, what are the responsibilities to the insurance company?

Has the therapist talked to a lawyer before co-signing or asking someone else to co-sign?

In all cases I have heard, both parties have been held responsible. It is the therapist's responsibility in the case of sign-off or co-signing to know the rules of the insurance company. Ignorance may result in paying legal costs, refunding all fees to the insurance company and client, losing the state license or provider status with the insurance company, or even being accused and found guilty of insurance fraud, as well as the enormous emotional price exacted. In the counseling profession, reputation is everything. When that gets tainted, whether rightly or wrongly, the effect can be devastating.

QUESTIONABLE BILLING PRACTICES

A private practitioner is free to charge whatever fee is felt to be appropriate for the services provided. Sliding scales, or different fees for families, groups, or children can be used as the practitioner sees fit. However, problems can arise with clients who use insurance, whether the therapist plans to collect directly from the insurance company, or to have the client pay first and receive reimbursement from the insurance company. It is wise to know what effect third-party reimbursement will have on the practice.

Insurance companies who pay a flat fee per session, regardless of what is charged, allow the most flexibility. With this type of policy, the company will pay a set amount—say, $25.00 per visit—with or without an annual cap, a predetermined annual maximum. The therapist must supply the company with a correctly completed claim form and an appropriate diagnosis and, if the company accepts the claim, it will pay its $25.00. It is the therapist's responsibility to collect the balance from the client. If desired, the practitioner can accept the insurance company's payment as full payment for services, or as partial payment; as long as the company's requirements are met, all will be fine. If there is an annual cap, the company or the client will make it known, and it will be up to the therapist to collect the fee from the client after the cap has been reached.

Problems can arise with policies under which the insurance company pays a percentage of the fee. With these policies, the company agrees to pay a percentage of the total fee charged. It is assumed that the payment the insurance company makes is only a partial payment, and the therapist must collect the remainder.

Here are some questions to ask when using third-party reimbursement.

Question 1

If a sliding scale based on income is used, can the therapist charge insurance clients the top of the scale, regardless of the clients' income?

The insurance company is basing its reimbursement on what the therapist states the full fee to be. If a sliding scale is used and the usual fee for a client at that income level is $40, whereas higher income clients are charged $80, the company will expect to pay its percentage of $40, not of $80. I have heard people wonder how the company would know that $80 is not the usual fee. How they would know is not the point. Such a practice is not only unethical, it also constitutes fraud, against which insurance companies are starting to take action. Although they don't want to pay less than they owe, they don't want to pay more, either.

Question 2

If the charge is $100 per session and the insurance company pays 50%, or $50.00 per session, can the therapist tell the client to forget the other $50?

Again, the question boils down to the usual and customary fee. If the usual fee is $100, the client should be billed for the difference, and all reasonable effort should be made to collect. If it is not collected because the therapist has made no attempt to collect, the company could audit and disallow the claim.

Question 3

A therapist usually charges $60 per session. Because of the increased paperwork, which means more time, can the clients with insurance be charged $85.00 per session?

The insurance company can claim that the fee is $60, not $85, and that the fee for their clients is not the usual and customary fee. This could be grounds for charging the therapist with fraud for misrepresenting the fee.

Question 4

When the therapist is paid in cash or by check, is it important to give a receipt to the client?

The insurance company has the right to audit a therapist's records to see that the fee charged their claimants is the usual and customary fee, and is consistent with the fee charged other clients. For the therapist's own protection and to justify the fee, good, clear records should be kept. If an insurance company demands an audit, the therapist's best protection is a book-keeping system that shows appointments, receipt systems, and posting of fees.

When a practitioner welcomes the involvement of an insurance company in a practice, the practitioner agrees to be bound by certain rules. The fee is critical to the financial health of the practice; the practitioner should not risk problems by not hav-ing, and adhering to, a clear fee policy. No company is going to question a fee that is clearly set forth in writing, and is collected fairly from all clients. Problems arise only when practitioners try to collect more from the company than their usual and custom-ary fee.

HOW TO COLLECT A FEE

To begin with, remember that the fee is part of the counseling/consulting process. Some would say that it is a critical part of the process. These guidelines and explanation should give a ba-sis for evaluating the collection process.

Collect the fee in person. This is one task that should not be delegated to the secretary, receptionist, or bookkeeper. The fee is part of the contractual arrangement. Asking and collecting the fee puts the therapist in the best position to evaluate any resistance, transference, or manipulation on the client's part.

Collect at each session. This will help avoid two potential problems. First, the client's debt does not have a chance to mount up, so the total is always manageable. Second, as an ongoing evaluation process, collecting the fee at each session means that any difficulties that arise are addressed immediately and not left to develop.

Collect at the close of the session. It has always been my policy to do 50-minute hours, and to stop the session after 45 minutes. I then use the last 5 minutes to collect the fee and set the next appointment.

Collect in a different area. Over the years I've learned that by physically getting up and moving to a different location to collect the fee, (my desk area, in a different part of the room from the area in which I counsel), enhances the break and establishes the transition between the counseling process and leaving the office.

Give a business receipt. All other professional offices give receipts for payment. By completing the receipt, I am able to record the client's payment, note the type of session, the length of the session, and the time of the next appointment. This also gives the client a tangible record of our transaction, whether cash or check, and a record of our next appointment.

Allowing Credit

Extending credit to clients has an adverse effect on cash flow and increases the chance of putting the practice at financial risk. Every dollar a practitioner allows a client not to pay at the time of service is a dollar worked for and not yet received, and potentially a dollar that will never be received. Take a look at these guidelines for extending credit.

It's advisable to not book a client for a second appointment if the checkbook was forgotten at the intake (first) appointment. If clients receive a copy of the self-disclosure brochure clearly stating the payment policy before the first session and don't read it, they are likely to continue ignoring or misunderstanding the policy and will leave the therapist unpaid for several sessions.

If a regular client decides to use insurance, let the client pay for the session, and have the reimbursement go directly to the client. This makes the client more responsible about filling in and sending the reimbursement forms right from the beginning, when it's the client's own money on the line. If the insurance company does not pay the claim, the client as policyholder has much more leverage than the therapist does. If there's a problem with payment forms, diagnosis, or whatever, the client is responsible, and is better able to deal with the carrier. Also, even if the insurance company refuses reimbursement, the therapist has received payment.

Continued insurance reimbursement. Once the client has been reimbursed by the insurance company, the claim will usually be honored by the company, and payments will be received from the company in reasonable time, based on the limits of coverage. At this point, it is appropriate to arrange for the client to pay only the insured's share of the fee because it is fairly certain the remainder will be paid by the insurance company.

Credit for a client in financial difficulties. A client whose financial status has changed due to divorce, job change, death of a spouse, or other trauma may need counseling more than ever, but have difficulty paying the full fee. Such situations should be considered on an individual basis. The client might pay a percentage of the fee at the time of therapy, with the remainder to be paid after therapy is over, but whatever the decision is, discuss the arrangement fully with the client. Make sure the client is aware of what the new arrangement entails and what the client's responsibility is. I have spoken to counselors who simply asked the client for half the regular fee, without telling them that the other half was being added to an account; at the end of therapy, the client was in for an unpleasant surprise.

Fee for missed or no-show appointments. This charge works better as a deterrent to no-shows than as a collectible fee. The therapist can charge the fee and hope to collect it, but if the client were to be taken to small-claims court, the therapist would probably find that, because he didn't perform the service, he should not expect to be paid for it. Being available is not performing the service.

USING A CHECKING SYSTEM

Sometimes, when I talk to people during my workshops, I am amazed and concerned by the "naive" attitude some people take toward doing business. The therapist is responsible for keeping records of all income and expenses for the Internal Revenue Service, and the IRS is responsible for making sure that all necessary taxes are paid. And yet, I often meet people who keep personal and business income in the same account, adding the spouse's income to the practice income, and paying both business and personal bills from the same account. I can see the attraction in doing this: There is only one set of charges for maintaining a checking account, and because the practice income eventually pays the wages, it seems far simpler to merge all the accounts right from the start, rather than doing a lot of bookkeeping to keep them separate.

Doing this opens the door for the IRS to question all the income and every deposit into the account. The easiest way to avoid this situation is by using a system that tracks all income going into the practice and all payments made from the practice. This involves keeping accounts separate. Start an account solely for the practice, and deposit each week's receipts from the practice into this account; then make all practice disbursements from this account.

Once this separate account has been set up, the practitioner must maintain records of deposits and disbursements. Of course, most standard statements received from the bank will allow tracking of deposits and disbursements. As deposits are made and checks are written, post all deposits as practice income and make a notation on all checks as to what the expense was for. It is then possible to go through the checkbooks and tally the expenses for each category.

The disadvantage to using this method is that it is time-consuming and adds a number of extra steps to keep an accounting of expenses. It can be very easy to put off making the notation until there is a little more time, and end up with a number of checks where it is impossible to remember what the expense was. Using a one-write system vastly simplifies the process and makes tracking disbursements straightforward. Many other one-write checking systems are available, at a variety of prices. Before purchasing one, it is important to know how it works and what the practitioner expects to accomplish with the system.

How It Works

A simple one-write system allows the practitioner to record the disbursement information on a ledger page while writing the check. This means that a check cannot be written without knowing the amount, nor can the practitioner "forget" to fill in the check stub.

A carbon strip on the back of the check automatically records the essential information about the check: to whom it was paid, for how much, and on what date. Then, before detaching the check, the practitioner may post the purpose of the check in one of a number of columns to track expenses (e.g., stationery, postage, printing, electricity, telephone, or other.) Then the check is placed in a double-window envelope and is mailed, eliminating three time-consuming and costly steps.

First, write the check and record all checking and bookkeeping information in one step. There is no longer a need to copy the amount and payee of a check onto the stub, because the carbon strip records this information on the ledger page.

Also eliminated is the need to do any kind of posting on a separate accounting ledger book. This gets rid of that "shoebox syndrome" so many of us have gone through where we simply write the check, then go back through the checks every 6 months or once a year to post everything under the correct categories for our accountants or bookkeepers to review.

Finally, because of the way the check is printed and written, the return address is already located in the upper left-hand corner of the check. When addressing information is completed on the check and it is inserted in the double-window envelope, the expense of printing a separate envelope with the return address and the time it takes to write out and address an envelope have been eliminated.

One-write systems are the most effective accounting systems for practice disbursements. This has been shown repeatedly in other small business enterprises such as medical practies, law firms, accounting firms, and small grocery stores. Paying with a one-write system also tells creditors that the practitioner is serious about being in business and is following the same procedures that they use.

MONEY MANAGEMENT

The one-write system helps manage money better by pinpointing how much was paid to whom for what. Whenever the checkbook is opened, it is evident what checks for expenses have been written and to whom. The system eliminates the errors that can happen with standard checking systems because all information written on the check is transcribed onto the ledger page. This reduces bookkeeping time. Check writing is easier because there is no longer a need to post expenditure information on a bookkeeping ledger page.

At the end of each month, bookkeeping can be done in less than an hour. The monthly statement received from the bank includes cancelled checks and indicates the present balance and which checks have cleared. With the one-write system, the balance in the checkbook needs to be compared only with the balance shown by the bank, deducting any service charges, uncleared checks, and other debits. As the checkbook is balanced, each of the expenses is also balanced. At the beginning of the year, or whenever the system is instituted, designate each column for one expense type, for example, column 1 is for rent, and column 2 for postage. When a check for rent is written, post the amount in column 1; when a check for postage is written, post it in column 2. At the end of the month total each column, and the figure obtained is the total amount paid that month for that expense. It is important to start a new month at the top of a new page. To balance the month's accounts, total the amounts of all checks written, then add the totals for each expense column. The two figures should be equal. If not, a very few minutes will reveal the error, thus giving accurate totals of expenditures for each month.

Adding the monthly totals to the balance forward figure carried over from the previous month gives a year-to-date total of expenditures in all expense categories. This running total serves two purposes. First, assuming that the therapist has budgeted expenses for each category, the year-to-date total keeps track of how well the therapist is doing in staying within that budget. Say, for example, that $720 has been budgeted for postage costs in a 1-year period, which breaks down to approximately $60 per month. At the end of March, the third month of the accounting year, the total expenditure on postage should be around $180. If almost $400 on postage has actually been spent, the practitioner should ask why. Perhaps the increased amount is due to one large mailing sent out; perhaps postage costs each month have been substantially higher than anticipated. Once this has been determined, it can be decided whether this higher cost is appropriate and whether the budget allotment in that category should be increased, or if postage is being wasted and how that wastage can be reduced or eliminated.

The other advantage of the running year-to-date totals is in tax preparation. At the end of the year, when the checkbook has been balanced for the month of December and each column has been tabulated, take only the ledger page for the month of December to the accountant or tax preparer. This gives all the information needed regarding expenditures made throughout the year, under each category. Taken in conjunction with the receipt system, this provides a check and balance of all income into the practice, all deposits made into the checking account, and all expenditures from the checking account.

Using a one-write system for the practice checking account is a simple way to track practice expenditures and conform to IRS regulations. It also cuts down the time spent on bookkeeping, and adds to the practitioner's knowledge of just where the money in the practice is going. One-write systems are available from a variety of sources, such as stationery stores and office supply outlets.

Tax Planning

Every practitioner faces the April 15th deadline. Throughout the whole year there has been a silent partner, the IRS, who shows up demanding wages on April 15th. The Internal Revenue Service is an active participant in every business and industry in the United States. Private practice is no exception. Tax planning and tax preparation begin at the beginning of each fiscal year and run through the full year. There are a number of factors to be aware of when planning taxes. An accountant is an extremely important member of the team, but the private practitioner must take care of the ongoing work and the decisions that must be made concerning taxes. The following information is designed to help in some of the areas of tax planning and tax awareness that are ongoing concerns of anyone in private practice. In the 14 years I have been in private practice, the tax codes have changed, and I constantly need to check with my accountant regarding how they affect me. There are some basic practices I must continually maintain, such as good record keeping and understanding what to do with the records once they are kept, staying aware of when I should or should not purchase equipment, knowing how to handle cash flow, when to do end-of-the-year billing, and retirement planning. All these things need to be considered in a successful practice.

Can I Barter in My Practice?

The IRS is becoming increasingly concerned about individuals who barter for services and assume that, because no cash changes hands, they do not have to declare that payment for service as income.

If a therapist sees a client and agrees to perform a service (counseling, consulting, or training), and exchange that for a service performed by the client, the cost for the services must be declared as income, and the client must declare the cost of the service performed as income. Here are two examples to illustrate this point.

A counselor agreed to see a couple for marriage counseling in exchange for the husband's supplying the counselor with firewood. The IRS would expect that the counselor list the normal fee for each session as income even if no cash were exchanged and the husband would be expected to list the value of the wood as income to his wood cutting business.

A consultant agreed to do a seminar for a manager of a computer firm in exchange for technical assistance in installing a new computer. The IRS would rule that both parties should list income for this exchange.

The clearest way to deal with bartering is not to do it. If the therapist wishes to exchange services, do it clearly and simply by exchanging checks.

The Business-Only Credit Card

My accountant often reminds me that the best way to be prepared when tax time comes is to follow two simple rules during the year: Keep clear and trackable records, and keep them simple. Following these rules will save both time and money, twice:

once when the tax return is prepared, and again if and when an audit takes place.

Most people use credit cards as a handy means of payment for subscriptions, workshops, and other business-related expenses. This is an excellent idea because it allows the practitioner to defer payment for 25–30 days without being charged interest.

However, a problem can arise if the card is not used only for business expenses, but for a combination of business and personal use. If the uses of the card are mixed, each item must have documentation to explain to the accountant and then the auditor why one item was charged to the business and another was not.

If the therapist doesn't have a card strictly for the business, one should be obtained. Add the name of the business to the card; it will help in marketing. (Potential clients work in stores and other places where credit cards are honored.) Having a business-use credit card will help in following the first accounting rule: Keep it clear and trackable. Credit card receipts from the business-use only credit card will clearly state a business purpose, and tracking will also be furthered. If a billing statement is produced as proof of expenses, only business expenses will be on the statement. Each entry should have a slip indicating on the back the purpose of the expense, the amount and, if the payment was for a meal, the purpose of the meeting. In this way, business and personal expenses will not have to be documented separately, nor explained to an accountant at tax time (when it's hard to rememeber why something was charged to the business on a mixed-use card).

When applying for a business-only credit card, ask for a $3,000 to $5,000 line, depending on the number of years the practice has been open and projected cash flow. Most banks are more liberal with credit cards for business than cards for personal use, and there is no reason not to ask for the largest line of credit possible.

Finally, to maintain the clarity needed from the card, use it only for business purposes. Whenever possible, pay off the balance each month; this way the card will work as a means of interest-free deferred payment, and a simple way of tracking business expenses.

Putting a Spouse or Child on the Payroll

One way to save on taxes while filling the office needs is for the therapist to employ a member of the family. Autumn and winter tend to be busy times in a practice. Summer vacation is over and the therapist is anxious to increase the client load, training opportunities, and workshop presentations. This involves mailing newsletters, getting back to referral sources, and preparing packets of material for presentations—all of which can take more time than the office staff has available. This is a good time to get a spouse or children involved to help with all those jobs.

If the therapist is self-employed, not a corporation, then hiring the family to help has extra advantages from the tax standpoint. First, if the family members are hired as independent contractors, they need not be put on the payroll, thus avoiding payroll and unemployment taxes. The real tax advantage is the savings that can be taken on the social security tax.

At the end of the year, the therapist will pay two taxes on the profit made in his practice—income tax and social security. Social security tax will be levied on the total profit for the year. For example, if the gross receipts for the year totalled $80,000 and the expenses (rent, office equipment, secretarial staff, and others) came to $50,000, there would be gross profits of $30,000. This is the amount on which social security tax would be paid.

To reduce the amount of social security tax paid, the gross profit must be reduced. Hiring a family member can help. If a spouse is hired, at a fair salary for the hours worked, for the period of September to December for a total of $5,000 for that period, the gross profit from the practice will be reduced by $5,000. Using the example of gross receipts of $80,000, with $50,000 in other expenses, this would mean the therapist would be liable to pay social security tax and other employment taxes on $25,000. The tax due on $30,000 would be $3,600; on $25,000 it would be $3,000, a savings of $600.

Of course, if a spouse is hired, the therapist will still pay income tax on the full $30,000: $25,000 will be the therapist's salary with $5,000 being the spouse's salary. If one of the children is also employed and is paid $1,000 (the limit for children under 14), there would be a double advantage. First, the $1,000 would lower the amount of income on which the therapist would have to pay social security tax (the tax on $24,000 in our example is $2,880), and as long as the child's income remained below the limit, no income tax would have to be paid on that $1,000.

As usual a few guidelines will simplify things. First, make sure to keep accurate records of the work performed and the hours, especially if the person is not on the payroll. The IRS is likely to question payment when there is no payroll card.

Second, remember the $1,000 limit on income paid to children under 14. A child earning over $1,000 will have the income taxed at the same rate as if it were added to the therapist's income. Children over 14 can work for a parent and be taxed at their own rate, possibly increasing the parent's tax advantage further.

Time is extremely important for this tax-saving idea. Employing a spouse and children can save money, but now is the time to call the accountant.

What Records Do I Need to Keep?

At the end of the year it is time to organize records preparatory to going over them with the accountant and lawyer. Over the year any practitioner will have accumulated a small mountain of papers referring to the practice, and decisions must now be made about what papers to keep, for what reason, and how long.

There is a saying that goes, "The longer a bill goes uncollected, the less likely it is that it will ever be collected." Think of paper retention the same way: The longer it is kept, the less likely it is to be needed. But if the therapist thinks that the obvious response is to give up on collecting bad bills and keeping papers, there could be trouble ahead for the practice. There are specific guidelines about both debt collection and document retention. That one piece of paper needed to answer a question about taxes, or to comply with the law, is indispensable, and often hard to identify in advance. The IRS does not say what books or papers must be kept; it simply requires that, when audited, the individual must be able to support what has been claimed. Here are some suggestions and guidelines that should be discussed in detail with an accountant and lawyer.

Time Line

Most people think that records need to be kept only for 3 years after the return is due, or has been filed. This is known as the statute of limitations, and it applies in most cases, but some documents must be kept for longer periods. (For example, if a piece of property is acquired and improved, all relevant material to prove the investment in the property needs to be kept, or the person could be taxed on the "profit" when it is resold.) If there is an omission from the gross income of 25% or more, the statute of limitations is 6 years; if there is reason to suspect fraud, there is no time limitation.

The private practitioner should also be aware that other branches of the government may have different requirements. If a practice falls under any other government regulations, the therapist should get specific advice and guidelines from a lawyer and accountant.

Suggestions

This is not a complete listing of records that should be kept, and it is offered only as a guideline. The accountant and lawyer should be the best judges.

Retain Indefinitely

Appointment book—The appointment book is central to all records, and should not be destroyed or discarded. Deductions and income will be based on this document.

Cash books—Records of each transaction or sale made.

Ledger cards—The posting card on each client from whom income was received, listing date, type of service, and amount.

Audit reports and financial statements.

Cancelled checks for taxes, capital purchases, and important contracts.

Contracts and leases in force—Keep from the time they are signed through duration and after as proof of deductions.

Corporation charter, minutes books and bylaws, as well as any stock or bond records.

Copyrights, patents, trademark registrations.

Correspondence on legal and tax matters.

Property reports—Keep deeds, mortgages, easements and appraisals even after the property has been sold.

Insurance records—Especially malpractice and liability records.

Tax returns and work papers—Especially documentation used to carry over or carry back a deduction.

Retain 7–8 Years

All other cancelled checks used in the business—Keeping all checks is recommended.

Vouchers for payment to vendors, employees, and basically any and all documentation to justify the check or cash spent for a deduction.

Records of inventories of products claimed at the end of the year.

Payroll records, especially time sheets with all deductions and appropriate tax tables used.

Expense reports with documentation receipts.

Payables and receivables ledgers—An accountant will give specific advice on this matter.

Purchase orders for any products or services sold, contracted for, or performed.

Expired contracts and leases.
Individual withholding tax statements for all employees.
Subcontractors' bills and payment records.
Monthly trial balances.
Employee disability benefits records.
All other employee insurance records.

Retain 3 Years

Personal files on any terminated employee with record of reasons and outcome of termination.

Bank reconciliations of checking and saving accounts including but not limited to any CD or other investments.

Petty cash vouchers and records.

Retain 2 Years

General correspondence not directly related to the deriving of income or expenses of the practice.

Requisition orders.

This information is offered as a rough guide to record retention. In no way should it be considered as an all-inclusive list. Use legal counsel and an accountant's advice before putting a record-retention schedule into effect. Documentation is the best protection in the case of a dispute or question by the IRS or any other government agency. The private practitioner is running a small business, which requires solid business practices. It's better to save too much than to be missing the one document out of a hundred that is needed.

Who Should Prepare the Taxes?

Early every spring, thoughts turn to taxes and preparing tax returns. The changes in the tax laws are prompting many individuals who have always prepared their own returns to opt for professional help, without being sure just how much help they need and how much it is going to cost. Enlisting the support of an accountant is one way to cope with tax preparation, but there are other options.

Tax Preparer

At the simplest end of the scale is the tax preparer, someone whose training is mostly in entering numbers correctly on tax returns. These preparers are usually either self-employed, or work for one of the big chains. They know the basics, and are perfectly competent to prepare the average individual tax return. However, if the practitioner expects to receive tax or financial planning advice for that fee, or if the return is more complex, most of these tax preparers do not have the experience to help.

Enrolled Agent

The enrolled agent is someone who has permission to represent taxpayers before the IRS. This means the agent has either passed a difficult test sponsored by the IRS, or has had at least 5 years' experience as an IRS auditor. Thus, the enrolled agent will have an excellent knowledge of tax laws, and will make sure the returns are in compliance with those laws. The enrolled agent will not necessarily aggressively interpret those laws to help the therapist save money. Fees for enrolled agents range from $25 to $150 an hour.

CPA

A certified public accountant (CPA) is someone who has passed a series of business and accounting courses. There is no guarantee, however, that a CPA is also a tax expert. Check on whether this is the CPA's area of expertise when contacting a CPA, and expect to pay from $50 to $200 an hour for services.

Tax Attorney

Unless there are legal complications to the tax return, hiring a tax attorney to prepare the taxes is overkill. If a lawyer's services are required, find one who acquired a master's degree in taxation after receiving a law degree, or one who is also a CPA.

Changes

The start of a new year is a good time to review and plan for a business, to make the new year as profitable and rewarding as possible. During the year changes will probably be made that will affect the business, including some changes in the therapist's personal life. The therapist should anticipate how these changes will affect the business and factor them into the business plan for the new year.

Here is a partial list of changes the therapist may be making. Treat this list as a checklist. Examine each item, and consider whether that change is likely to be made during the coming year. If the answer is yes, give a brief description of why, and what the desired effect of that change would be for the business. This will yield a list of possible and probable changes that should be discussed with the three major advisers, lawyer, accountant, and banker, to make sure that each possibility is taken into consideration in planning for the new business year.

People

Are any of the following personnel changes likely to happen in the new year?

Accountant;
Lawyer;
Secretary;
Office manager;
Answering service;
Taking on or losing business partner(s);
Taking on or losing stock partner(s);
Taking on or losing associates;
Taking on or losing subletters; and
Taking on or losing psychometric examiner.

Places

A change in the primary business location;
Up for renewal of the lease;
Planning on purchasing a building or condominium for the office;
Expanding and developing satellite locations;
Subletting from someone; and
Planning on traveling more extensively for training or consulting contracts.

Things

Is there any chance of purchasing or changing any of the following:

Computer;
Copy machine;
Office equipment;
Office furniture; and
New accounting/bookkeeping system.

Services Added or Changed

New product for direct sale;
Testing service;
Book or monograph for sale;
Increase in workshop or training activity;

Increase in consulting services;

Becoming an EAP provider;

Becoming a franchised deliverer of services or products;

Marketing a franchised product;

Adding groups, weekend retreats, or intensive therapy activities to the clinical practice;

Becoming a supervisor; and

Teaching at a college or university.

Personal

The following changes in the personal life can also affect the business:

Marriage;

Divorce;

Birth of child;

Child going to college or leaving home;

Pending death of loved one;

Change from full-time paid job to sole practitioner whether clinical, consulting, or training;

Major purchase of property for personal use; and

Geographic move of primary personal residence.

Any of these factors could have financial, tax or personal effects on the business and should, inasmuch as possible, be factored into the business plan for the new year (see appendix A, form 17).

EVALUATION OF THE PRACTICE

To run a successful business requires a certain amount of time in evaluating the direction, scope, cash flow, and important factors of the business. This evaluation is usually done monthly, quarterly, and yearly. In my experience, to successfully manage my practice, I need to review the broader picture of my practice at specific, periodic times.

This evaluation is broken down as follows:

Monthly Review of Income and Expenses

The form will give you some idea of how to lay out this information. The various components of the form may vary, depending on the nature of the individual practice, but the format should be the same. It is basically a statement of income and cash flow that is compiled at the end of each month to give an overview of what is happening within the practice (see appendix A, form 18).

At the top of the form is information regarding the income from the practice. This is usually divided into income from clinical fees, consultations, workshops and trainings, rental income and any other income sources, creating a total income figure.

Next would be the operating expenses. Listing from the checkbook accounting page all the operating expenses for the month will give a sense of what is happening in the practice. This can be best accomplished at the end of the month when the checking statement comes from the bank. Taking the information from the checking statement and the accounting pages (as indicated in the section on a one-write checking system) allows the information to be condensed to a one-page summary. With this in mind, as the practice builds each year, the total picture for a given month (first column) can be compared with the total picture for the same month of the preceding year. This allows an evaluation of how much progress in income has been made and how the expenses have changed. The third column is a year-to-date breakdown. This gives a picture of how the income and expenses are moving throughout the year. If the statement is prepared on a monthly basis, it is easy to evaluate exactly how the practice is progressing from one year to the next.

Once a system like this has been implemented, it takes a minimal time effort, usually at the time the checkbook is balanced, allowing a full overview of the cash flow of the practice. This overview reveals whether the profit or loss for a given month is comparable to the same month of the previous year, and whether that is typical for that month. If the same month is different each year, it may be possible to determine the factors causing the fluctuation.

Monthly Review of Clients

The second review would be a monthly, quarterly, and yearly review of the practice's client population. If the practitioner is using a receipt system (explained elsewhere in this section), it becomes possible and helpful to be able to condense this information into a simple analysis of what has been done in the practice for a given month and the same month the previous year, as well as year-to-date figures for both years. This review process gives a clear way to evaluate the overall direction of the practice regarding the client population being served and the services offered (see appendix A, form 19).

Without a marketing analysis I would not be able to project or plan my expenses, my marketing, and the specific directions in which the practice will be moving in during the coming months. This evaluation and review process does not need to be lengthy nor take a great deal of time. Doing it on a systematic basis provides a clear and specific way to approach an expansion of the practice. This evaluation and review process also serves to collect the necessary documentation for any type of bank financing or expansion that may be necessary in the future.

SUMMARY

A successful practice is based on a steady flow of clients to the practice. The need for an intake process that projects the professional relationship with the client is a necessity. Sending a letter confirming the appointment, as well as an intake form and self-disclosure brochure, increases the success of the first session.

The many issues surrounding fee collection and billing are addressed by knowing how to establish an appropriate fee. The therapist needs to have a clear response to the many gray areas such as missed appointments, phone consultations, late charges, and insurance forms. Knowing how to collect when a client owes for sessions will save confusion and manipulation by the therapist or the client.

Often practitioners fail to realize that as a business, all income to the practice must be recorded in a businesslike manner. The use of a receipt system that not only gives a client a clear impression that he or she is seeing a professional business person, but also provides an accounting system for all income, will enhance the image of the practice and simplify the bookkeeping necessary to comply with IRS rules.

The confusion about third-party reimbursement as well as the many hazards of co-signing must be understood before anyone accepts or attempts to seek reimbursement for clients. Insurance billing accounts for a great deal of the paperwork in a practice. Becoming overly dependent on insurance reimbursement can also cause a great deal of burden in the cash flow of a practice. With the many changes in insurance reimbursement policies, every practitioner needs to understand the system.

Cash dispersement to pay bills is another area where new practitioners can jeopardize their position with the IRS if they are not using a checking system specifically designed for the practice. The need for a clearly documented process, beginning with the payment from the client and ending with a check to pay for expenses, will save untold hours if an IRS audit is requested. Proper records must be retained because a private practice is a cash business. There are specific requirements regarding which records must be kept and for how long.

Finally, a well-planned monthly review of the health of the practice with regard to income, clients, and expenses will become the basis for growth in the practice. Being in private practice means treating the practice like a business and following sound, proven business principles.

Expanding the Practice

Inevitably as time goes on, each practitioner faces the question of whether the practice should be expanded. To a successful practitioner, it becomes important to broaden the financial base and guarantee long-term stability. The particular way in which a practice is expanded can be both positive and negative for the practice. In my own particular case, I have gone through a number of different practice expansions, some of which have proven very successful to my practice and some of which have not.

Basically there are three areas of practice expansion: people, places, and things. The three major questions the private practitioner who is contemplating expansion confronts are centered around when, where, and how:

- When is it appropriate to expand a practice?
- Where should it be attempted?
- How does the private practitioner go about expansion?

Let's begin with the "how" first.

HOW TO EXPAND A CLINICAL PRACTICE

Any expansion of a business venture a practitioner enters into designed to increase the profitability or long-term stability of the practice should be based on a plan. This plan should be a clearly written and developed objective, after consultations with an attorney and an accountant, to make sure that all factors have been considered. This plan should follow the standard format of a business plan. The discipline and process of developing a business plan will help the practitioner better to understand whether the contemplated expansion is appropriate. A business plan consists of:

History of the business, stating when and why it was formed and tracing the history from that time to the present.

Present condition would include an analysis of the cash flow over the last 12 months, stating income, expenses, and sources for income. In the case of a mental health service, it is important to delineate how much of the income is received on a direct basis from clients and how much is received through insurance reimbursement. In the case of insurance reimbursement, it is important to note the average length of time between billing for the service and receiving payment.

Space, either leased or owned, should be inventoried, with an analysis of the leasing or purchasing agreement of that space and projected increases in cost of the lease or property.

Inventory of all goods and equipment used in the practice is an analysis of all furniture and depreciated items in the practice as well as any computer or testing equipment.

Personnel analysis of the staff in the practice, either part-time or full-time, should include pay rate, benefits, and projection of increase over the next 12-month period.

Expansion objectives are a specific outline, stating why the expansion is needed, what will be accomplished when the expansion is complete, and what impact it will have on the practice.

Expansion cost will need to be worked out with the accountant, and specific costs involved will need to be addressed, both immediate and long-range financing costs, projected over a 3- to 7-year period.

Expansion outcome must be envisioned in terms of the expected outcome. How will this outcome directly benefit the practice? What objectives will have been met?

Preparing such a document in advance will allow the practitioner to make moves expected to enhance the stability of the practice. It's important in considering a practice expansion that the necessary cash flow and stability be there to sustain the costs the expansion will entail. If the practitioner has gone through the analysis, it will be evident whether he or she is prepared to take the risk or not. Practice expansion is a risky endeavor.

People

Most clinicians think of practice expansion with the focus on people. In section one, I addressed the issue of subletting. Subletting is workable and profitable, but a few guidelines will be helpful. These conclusions were drawn from two areas: my own experiences of having a counseling center of 11 therapists, and my discussions with other therapists across the country. These guidelines are offered for subletting arrangements that are not partnerships, but attempt to act as group practices.

- **The therapist must clearly understand the personal family of origin issues.** An unawareness of the personal family issues can deeply affect the working relationship required in a group practice.

- **The therapist must be ready, willing, and financially able to spend time processing the issues** that will arise between each of the renters or members of the practice and the therapist.
- **The therapist must screen the members of the group well,** not only for their match with the therapist, but with each other. It is important not to grow too quickly.
- **The therapist should get outside help.** Bringing someone in on a regular basis to consult and process the group's intraction with each other is a good idea.

Few group practices have made it past 3 years. Being successful is not based on what is done correctly; it's based on what is learned from mistakes and failures. With that in mind, let me offer some ideas about partnerships and corporations.

Partnerships

The basic purpose of a partnership or S corporation partnership is to strengthen and expand a business. I often hear stories about colleagues who work for the same agency, and feel that a partnership with each other would be just the thing to start their practice. They work out a few details—what they'll call the practice, whose name will be first, and how to arrange the office lease—but they tend to forget about the key financial and personal questions.

- What financial commitment will each make?
- What are each partner's individual strengths?
- What are their expectations from each other in terms of marketing or time spent in the office?

Other issues to consider might be:

- What are the partners' expectations about cross-referrals?
- What about peer supervision and outside supervision?
- Are there assumptions about insurance reimbursement and co-signing?
- What are the expectations for growth and change in the future?

Some factors to consider before forming a partnership follow.

Why a Partnership?

Know why a partnership is the choice. Private practice is a lonely business, but a partner shouldn't be selected just in order to have someone with whom to discuss business problems. The risk in a practice is enormous, but if the benefits of a successful practice are to be enjoyed, the practitioner has to be willing to take that risk. Starting out with a partner who doesn't measure up can increase the risk; it could even overburden the practice. If the practice is already established and has gotten over the most risky beginning 2- to 3-year period, taking on a partner could be a setback for the stability of the practice. Think carefully about the reasons; there is a lot at stake.

Part of the Plan

Have a specific goal in mind. Deciding to form a partnership because a colleague suggests it is similar to agreeing to buy advertising time from the local radio because it offers a special rate for mental health practitioners. Advertising should be part of a plan with a specific goal in view. Bringing in a partner should also be part of an overall scheme designed to strengthen the business.

First, a partnership should be the private practitioner's own idea and decision, and second, that decision should be based on a clearly thought-out plan in which the practice will be enhanced by forming a partnership, the practitioner's income will be increased, and the stability of the business will be assured. Decide in advance what the benefits of a partnership would be. Some aspects that might look like benefits in a discussion with a colleague could turn out, on later consideration, to be actual disadvantages. Don't be talked into partnership by someone else.

Partner or Pal?

What is proposed is a partner, not a pal. Forming a partnership because one likes the other person may be very nice, but personality is definitely not the most important reason for choosing a partner. Many highly effective partners never socialize outside the office. Partnerships are formed for business purposes and friends are for social purposes; don't look for both in the same person. The best rule to follow is that partners are there to help make business decisions, and pals are to share good times. Pals who become partners almost always find that one aspect of the relationship, pal or partner, suffers.

Business Goals

The business goals of both parties clearly need to be the same. The partnership is being formed to expand the business. The partner must be as enthusiastic as the practitioner is about expanding the practice and improving the services. When two competent, busy therapists go into partnership to reduce costs, without planning the effect such a move will have on their practices, what the response of the community will be to the change, or their increased liability, the result is often that costs go up, not down.

Delegate

The private practitioner must ask if the time is really right for a partner. If a therapist has been running a solo practice, with no secretary or other personnel in the office, it might be difficult to delegate responsibility. Before going into partnership, consider hiring a secretary, or another therapist or consultant, to see what it's like to let others make decisions that affect the practice.

Capital and Skills

Look for two key attributes, capital and skill supplement. The first attribute the prospective partner needs to bring to the partnership is capital. A partnership is based on expanding the profit of a practice, so if the plan is to share the profit, the new partner should pay for what has already been built up: the name, reputation, location, and good will. Discuss the value of the practice with an accountant, and establish what can be expected from selling a share to a partner before making any commitment.

Next, the accountant should review the prospective partner's tax returns for the last 3 years to be sure that the person is financially stable. Again, it would be nice just to have the prospective partner say everything is OK, but for the therapist's sake, documentation is the key. Also, if there is a later need to apply to a bank to finance expansion, such as buying a building or purchasing new equipment, the bank will want to examine both partners' financial records. If the new partner's records do not stand up to scrutiny, financing may be refused, or the therapist may be held wholly responsible by the bank for any money borrowed. Be sure of the new partner's finances from the beginning.

The prospective partner's skills or knowledge should supplement the therapist's own. For example, the therapist might choose someone with excellent financial or marketing ability, someone who works with a different client population than the therapist does, or someone familiar with a new product or service that will expand the services the practice offers. The partner should do more than pick up the client overload; the partner should enhance and expand the practice's services. If a long waiting list is the only issue that needs to be addressed, hiring employees or associates would probably be a simpler solution than going into partnership.

Make It Legal

The practitioner should leave an out. Once it has been decided to invite someone to join the practice, the practitioner should talk to a lawyer about the legal steps to follow and then develop a contract. A partnership should never be formed on a handshake; save the handshake until after the closing. The practitioner should have the attorney contact the prospective partner's attorney to draw up the formal agreement. Yes, I did say attorney: A partnership is a legal agreement, and that should be done between the two people best able to negotiate such an agreement—attorneys. The hardest issue to settle is not how the partnership will be formed; that can be discussed together and then the attorney can draw it up in legal terms. But what will happen if the partnership doesn't work out? Look at every eventuality. What will be the provisions for the division of profits, leases, or referral sources? Remember, like marriages, business relationships don't usually end when everything is going smoothly, but when a great deal of stress has been generated. At that stage, good intentions don't count for much. Work it all out in advance, and remember to include provisions for the death, retirement, or incapacitation of either partner, with clearly stated buyout and insurance agreements.

Going into partnership resembles getting married in many ways, but it does have one distinct advantage. The outcome doesn't have to be guesswork. With a partnership, the right person can be chosen, and the two parties can agree on a course of action if it doesn't work. A partnership is a sharing of the responsibilities, growth, and profits of a business. Don't be afraid to do it, but don't rush into partnership until you've found the right person.

In summary, it is important that everything be done in writing and that an attorney be involved. Any practice expansion involves the potential liability of the practice, especially the goodwill of the practice. Involving other people in the practice can jeopardize the good-will, marketing, and reputation that has been built. It is important that all arrangements be done in a legal and ethical way with everything in writing and under the supervision of an attorney.

Places

Sometimes a practice has simply outgrown its space, and often therapists do not realize that moving can also be considered practice expansion. Relocating one's office often means that the office moves to a larger space where the temptations of subletting or renting space to other therapists becomes a factor to consider. Sometimes moving a practice may necessitate the purchase of property; practice expansion can occur by purchasing a condo or office building. In my particular case, that is what I have done to stabilize my practice in one way. I moved from rented space into space that I purchased. Increasing the stability of my practice by allowing myself to have a depreciation expense versus a simple rent expense, and the aspect of increasing my investment by owning property, was an attractive option for me. But purchasing property without a proper business plan can be a financial nightmare.

If purchasing property is being considered, it should be approached with a business plan, as with any other expansion. Time needs to be taken to find the proper location. The amount of time that will be needed to renovate new space and do the necessary negotiating and financing must be considered. Purchasing office space in either a free-standing building or a condominium requires time away from the clinical practice. During the purchasing and renovation time, there is apt to be a dip in the billable clinical time. It's important that this be factored into any practice expansion as a cost. It is impossible to go through the purchasing of property and still be able to continue a full clinical and billable practice.

Purchasing property can also be a long process requiring many hours of consultation about the many elements of finding property, negotiating the contract, and obtaining financing, and the supervision of renovation work that is often needed once the property has been purchased. Often successful practitioners who need to divert cash flow will purchase property for rental rather than clinical purposes. If the income is in excess of $100,000, sometimes a practitioner will form a corporation for the sole purpose of being able to purchase rental property. Because this property is then listed in the corporation's name, the corporation receives the tax benefits of property ownership.

If a practitioner forms a corporation to purchase a house for a reasonable price, finances the house, and takes on the debt service repayment through the corporation, the corporation receives a tax write-off for the depreciation of the house and all expenses, which, in turn, lowers the practitioner's tax liability.

Practitioners who do not choose to add other therapists to their practices often do that, but they need a way to create passive income and to protect their long-term retirement goals.

Products

Selling products that the practitioner believes in or has created is the third way of expanding a practice. I have met a number of practitioners who have created a product that could be sold. These types of products include audio or visual tapes used in stress reduction, parenting, guided imagery, or meditation; puppets or toys for use with children; and written materials such as booklets or pamphlets, testing materials, and newsletters to be sold to other therapists for use with their clients. I once met a therapist in California who had an exhibit booth next to mine where I was offering products from my Private Practice Institute. She was selling puppets. She did a lot of incest and victimization work and had developed the use of puppets in her practice. Her clients had enjoyed them and had asked to buy them for members of the family. She began marketing them and attending state and national conferences to do so. This proved to be highly successful. I personally purchased quite a few for my practice. I have also met therapists who have produced audio or visual tapes that they marketed to the general public as another income-producing method. Writing a book is another example of things that practitioners can do to expand their practice. The income from the book sales is added income to the private practice, so that the expenses involved in the creation of the book can be deducted from the private practice.

SUMMARY

Building a successful private practice not only involves building a private practice but also a long-term commitment to developing a strong financial base from a variety of other sources. Simply building a practice on the assumption that direct billable clinical hours will be the stability of the practice puts the practice in jeopardy. Finding a number of income sources that will provide revenue over lean periods will protect the practice over the long haul and will more comfortably ensure the long-term stability needed. Considering expanding the practice is important, but should never be entered into lightly. Any choice to move a practice, to increase the overhead costs of a practice, or to bring in other personnel to the practice, should be done with the full consultation of both legal and tax advisors. It should be done with a clearly delineated plan, and with the anticipation of the time and effort it will take. Expansions do not always work, but they always teach the practitioner more about the business world and how to be successful in it.

SECTION EIGHT

Reflections

As I finish this book I'm reminded of why I've written it. I'm reminded why I have traveled across the country and lectured so much on private practice, of why I've spent 3 years of my life putting together a newsletter for people in private practice, and why I've gone through the labor of creating this book. And as I think of those things I remind myself of the gift that I have to do the work that I do. As a private practitioner, as a therapist, as a man, as a human being, I have a commitment to this world. I have a responsibility to help make this life better for those whose paths I cross. I'm reminded so often as I work with my clients, talk to other therapists across the country, or talk with someone who approaches me during one of my workshops that I am but a wounded healer. I am but someone who, by the very nature of the course that I have chosen to take, will experience within myself levels of being wounded that cannot often be easily or readily described. But I am aware that as my own journey has gone on that it is **from** my journey that I can help others.

When I first began my private practice, I knew that I didn't know what it would take to be successful, but I had a longing to learn and to grow. Over the years of being in private practice I have made what many might consider mistakes, some of which were very costly either to myself or my family. But I know that because of the work that I do, had I not taken those risks, had I not taken those chances, had I not experienced both the ecstasy of success and the depression of failure, I would not have been able to write this book or share those experiences. Had I stayed in the practice I first began with its limitations and confines, with my clinging to outdated ideas, without the personal growth and knowledge I have had to obtain, I would not be able to do the effective work that I do today. My own personal background of life experiences is what I bring to those individuals who choose to journey with me, whether in the brief moments that we may spend at a workshop, lecture, or presentation I am doing, or the many countless hours we spend together in that scariest of all human intimacy commitments known as therapy. But it is that

231

process, it is that commitment to the process that is my strength and is my journey.

When one chooses to become a therapist, to offer that service to the public, one is choosing to face one's own wounds. The blind spots that each and every one of us has, the blind spots to which our clients will expose us, are just the elements that are causing that client and that therapist to come together and journey. In this book I have attempted to explain in detail the elements I feel constitute running a successful private practice. I have emphasized the personal aspect of it, the requirements, the proper facilities, marketing, financial endeavors, and ulti- mate expansion. But the one element I hope you have seen through this book is the one I feel so strongly about: that I am but a human being and when I do this work, whether in front of hundreds or face-to-face, it is my oneness that is brought to bear in that process. I want to leave you with one thought:

To climb a mountain is to find a path. And each and every one of us must take our own path up our own mountain. We may ask for help and will, at different times, receive it, but the path and the journey are our own. We can help others as we go. This book is my attempt to help you find your path up that mountain. It is my attempt to share the experiences and the knowledge I've acquired in this process that I call private practice. As I have carved my path up my own mountain, I hope this book will help you carve your path up yours. For each of us must climb our own mountain, and each of us is the only one who knows where he or she is on that path.

Let me get personal now and ask you a pointed question: Why are you in practice? Is it the money, the control of your life, the need to help? What and why do you judge? Do you judge your clients, your fellow professionals, yourself? What energy does judging take from your practice? Let me share a story with you.

There was once a pilgrim who stopped on his journey and saw that some people were standing on the side, attempting to help fellow pilgrims along the way. The pilgrim wondered about these helpers: What did they do to help others? How did it help? Why did they charge for the help they gave? What did it take to do what they did? What would it be like to be a helper himself? He was filled with questions, and curious to learn.

As he journeyed on, he began to ask the helpers those ques- tions that kept nagging him; he was surprised and confused by what he found. Everyone he spoke to was willing to help him on his journey, but when he inquired about them and sought an- swers to his questions, the response was different. Some seemed hesitant to talk about themselves and what they did. Some seemed angered by his questions, telling him that there were already too many helpers and he couldn't possibly do what they did. But some welcomed him warmly. They freely shared with him how they became helpers, what they did, and why they charged a fee for their services.

After talking with many helpers, our pilgrim stopped on his journey and thought about what he'd learned. He realized that helpers were also pilgrims on their own journey, that some were timid, unsure, and lacking in confidence, others were scared and resentful, hiding from themselves and others, and some were warm and confident, true helpers who liked themselves and knew who they were and truly wanted to help any pilgrim.

What help would you be to the pilgrim who came to your door? Would you be willing to share what makes you qualified to do what you do and why you charge what you do without judging him or his motives, or judging the right of others to call themselves helpers?

I'm often struck by the lack of openness, dialogue, and encouragement of fellow helpers. It pains me to hear of helpers who lack the confidence and compassion to be nonjudgmental. It confuses me when fellow helpers attack each other's credentials, professionalism, and judgment. As I grow in my own understanding of what it means to be a helper, as I confront my own judgments and control issues, I realize just how hard it is to be a helper. I also realize that no one person is the perfect helper. My humanness and my quest to understand myself give me the strength to struggle with those pilgrims who stop at my door.

APPENDIX A

Business Forms

Form 1	Office Lease Agreement
Form 2	Fee Per Session Rate
Form 3	Checklist for Evaluating Rental Space
Form 4	New Equipment List
Form 5	Survey of Fees Charged
Form 6	Sample Budget
Form 7	Projected Budget
Form 8	Summary of Sample Costs/Session
Form 9	Summary of Sample Fees/Session
Form 10	Sample Self-Disclosure Brochure
Form 11	Marketing Analysis
Form 12	Sample Feedback Form
Form 13	Sample End-of-Year Statement
Form 14	Sample Confirmation Letter
Form 15	Sample Intake Form
Form 16	Sample Release Form
Form 17	Personal Change Form
Form 18	Monthly Review of Income and Expenses
Form 19	Monthly Review of Clients

Form 1
Office Lease Agreement

OFFICE LEASE AGREEMENT made this ____ day of _____, 19 ____, by and between Southern Maine Counseling Center, Inc., a Maine business corporation, with its principal place of business at 581 Forest Avenue, City of Portland, County of Cumberland and State of Maine (hereinafter "Landlord") and John Doe (hereinafter "Tenant").

WITNESSETH

1. *Premises.* Landlord does hereby agree to provide space for Tenant, and Tenant does hereby agree to accept such space from Landlord, which space is currently leased by Landlord pursuant to a certain lease between Foxbrook Realty, a Maine business, and Southern Maine Counseling Center, Inc., dated _____, of a certain building located at 581 Forest Avenue, Portland, Maine. Space is hereinafter referred to as "Premises" and said building, including the land on which it is located and all exterior areas and appurtenances related thereto, is hereinafter referred to as "the Building."

2. *Commencement and Ending Date of Term.* The term of this Agreement shall be for a period of two (2) years commencing ____ and terminating on ____ unless mutually extended in writing by either party, or unless terminated earlier pursuant to Paragraph 3 hereof.

3. *Termination.* This Agreement may be terminated by either party upon thirty (30) days written notice.

4. *Payment Schedule.* Tenant covenants and agrees to pay to Landlord, or to such appointees of Landlord, as Landlord may from time to time designate, total rental during the initial two-year term in the amount of Fifteen thousand, six hundred dollars ($15,600) payable during the twenty-four months in monthly rental installments of six hundred fifty dollars ($650.00) per month.

5. *Operation and Maintenance.* Landlord shall be responsible for all costs of maintenance and operation of the Premises.

6. *Covenants by Landlord.* Landlord covenants and agrees with Tenant as follows:

(a) Landlord shall advertise that Tenant is locating at Southern Maine Counseling Center in the following manner: in a local newspaper of general circulation, through Landlord's mailing list, by correspondence with members of the medical community chosen by Landlord, and by correspondence with various educational institutions chosen by Landlord;

(b) Landlord shall provide letterhead and stationery for Southern Maine Counseling Center, which letterhead will include Tenant's name;

(c) Landlord shall provide an answering service for Tenant;

(d) Landlord shall provide a secretary to book Tenant's appointments, on hours set by Landlord.

(e) Landlord shall provide a phone for local use by Tenant.

(f) Landlord shall provide off-street parking.

(g) Landlord shall provide four (4) hours of typing per month, non-accumulative.

(h) Landlord shall provide up to 100 pages of photocopying per month, non-accumulative.

(i) Landlord shall provide one single line listing of Tenant in yellow pages as well as name listing in large Southern Maine Counseling Center yellow page advertisement.

7. *Covenants by Tenant.* Tenant covenants and agrees with Landlord as follows:

(a) Tenant shall be responsible for all long-distance telephone calls, charging those calls to Tenant's personal credit card. Any call not charged will be billed to Tenant with an additional $5.00 per month service charge.

(b) Tenant shall perform or cause to be performed all of his/her own billing or record keeping;

(c) Tenant shall pay Landlord for all secretarial services performed by Landlord's staff at a rate of $8.00 per hour for secretarial work and $10.00 per hour for service done on the word processor or computer. This time will be computed on quarter hour intervals. This amount is payable at the end of each month for any secretarial services performed by Landlord's staff besides booking appointments, and not covered under Paragraph 6, item (g).

(d) Tenant shall pay all charges for use of the premises as set forth above in Paragraph 4 hereof.

(e) Tenant agrees that he will maintain throughout the term of this Lease and any renewal, a policy or policies of general liability insurance indemnifying Landlord and Tenant against all claims and demands for any personal injuries to or death of any persons and damage to or destruction or loss of property which may have or be claimed to have occurred on or about the demised premises, including the areas which the Tenant has a right hereunder to use in common with others, in an amount not less than One Hundred Thousand dollars ($100,000) for injury to or death of one person, Three Hundred Thousand Dollars ($300,00) for injury to or death of more than one person in any single accident and Fifty Thousand Dollars ($50,000) for damages to or destruction or loss of property. Tenant shall deliver to Landlord a certificate of such insurance coverage. Such policies of insurance shall name Landlord and its mortgagees, if any, as additional insureds and provide that they shall not be cancelled without at least ten (10) days prior written notice to Landlord.

(f) Tenant shall maintain and pay all premiums for his/ her own malpractice insurance, and copy shall be given to Landlord.

(g) Upon the termination of this Agreement, Tenant shall immediately cease using the Premises and shall remove its goods and effects and yield and deliver up peaceably to Landlord the Premises in good order, repair and condition.

(h) Tenant shall have exclusive use of office number three and four (#3 and 4) for counseling and consulting activities, as well as other space as agreed between Landlord and Tenant.

(i) Upon the termination of this Agreement, Tenant shall not practice under the name of Southern Maine Counseling Center.

8. *Default and Landlord's Remedies.* It is covenanted and agreed that if Tenant shall fail to neglect to perform or observe any of the covenants, terms, provisions, conditions, contained in this Agreement on his/her part to be performed or observed, Landlord may lawfully immediately or at any time thereafter, and without demand or notice, enter into the Premises and expel the Tenant and

those claiming through or under him and remove their effects without being deemed guilty of any manner of trespass, and without prejudice to any remedies which might otherwise be used by Landlord, for arrears under this Agreement or proceeding under breach of covenant, and upon entry, as aforesaid, this Agreement will terminate.

9. *Breach.* Any breach to Tenant of this Agreement shall entitle Landlord to commence an action against Tenant for damages and/or for an injunction to enjoin and restrain Tenant from any breach of this Agreement, and if Landlord is successful in such action, Tenant agrees to pay Landlord's attorney such reasonable legal fees as the court may fix in said action.

10. *Assignment.* Tenant may not assign this Agreement or any part thereof to any person without Landlord's express written consent.

11. *General.* This Agreement shall inure and be binding upon the respective successors, heirs, executors, administrators and assigns of Landlord and Tenant. This Agreement is made in and shall be governed by and construed in accordance with the laws of the State of Maine. The captions and headings contained in this Agreement are for convenience only and shall not be taken into account in construing the meaning of this Agreement or any part thereof. As to the obligations of each party hereunder to perform his or her undertaking, promises, covenants and obligations hereunder, time is of the essence. If any term or provision of this Agreement or the application thereof to any person or circumstance shall, to any extent, be invalid or unenforceable, the remainder of this Agreement, or the application of such term or provision to persons or circumstances other than those to which it is held invalid or unenforceable, shall not be affected thereby, and each term and provision of this Agreement shall be valid and enforced to the fullest extent provided by law. Wherever by the terms of this Agreement notice shall or may be given to either Landlord or Tenant, such notice shall be in writing and shall be sent by certified mail, return receipt requested, postage prepaid, to Landlord and Tenant's addresses as set forth below. Said notices shall be deemed to have been given when mailed.

If to Landlord: **Southern Maine Counseling Center**
                         581 Forest Avenue
                         Portland, ME 04101

If to Tenant:

IN WITNESS WHEREOF, Landlord and Tenant have caused this Agreement to be executed in duplicate under seal the day and year first above written.

Signed, Sealed and Delivered in the presence of:

_____   _____

_____   _____

_____   _____

_____

Form 2
Fee Per Session Rate

Number of Sessions/Month	Rate Charged per Session	Income Range
1 to 20	× $14	= $14 to $280
21 to 40	× $13	= $273 to $520
41 to 60	× $12	= $492 to $720
61 to 80	× $11	= $671 to $880
81 to 100	× $10	= $810 to $1,000
101 to ?	× $9	= $909 to ?

Form 3
Checklist for Evaluating Rental Space
Rated on a Scale of 1 [poor] to 10 [excellent]

	Location 1	Location 2	Location 3	Location 4
other professionals				
parking				
bus routes				
freeways				
easy to find				
lighting for night				
entrance				
Actual Space				
soundproofing				
size of space				
lighting				
natural				
indirect				
private work area				
waiting room				
bathroom space				
client				
personal				
private entrance				
secretarial space				
phone location				
location of the				
therapist's name				
furnished				
unfurnished				

Form 4
New Equipment List

Tables
Chairs
Paintings
Desk and chair for own personal use
Desk and chair for secretarial use
Lamps
Telephones
Typewriters
Computers
File cabinets
Storage stands
Sofas
End tables
Coat racks
Copy machine

Form 5
Survey of Fees Charged

Name	Length of time in practice	Sliding	Fee range	Fixed	Insurance client payment	% of clients	Waiting time
Psychiatrist							
1)							
2)							
3)							
4)							
5)							
Psychologist							
1)							
2)							
3)							
4)							
5)							
Counselor							
1)							
2)							
3)							
4)							
5)							
Social Worker							
1)							
2)							
3)							
4)							
5)							
Psychiatric Nurse							
1)							
2)							
3)							
4)							
5)							

Form 6
Sample Budget

Consulting/supervision	$1,100
Wages	4,732
Travel	550
Dues/publications	300
Telephone	2,000
Supplies	300
Payroll taxes	200
Rent	7,500
Postage	200
Miscellaneous	768
Insurance	1,000
Advertising	2,000
Professional fees	750
Interest	200
Total per year	$21,600
Total per month	$1,800

Form 7
Projected Budget

Consulting/supervision _____	Rent/wages _____
Wages _____	Postage _____
Travel _____	Miscellaneous _____
Dues/subscriptions _____	Insurance _____
Telephone _____	Advertising _____
Supplies _____	Professional fees _____
Payroll tax _____	Interest _____

Form 8
Summary of Sample Costs/Session

	Dr. Acton	Dr. Currer	Dr. Ellis
Monthly expenses	$1,800	$1,800	$1,800
Minus other income		−$800	
Divide by monthly billable hours	100	100	120
Average cost per hour	$18	$10	$15

Form 9
Summary of Sample Fees/Session

	Dr. Acton	Dr. Currer	Dr. Ellis
Business expenses	$1,800	$1,800	$1,800
Personal expenses	$2,000	$2,000	$2,000
Profit	$500	$500	$500
Individual investment	$500	$500	$500
	$4,800	$4,800	$4,800
Minus other income		– $800	
Divided by billable			
hours	100	100	120
Per session	$48	$40	$40

Form 10
Self-Disclosure Brochure

I am pleased that you have considered coming to me for counseling. Counseling is a very personal shared interaction between two people and should not be entered into lightly. The following information is designed to help you know me and what you can expect from the counseling.

I am married and have two children. My highest degree is a Ph.D. in Counseling from the State University of New York at Buffalo. I have been in private practice for fourteen years. I presently hold certification with the National Board of Certified Counselors, and the American Association of Sex Educators, Counselors and Therapists. I've served as president of the Maine Association for Counseling and Development and the Maine Mental Health Counselors' Association. I have also served as an officer of various regional and national professional organizations. I've lectured and given workshops in the United States and Canada on private practice, counseling, sexuality, addiction, and codependency, and have published a number of articles on these topics.

Daniel L. Richards, Ph.D., N.C.C.
Southern Maine
Counseling Center
581 Forest Avenue
Portland, Maine 04101
(207) 772-2404

Counseling Approach

Counseling cannot be effective if you only concentrate on the issues and concerns once a week. Therefore, as part of my approach, I will ask that you bring a tape recorder to all sessions. I ask all of my clients to tape each session and go over the tape at least once between sessions.

I will also ask that you do specific activities and/or read specific books that will help to speed up the time it takes for you to work out your concerns and problems.

The process of recovery requires a great deal of work and understanding. To help accomplish this, I offer a variety of methods to assist you:

☐ Individual Counseling

☐ Group Counseling

☐ Weekend Workshops
   Healing the Child Within
   Advanced Child Within
☐ Couples' Counseling

To be able to change behaviors which lead to healthy outcomes and consequences, you will need to understand your experiences and learnings.

Growing up in a dysfunctional family can be the cause of many of today's problems. This is because:

what you experienced
growing up
is what you learned;
what you learned shaped your
behaviors; your behaviors have
outcomes and
consequences.

A dysfunctional family is one where one or more of these conditions were present:

- ☐ Alcohol Addiction
- ☐ Drug Addiction
- ☐ Food Addiction
- ☐ Gambling Addiction
- ☐ Religious Addiction
- ☐ Work Addiction
- ☐ Emotional Abuse
- ☐ Mental Abuse
- ☐ Physical Abuse
- ☐ Sexual Abuse

If you are coming for counseling because of an abusive or addictive relationship you have just left, or if you are in an abusive or addictive situation, or you are afraid you are abusive or addicted, help is possible and counseling is effective.

Fee

My fee is $65.00, payable at each visit. Due to the vast number of insurance companies, each having separate forms and procedures, I do not bill insurance companies for your visits. If you are considering insurance companies for reimbursement, you should discuss this option at your first visit with me. However, you will be responsible for paying for each visit, each time, including the first visit.

Helpful Hints for Your First Session:

- ☐ Fill out the questionnaire I've sent you.
- ☐ Make a list of ideas you want to talk about.
- ☐ Don't be afraid to ask me questions.
- ☐ If feelings come up, stay with them and express them.
- ☐ You are interviewing me when I am interviewing you.
- ☐ When the session is over, you should feel you were heard.

Broken Appointments

Due to the time commitment I make to you, if you fail to show without having given at least 24 hours notice, you will be charged the full $65.00 appointment fee. I maintain a 24-hour answering service at (207) 772-2404 in case an appointment must be broken.

Form 11
Marketing Analysis

What are the typical demographics around the client base?

Men _____%

Age   under 18 = _____%
       18–29 = _____%
       30–45 = _____%
       45–59 = _____%
       60+ = _____%

Women _____%

   under 18 = _____%
   18–29 = _____%
   30–45 = _____%
   45–59 = _____%
   60+ = _____%

Income level
   under $20,000 = _____%
   20–35,000 = _____%
   35–45,000 = _____%
   45,000 + = _____%

   under $20,000 = _____%
   20–35,000 = _____%
   35–45,000 = _____%
   45,000 + = _____%

Education level
   high school = _____%
   2 yrs college = _____%
   4 yrs college = _____%
   4 yrs college + = _____%

   high school = _____%
   2 yrs college = _____%
   4 yrs college = _____%
   4 yrs college + = _____%

Single = _____%
Married = _____%
Divorced = _____%

Single = _____%
Married = _____%
Divorced = _____%

Listing of communities or parts of communities where 70% of clients come from: _____

_____

_____

Promotional Budget

	Present Year		Projected	
	Fixed	**Specific**	**Fixed**	**Specific**
Jan				
Feb				
Mar				
Apr				
May				
Jun				
Jul				
Aug				
Sept				
Oct				
Nov				
Dec				

Promotional activities
Yellow page(s)
Present size(s)
Section(s)
Cost per ad
Average number of calls per month

Internal

Business cards, cost	Number used
Practice brochure, cost	Number used
Stationery, cost	Number used
Handout office material, cost	Number used
Others:	

External

Newsletters, cost	Number used	frequency
Promotional fliers, cost	Number used	frequency
Paid advertisements, cost	Number of times	

Competition analysis

Name of major competitors (list four)

1.

2.

3.

4.

Types of marketing used (list for each one)

1.

2.

3.

4.

Strengths each offers the public (what you like about each
  one)

1.

2.

3.

4.

Marketable strengths (four specific words or three-word
  concepts desirable by the public)

1.

2.

3.

4.

Personal assessment

What makes you qualified to do what you do?

What makes your approach different from others'?

What type of clients do you work best with?

What type of clients do you refer out to other therapists?

What are your strengths as a therapist?

What are your weaknesses as a therapist?

What are your latest awards, degrees, certifications, or
  recognitions?

Types of client problems presented on first session:

Types of client problems worked with in therapy:

Average number of sessions

Number of intakes per month:

Jan ___	Apr ___	Jul ___	Oct ___
Feb ___	May ___	Aug ___	Nov ___
Mar ___	Jun ___	Sep ___	Dec ___

Number of second sessions per month:

Jan ___	Apr ___	Jul ___	Oct ___
Feb ___	May ___	Aug ___	Nov ___
Mar ___	Jun ___	Sep ___	Dec ___

Referral sources:

Professional ___

MDs ___	DOs ___	Dentists ___
Clergy ___	Chiropractors ___	Lawyers ___
Social workers ___	Psychiatrists ___	Psychologists ___
EAP providers ___	Nurses ___	Counselors ___
Social welfare personnel ___	Police ___	School personnel ___

Personal ___

| Present clients ___ | Former clients ___ | Friends ___ |

Form 12
Sample Feedback Form

Daniel L. Richards, Ph.D., N.C.C.
Southern Maine Counseling Center
581 Forest Avenue
Portland, Maine 04101
(207) 772-2404

Re: _____   Age: _____

Dear Dr. _____   Date: _____

Thank you for referring your patient. The following is a summary of essential findings.

History:

Diagnostic Impression:

Treatment or Disposition:

Remarks:

Signed: _____

_____

Form 13
Sample End-of-Year Statement

Daniel L. Richards, Ph.D., N.C.C.
Southern Maine Counseling Center
581 Forest Avenue
Portland, Maine 04101
(207) 772-2404

Dear   :

For your records and tax purposes, the following is a summary of your counseling visits for the year of 19____.

        # of visits   Total amount paid

                        Sincerely,

                        Daniel L. Richards, Ph.D.

Form 14
Sample Confirmation Letter

Daniel L. Richards, Ph.D., N.C.C.
Southern Maine Counseling Center
581 Forest Avenue
Portland, Maine 04101
(207) 772-2404

January 1, 1999

Dear

In following up on your recent phone call, I'm confirming your appointment on _____. If you find that you cannot keep this appointment, please notify the office as soon as possible.

Enclosed you will find a brochure explaining my service, plus an intake form. If you would please complete the intake form and bring it with you to your first appointment, it would be greatly appreciated.

I look forward to meeting with you.

Sincerely,

Daniel L. Richards, Ph.D., N.C.C.

DLR/sos

Form 15
Sample Intake Form

To help me with our first session, please fill out the following information as completely as possible:

Date: _____

Name: _____
         First   Middle Initial   Last

Address: _____
                                    Street

_____
         City   State   Zip Code

Date of Birth: _____ Age: _____

Place of Birth: _____

Phone: (h) _____ (w) _____ (other) _____

Marital Status:

single _____ married _____ separated _____ divorced _____

   If married, spouse's name _____

   Age: _____ Place of Employment: _____

   Number of Years Married: _____

   If divorced, ex-spouse's name: _____

   Age: _____   Number of Years Divorced _____

Children:

   Name _____ Age _____
   Name _____ Age _____
   Name _____ Age _____
   Name _____ Age _____

   Employment: Job Title _____

   Place: _____

Family Physician:

   Name _____
   Address _____

Urologist:

   Name _____
   Address _____

Gynecologist:
  Name _____

  Address _____

Are you taking any prescription drugs at this time?
  Yes __ No __

  If yes, what type and for what purpose _____

Referral Source: _____

The following questions are designed to help me understand
your background. Please complete them as they apply to
you. Thank you.

Parents' Names: (F) _____ Age: __ (M)_____ Age: __
  Married ____ Divorced ____ Widowed ____ Separated ____
Number of brothers _____ sisters _____
Have any of them had counseling before: If so, for what? ____
_____

Any history of drug/alcohol abuse?
  In father's family: Yes ____ No ____
  If yes, please describe _____
_____

  In mother's family: Yes ____ No ____
  If yes, please describe _____
_____

Any history of drug or alcohol abuse with mother:
  Yes ____ No ____
  If yes, please describe _____
_____

Any history of drug or alcohol abuse with father:
  Yes ____ No ____
  If yes, please describe _____
_____

Any history of physical abuse to you or brothers/sisters:
   Yes _____ No _____
   If yes, please describe _____

Any history of sexual abuse to you or brothers/sisters:
   Yes _____ No _____
   If yes, please note person abused and by
   whom: _____

Do you use alcohol or drugs: Yes _____ No _____ If yes, please
describe frequency and type _____
_____

Have you any physical problems now or in the past that you
feel have affected your life: Yes _____ No _____ If yes, please
describe what and when: _____

Have you ever experienced any sexual difficulties:
   Yes _____ No _____
   If yes, please describe _____
_____

Have you ever had counseling before: Yes _____ No _____
If yes, please describe and list name of person(s): _____
_____

Please make note of any other comments that you feel are
important to this counseling process: _____
_____

Form 16
Sample Release Form

To Whom It May Concern:

I, _____, D.O.B., _____
hereby authorize any mental health facility, counseling center,
physician, psychiatrist, psychologist, or counselor to disclose,
when requested to do so by Daniel L. Richards, Ph.D., any and
all information concerning myself with respect to any illness
of injury, medical history, consultation, prescription or treatment, and copies of any medical, or social service records.

A photostatic copy of this authorization shall be considered
as effective and valid as the original.

_____
Signature

_____
Date

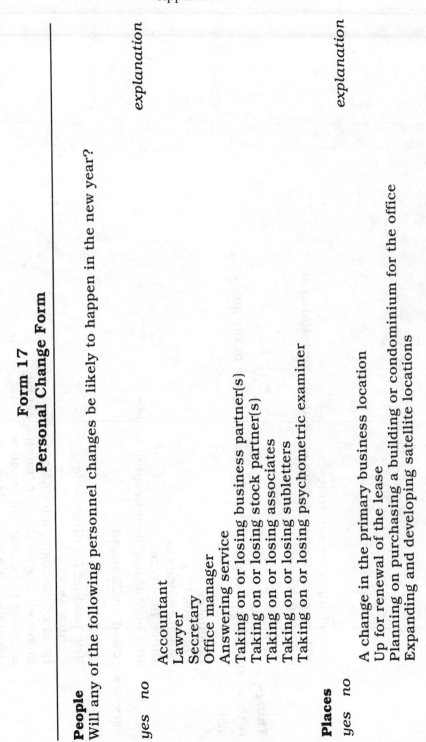

Form 17
Personal Change Form

People
Will any of the following personnel changes be likely to happen in the new year?

yes   no   *explanation*

Accountant
Lawyer
Secretary
Office manager
Answering service
Taking on or losing business partner(s)
Taking on or losing stock partner(s)
Taking on or losing associates
Taking on or losing subletters
Taking on or losing psychometric examiner

Places
yes   no   *explanation*

A change in the primary business location
Up for renewal of the lease
Planning on purchasing a building or condominium for the office
Expanding and developing satellite locations

Subletting from someone
Planning on traveling more extensively for training or consulting contracts

Things

Is there any chance of purchasing or changing any of the following:

yes no   *explanation*

Computer
Copy machine
Office equipment
Office furniture
New accounting/bookkeeping system

Services Added or Changed

yes no   *explanation*

New product for direct sale
Testing service
Book or monograph for sale
Increase in workshop or training activity
Increase in consulting services
Becoming an EAP provider
Becoming a franchised deliverer of services or products

Marketing a franchised product
Adding groups, weekend retreats, or intensive therapy activities
    to the clinical practice
Becoming a supervisor
Teaching at a college or university

Personal
The following changes in the personal life can also affect the business:

yes no   *explanation*

Marriage
Divorce
Birth of child
Child going to college or leaving home
Pending death of loved one
Change from full-time paid job to sole practitioner whether
    clinical, consulting, or training
Major purchase of property for personal use
Geographic move of primary personal residence

Form 18
Monthly Review of Income and Expenses

	Month Previous Yr.	Current Month of _____	Year to Date 19___
INCOME FROM THE PRACTICE			
Fee income			
Rental income			
Other income			
Total income			
OPERATING EXPENSES			
Consultation			
Wages			
Travel			
Dues/publications			
Telephone			
Office supplies			
Payroll taxes			
Rent			
Postage			
Miscellaneous			
Insurance			
Advertising			
Professional fees			
Interest			
Total Operating Expenses			
Operating Income			

Form 19
Monthly Review of Clients

Types of Clients	This month's total	Same month previous year	Year-to-Date Total
Total intakes (1st appointment)			
Evaluation (2nd appointment)			
Marriage			
Individual			
Group			
Testing/assessments			
Consultations			
Workshops			

APPENDIX B

References

American Psychiatric Association. (1987). *Diagnostic and statistical manual of mental disorders, Third edition, Revised.* Washington, DC: Author.

Beck, E. (1988a). Response to Jim Wiggins. *Private Practice News,* 2(9).

Beck, E. (1988b). Thoughts upon entering HMO and PPO. *Private Practice News,* 2(11).

Dwinell, M. (1987). Private practice: A three-legged stool. *Private Practice News,* 1(11).

Kopp, S. (1985). *If you meet the Buddha on the road, kill him.* New York: Bantam Books.

Kouzmanoff, K. (1988). Private practice: Life on the edge. *Private Practice News,* 2(6).

Lerner, H. (1985). *The dance of anger.* New York: Harper & Row.

Levine, S. (1982). *Who dies: An investigation of conscious living and conscious dying.* New York: Anchor Books.

Lew, M. (1988). *Victims no longer.* New York: Neuraumont Press.

Remley, T. (1988). The legal basis of health insurance and insurance fraud. *Private Practice News,* 2(7).

Richards, D. (1988). Third-party reimbursement: Big brother is watching. *Private Practice News,* 2(1).

Richards, D. (1989). There's an elephant in the living room: Does anyone see it? Money in therapy. *Private Practice News,* 3(1).

Schoff, J.S. (1988). The impact of private practice on our personal lives and relationships. *Private Practice News,* 2(8).

Small, J. (1982). *Transformers.* Marina del Ray, CA: DeVorss.

Wiggins, J. (1988). Counselor survival in the next five years, *Private Practice News*, 2(7).

World Health Organization. (1978). *Manual of the international statistical classification of diseases, injuries and causes of death*. ICD-9. Albany, NY: World Health Organization Publication Center.

APPENDIX C

Supplemental Reading List

Browning, C.H. (1982). *Private practice handbook*. Los Angeles, CA: Duncliff's International.

Connor, R.A., & Davidson, J.P. (1985). *Marketing your consulting and professional services*. New York: Wiley.

Forman, B.D., & Forman, K.S. (1987). *Fundamentals of marketing the private psychotherapy practice*. Muncie, IN: Professional Consultants Associates.

Mone, L.C. (1983). *Private practice: A professional business*. La Jolla, CA: Elm Press.

Richards, D.L. (1987–1989). *Private Practice News*. Portland, ME: Private Practice Institute.

Schechtman, M.R. (1977). *Private practice manual*. Chicago, IL: The Center for the Study of Private Practice.

Shenson, H.L. (1990). *The contract and fee-setting guide for consultants & professionals*. New York: Wiley.

NOTES

NOTES